Robert Watson, William Thomson

The History of the Reign of Philip the Third

King of Spain - Vol. 2

Robert Watson, William Thomson

The History of the Reign of Philip the Third
King of Spain - Vol. 2

ISBN/EAN: 9783337230227

Printed in Europe, USA, Canada, Australia, Japan

Cover: Foto ©ninafisch / pixelio.de

More available books at **www.hansebooks.com**

THE HISTORY

OF THE REIGN OF

PHILIP THE THIRD,

KING OF SPAIN.

THE FIRST FOUR BOOKS.

By ROBERT WATSON, LL. D.

Principal of the United College in the Univerfity of St. Andrew's.

THE TWO LAST

BY WILLIAM THOMSON, LL. D.

A NEW EDITION.

VOL. II.

BASIL:

Printed and fold by J. J. TOURNEISEN.

MDCCXCII.

THE HISTORY

OF THE REIGN OF

PHILIP THE THIRD,

KING OF SPAIN.

BOOK V.

ABOUT the end of the fifteenth century, the several kingdoms of Spain formed one powerful monarchy, containing above twenty millions of inhabitants. It was well cultivated, abounded in flourishing manufactures, and was governed with equal vigor and prudence by the joint authority of Ferdinand and Isabella. These princes, agreeably to the natural progress of ambition, extended their united power, by the superiority of their policy and arms, in Europe, while the inventive and daring genius of Columbus opened to their aspiring views an immense field of conquest by the discovery of a new world. An object so animating, by its novelty as well as grandeur, nourished those seeds of ambition which had taken root in the court of Spain, and roused a spirit of enterprise among the people. A succession of bold leaders followed by numerous adventurers, allured to their standards by the love of change, or the hope of

1609. Ambition of Spain accounted for.

BOOK
V.
1609.

plunder, united to the Spanish empire almost the whole of those vast regions which extend from the Gulf of Mexico to the Straits of Magellan.

The collected treasures of America, over which the cortes had not any control, enabled Charles V. to trample on the liberties of his own subjects, and to threaten neighbouring states with universal dominion. The ambition of the emperor descended, together with his immense resources, to his son, Philip II. and engaged him in projects beyond his abilities. The monarch was governed by a lust of power, and the people were seized with a spirit of emigration. The energy of the nation was diverted from domestic industry, the true source of national wealth and grandeur, and turned to distant enterprises of colonization and of war. The monarchy became faint through the loss of its blood and treasure; and the power, on which its vast ambition had been originally founded, was subverted. But ideas of uncontrolable dominion were by this time deeply impressed on the Austrian race; and Philip III. with exhausted resources, and a feeble mind, faintly pursued the same ambitious plan that had been formed or adopted by his predecessors on the Spanish throne, not more formidable for their extensive revenues, than for the vigilance, vigor, and perseverance of their nature.

It is so natural for sovereign princes to exert every nerve to reclaim the obedience of revolted subjects, that the continuance of the war in the Netherlands till the late truce, ought not, indeed, to be accounted any proof of extraordinary ambition; and the expulsion of the Morescoes, a people industrious in an indolent climate, seemed an act by which the Spanish crown voluntarily sought its own degradation. The ambitious schemes, however, of the court of Madrid, though better concealed, and apparently suspended, were not wholly abandoned. The aggrandizement of the house of Austria was still the first object in the counsels of Spain. But her power corresponded not with her inclination; and her pursuit of greatness was sullied by those machinations which are the usual resources of impotent ambition, and which mark a declining empire.

The peace of Vervins restored the appearance, but did not establish the confidence of friendship between two great and rival kingdoms. The court of Spain continued to encourage and support the enemies of the crown of France: and the French monarch, in return, encouraged and supported the enemies of Spain. Thus the ancient antipathies of these neighbouring kingdoms were still kept alive by reciprocal injuries. But, while the intrigues of Philip were dark and treacherous, the hostilities of Henry were ennobled by the occasions on which they were exercised, and the part which sound policy required him to act, was consonant to the natural generosity of his temper. This magnanimous prince, enraged at the repeated injuries he had suffered from the ambition of the Spaniards, apprized of their intrigues and influence with the discontented nobles

BOOK V.
1609.

Jealousies continue between the courts of France and Spain.

BOOK V.
1609.

Great plan of Henry IV.

of France, and alarmed at the dangers which threatened both his life and his crown, conceived a project of uniting different powers in a league againſt the encroachments of a nation which ſeemed ſtill to aim at univerſal monarchy. His ultimate deſign, in the formation of ſuch a confederacy, was to eſtabliſh among the nations of Europe a new ſyſtem, and to fix a durable balance of power, by the exaltation of other ſtates on the ruins of the houſe of Auſtria [1].

[1] See Sully's Memoirs. — The ſcheme, which was aſcribed to Henry, of uniting all Chriſtendom in one great republic, for the promotion of general happineſs, and the eſtabliſhment of general tranquillity, has afforded matter of great ſpeculation and conjecture. Although it is impoſſible to penetrate into the receſſes of the minds of princes, and that hiſtory is more ſucceſsfully employed in tracing the conſequences than in exploring the ſprings of events and actions; yet, in every deſign of ſo great a man as Henry IV. we are deeply intereſted, and it is with difficulty that we can refrain from indulging conjectures concerning whatever appears myſterious or doubtful in his conduct.

The project of uniting the Chriſtian powers into one general republic, as it was not unworthy, ſo neither was it too great for the mind of Henry. It was the perfection and juſt completion of his plan. Nor is it improbable, that at certain times, he amuſed his fancy with the contemplation of ſo grand an object. But, on the other hand, it is almoſt certain that it was not the contemplation of this great end that firſt ſuggeſted the idea of the confederacy, and firſt rouſed him to action. A more natural or probable account of his original motives, in his intended enterpriſe, there cannot be given than what we have in Sully's Memoirs. " Henry IV. recollecting the intrigues of Spain, ſaid, I ſee theſe people will never let me alone while it is in their power to diſturb

PHILIP III. KING OF SPAIN. 5

BOOK V.
1609.

At this time religion was the moſt powerful band of union among men; and, conſequently, religious ſympathies and antipathies were the great engines that governed the world. The Auſtrians gloried in patronizing the church of Rome. Henry, from the moſt urgent motives of policy, had changed the profeſſion of his faith, and embraced the catholic religion, but ſtill poſſeſſed and deſerved the confidence of the Proteſtants. The French monarch, of courſe, in a conteſt with the houſe of Auſtria, could depend on the good wiſhes of all, as he was aſſured of aſſiſtance from moſt of the princes and ſtates of the reformed religion. With England he entered into a league for the mutual defence of that kingdom and of France. The United Provinces of the Low Countries, the Proteſtant princes of Germany, the greater part of the imperial towns, were ready to take an active part in his intended enterpriſe. And Denmark and Sweden, although from their remote ſituations they were not ſo nearly inteſtered in his deſigns, if they ſhould be involved in the flames of a general war, it was eaſy to foreſee,

me. And that the different jealouſies of honor, of reputation, and of the intereſts of ſtate, render all confidence and harmony between France and Spain impoſſible. Other foundations of ſecurity muſt be ſought for than words. They will conſtrain me to do what I never intended. But I ſwear by God, that if I have once put my affairs in order, and raiſed money and all neceſſary ſupplies, I will make them repent that they have rouſed me to arms.". Vol. iii. p. 33. duodecimo, Paris, 1663.

would espouse the cause of their Protestant brethren.

But the catholic powers were not in like manner disposed to favor the house of Austria. For neither was the veneration for the ancient equal to the zeal which appeared for the new doctrines and forms of worship, nor were political motives wanting, which in certain catholic governments counterbalanced those of religion. The princes and states of Italy, who generally looked up to Henry as their protector, favored his views secretly. But the Venetians entered openly into a league offensive and defensive, with a monarch through whose mediation they had been enabled to maintain the civil authority of the republic in opposition to the spiritual jurisdiction of the pope, and whom they regarded as a bulwark against the encroachments of the Spanish governors of Milan. The Swiss cantons too, catholic as well as protestant, either actuated by a dread of the power of Austria, or, as other historians affirm, induced by a promise of Franche Compté, Alsace, and Tirol, embarked in this confederacy [2]. The duke of Savoy also, a catholic prince, but who never professed an inordinate zeal for the Romish faith, Henry drew over to his side, by a promise of his eldest daughter in marriage to the prince of Piedmont, and by holding up to his ambition the sovereignty of Milan. That sovereignty the duke had in vain expected to receive

---

[a] Mezeray, abrégé chronologique, 1609.

in partage with Catherine, a daughter of Spain; a mortincation the more severe, that the joint authority of the archduke Albert and the infanta Isabella governed the Auftrian Netherlands.

The high esteem in which Henry held this new ally, appears from the terms on which he purchased his alliance. The general voice of admiration had bestowed on both these princes the title of great: and their respective talents and virtues, so formidable to each other when in a state of mutual hostility, inspired them now with reciprocal confidence.

While Henry thus prepared to carry his intentions into execution, an event happened which, according to his usual good fortune, gave him an opportunity of covering his real designs, under the veil of redressing injuries, and supporting the cause of justice.

John William, duke of Cleves and Juliers, having died without children the right of succession to the sovereignty of those states was claimed by different princes. The most powerful of these prepared to maintain their pretensions by arms. But the emperor Rhodolphus II. as well to support his own authority, as to prevent the calamities of war, summoned the several competitors to appear before him, to explain the nature of their particular claims. In the mean time, he sequestered the fiefs in dispute, the administration of which he bestowed on his brother Leopold, bishop of Stralburgh and Passau. The administrator,

Succession of Cleves and Juliers.

seizing Juliers, levied troops, and began to extend his territories around that city.

Two of the competitors, the marquis of Brandenburgh, and the count Palatine of Neuburgh, proteſtant princes, alarmed at the conduct of the emperor, agreed to make a fair partition of that ſovereignty to which they ſeverally made pretenſions, until their differences ſhould be terminated in an amicable manner by arbitration.

The count Palatine took the field with an army, and aſſembling the ſtates of Cleves and Juliers at Duſſeldorp, engaged them to acknowledge himſelf and the elector of Brandenburgh as the lawful hereditary ſovereigns of Cleves, and all the other principalities that had been poſſeſſed by John William beyond the Rhine. Alarmed at theſe proceedings, the Catholic princes of the empire formed a league for the defence of the ancient faith, and ſent deputies to demand aſſiſtance from Madrid and from Rome. The princes of Brandenburgh and Neuburgh, on the other hand, endeavoured to fortify themſelves in the ſtates of which they had taken poſſeſſion, by adding to the ſupport they received from the princes of the evangelical union, the powerful aid of the king of France. The ſtates of Cleves and Juliers annexed to the Auſtrian Netherlands, on which they bordered, would have extended the dominions of Spain beyond the Rhine, and bridled the power of the ſeven United Provinces. It was not therefore with difficulty that the Protestant princes prevailed on Henry to espouse their cause. To the prince of Anhalt, whom they had sent to Paris, he readily replied, and in the most obliging manner, that he would not only assist them with all his strength, but would himself march for their protection at the head of his army. This army consisted of thirty thousand foot, and six thousand horse, a great proportion of which troops were veterans, commanded by officers formed for war under his own standard. He had a train of artillery superior to any that had ever before been brought into the field, and provided with ammunition for sixty thousand round of shot. And so great and judicious had been the economy of Henry, that he possessed treasures sufficient to keep on foot so great a military force for ten years, without the least oppression or injury to his subjects [1]. Besides this, there was an army in Dauphiny, of twelve thousand foot and two thousand horse, under the command of the marshal Lesdiguieres, ready to join the duke of Savoy in an attack upon the Spanish dominions in Lombardy. Europe had not seen military preparations so great, or known a juncture apparently so big with revolution. The wealth of Venice, the valor of the Swiss, the impetuosity of the Savoyards, the juvenile ardor of the United Provinces, the active zeal of the Protestant princes and states of Germany, the disciplined bravery of

[1] Duke of Rohan's Discourse on the Death of Henry the Great. Mémoires de Sully, Mezeray.

BOOK
V.
1610.

France, the good wishes of all who professed the reformed religion: these, in the hands of a warlike and political prince, formed an engine fitted to subvert kingdoms, and to change the face of the world. The force of the means he possessed, and the grandeur of the end he had in view, were a source of delight to the martial and sanguine disposition of Henry. Sometimes he would take pleasure in reviewing his troops, at others, in trying the arms he designed to wear in the day of battle. He slept but little, was constantly in motion, and conversed much with the ministers and officers in whom he most confided. He burned with impatience to exchange the luxury of a palace for the dangers and hardships of the field, and was eager to retaliate on the marquis of Spinola, the advantages that had been gained over himself by the duke of Parma. He had already strengthened the garrison in his frontier towns, and his troops began to file off in separate divisions towards the general rendezvous in Champagne. He acquainted the archduke Albert at Brussels of his intended march through part of his territories, and desired to be informed whether he should be received as an enemy or as a friend. Nothing detained him in Paris but a desire to be present at the coronation of Mary de Medicis, his queen, whom he had appointed during his absence regent of France.

The house of Austria, against which this gathering storm was directed, beheld it with astonishing indifference. The emperor, Rhodolphus, more intent on obferving the motions of the heavenly bodies, than on watching the movements of his enemies, indulged a natural love of fcience, the only paffion that is able to extinguifh the pride of power in the breafts of princes. He had given up, with little reluctance, to his brother Matthias, the government of Hungary, Moravia, and Auftria, and foon after he alfo refigned that of Bohemia. With the title of emperor, he lived a private man. It is matter of greater wonder that the king of Spain, in whom the paffion of religion did not eradicate all the feeds of ambition, appeared unconcerned at the warlike preparations of an inveterate enemy. Whether the minifters of Spain trufted to the fuccefs of thofe plots they had formed againft Henry in his own palace; or, that with the fuperftitious credulity of the age in which they lived, they confided in the completion of thofe predictions that about this time were fo frequent in the mouths of Catholics concerning the fudden death of the king of France*; or that they weakly imagined this

---

* This conjecture may appear at firft fight, to certain readers, wholly abfurd and groundlefs. Neverthelefs it will not feem altogether extravagant, if we reflect on the power of univerfally received prejudices on even the ftrongeft minds.

About this time, and even long after it, the fcience of Judicial aftrology was ftudied by philofophers of the higheft reputation, with great gravity, and, as they firmly believed, with great fuccefs. There is in the univerfity of Peterfburgh, a very able mathematician, who is making great

BOOK V.
1610.

monarch had no other object in view than the expulsion of Leopold from the states of Juliers; or from whatever secret cause, it is certain, that amidst a general and anxious suspense, the court of Madrid discovered not any symptoms of alarm. The world, struck with the mighty preparations of France, wondered at the serenity of Spain, when an event happened which proved how much human affairs are governed by causes beyond the reach of princes; which frustrated the well laid designs of the great Henry, and supplied the want of vigilance and wisdom in the counsels of Philip.

Death of Henry IV. of France.

On the eve of the day fixed for the coronation of Mary de Medicis, Henry IV. was going in his coach to the arsenal, to converse, according to his custom, with the duke of Sully, superintendant of the finances, and grand master of the

progress in judicial astrology at this very day. It is certain that the duke of Lerma was a firm believer in the doctrines of this science. See Anecdotes du Ministère du Comte Duc d'Olivarez.

Men of sense, of the present times, struck with that mixture of genius and extravagance which distinguishes the writings of antiquity, are at a loss how to reconcile so much reason with such great extravagance; and suspect that many of the opinions delivered in those writings were not real, but popular and affected. There is not a doubt but posterity will entertain similar doubts concerning some of the doctrines of the seventeenth and even eighteenth century. Men are ever changing their opinions, yet ever wondering that the world did not always think as they do now.

PHILIP III. KING OF SPAIN.

artillery, when he received two ſtabs with a knife, one of which pierced through the great canal which conveys the blood from the heart to the other parts of the body. The king fell dead on the duke of Epernon, who was on one ſide of him, and in whoſe ear he was whiſpering when he received the firſt wound. This parricide was committed by Francis Ravaillac, a native and ſchoolmaſter of Angoulême, on the 14th day of May, 1610. The miniſters of France conceiving that this execrable deed might have been the effect of ſome ſecret conſpiracy, put Ravaillac to the torture, not only as a puniſhment due to his crime, but as a means of diſcovering his abettors and accomplices. But that miſerable fanatic had no accomplices; and his only abettors were the prieſts of the Catholic ſuperſtition, whoſe writings and diſcourſes had fully perſuaded him that by murdering the Protector of the Proteſtants, and the enemy of the pope, he would ſave his own ſoul from perdition, and obtain, as a reward, eternal life.

BOOK V.
1610.

The tragical end of Henry filled one half of Europe with exultation, and the other with horror. The houſe of Auſtria rejoiced at the deſtruction of a formidable enemy; and the votaries of that religion which they patronized, applauded the pious zeal of Ravaillac, which they compared to whatever is moſt heroic in the lives or deaths of ſaints, martyrs, and confeſſors. But a general conſternation ſeized not only the Hugonots of France, but every ſtate profeſſing the

Effects of the death of Henry.

BOOK
V.
1610.

reformed religion. The whole proteſtant world deplored the untimely fate of the patron of religious toleration: and nations differing in matters of religion, united in bewailing the loſs of the illuſtrious guardian of the liberties of Europe. They indulged the melancholy recollection of his amiable and heroic virtues; his compaſſion; to which, on different occaſions, he had ſacrificed his ambition; the boldneſs and vigor of his genius; which diſdaining the windings of ſubtilty and refinement, purſued the paths that led directly to ſucceſs; his courage, which never forſook him in the moſt depreſſing circumſtances; his bravery in the field; which by a powerful contagion inſpired throughout his whole army irreſiſtible intrepidity; his patience under hardſhips, and affability in every fortune, which ſo won on the hearts of his ſoldiers, that they ſerved him not only with the loyalty of ſubjects, but the affection of friends. But the celebrated Benjamin, duke of Rohan, not content with mingling his own with the groans of nations, found a melancholy ſatisfaction in pouring forth the ſentiments of his heart in a pathetic compoſition, and tranſmitting to poſterity a memorial of his devotion to his beloved ſovereign. This elegy, written in a ſtrain of paſſion which nothing could have inſpired but the deepeſt ſorrow, is a lively picture of the grief and conſternation which followed the death of Henry, and exhibits a conſpicuous proof of that ascendant which he had acquired over the greatest minds [1].

[1] I deplore, says Rohan, among other expressions of extreme and vehement grief, I deplore in the loss of our invincible king, that of France, and from the bottom of my soul grieve at the manner of his death. Our own experience will soon inform us how fit a subject he is for our tears: the people are alarmed and filled with melancholy presages of future calamities; the towns are guarded as if they expected a siege; the nobility seek their safety amongst the most eminent of their own order, whose factions rather threaten them with danger, than console them with any hopes of safety. Together with the loss of his person, I bewail that of his courtesy and affability, his sweet and obliging conversation, the honor he did me, the admittance he deigned to grant me even to his most private recesses, oblige me not only to mourn for him, but even not to love myself in those places where the light of my good prince once afforded me such infinite happiness. I regret the disappointment of the most noble and heroic enterprise that was ever yet conceived. It is not credible that a military force of thirty thousand foot, six thousand horse, a train of artillery of sixty guns, and ammunition for sixty thousand round of shot, besides the army then in Dauphiny, should be destined for the siege of Juliers, which was since undertaken with eight thousand foot, and one thousand horse. Have I not good reason to lament the loss of such an opportunity of proving my courage, zeal, and fidelity to my king? One push of a pike given in his presence, would have been a greater satisfaction to me, than I should have now in obtaining a victory. Much more should I have valued the least praise in that art of which he was the greatest master of his time, than the approbation and applause of all other captains now alive. I grieve at the manner of his deplorable death: a prince composed of sweetness and clemency; who never condemned an innocent person to death; whose

BOOK V.
1610.

After the death of Henry, his friends and allies had reason to apprehend that the vindictive passions of the house of Austria would be heightened and inflamed by the hope of gratification [c]. The Italian states especially, overawed by the power of Philip in Naples and in Lombardy, trembled lest the Spanish arms should over-run all Italy. But Charles Emanuel, duke of Savoy, whose noble mind was inspired with the pride rather than the despondency of grief, endeavoured to rally the broken forces of the league, and to unite them once more into a compact and formidable body.

Character of the duke of Savoy.

The house of Savoy, one of the most illustrious in Europe on account of its antiquity, is more nobly distinguished for wisdom of policy, and valor of arms. Environed by the dominions of victories were never stained with blood; who having once reclaimed his enemies to their duty, cherished them as friends, and loaded them with favors. Who that ever lived under this most august prince, as I have done, can take pleasure in these present times? I will therefore divide my life into two parts, and call that part of it I have already passed, *happy*, since it was employed in the service of Henry the Great; and that which is yet to come, *unfortunate*, and spend it in lamentations, tears, sighs, and complaints: and out of the honor which I owe to his memory, I will devote the remainder of my days (the kingdom of God being preserved entire) to the service of France, because it was his kingdom; to the king, because he is his son; and to the queen, because she was once his dear companion and spouse.

[c] Spes addita suscitat iras. VIRGIL.

the

the empire, France, and Spain, the princes of Savoy are under a conſtant neceſſity of watching the balance of power among their ambitious neighbours, and of penetrating early into their deſigns, that, by affording timely ſupport to the weaker againſt the ſtronger party, they may be enabled to preſerve their own independence. And, if Providence has placed this family in a ſituation in which it is neceſſary to guard againſt the encroachments of ſuperior power; the nature of their country, bold, abrupt, and ſublime, inſpires that confidence which is neceſſary effectually to reſiſt them. The faſtneſſes and narrow defiles of the Alps, together with a hardy race of men inhabiting a mountainous and ſnowy region, encourage the dukes of Savoy boldly to enter on war, whenever the complexion of the times demonſtrates its expedience. Thus natural have conſpired with moral cauſes to form that illuſtrious character which the race of Savoy has juſtly obtained in the world.

Charles Emanuel did not diſgrace, but, on the contrary, added luſtre to the dignity of his birth. Nature, which had formed this prince of a weakly conſtitution of body, adorned his ſoul with a ſplendid variety of talents and virtues; and theſe the parental care of Philibert, renowned for his victory over the French at St. Quentin, exalted and matured by a learned and liberal education. The writings of antiquity, ſo full of heroic actions and rapid conqueſts, nouriſhed the natural ardor of his mind, and inſpired an emulation of the ancient heroes of Italy. Together with that intrepidity of spirit which delights in pursuing great designs, he possessed in an eminent degree those qualities which are requisite in order to carry them into execution; political conduct, and military prowess. His courage was not of that calm and equal kind which is connected with firmness of nerves, and which characterizes the warriors of the North. But, being derived from that vigor of imagination, and sensibility of frame peculiar to southern climates, it was ardent and impetuous. His genius also like that of the warmer climates, was fertile even to excess, and prone to subtilty and refinement. From a temper so sanguine, and an imagination so luxuriant, he derived an elasticity of spirit that rose under misfortunes; whence, though sometimes defeated, and often disappointed, he was never discouraged. His resources were endless: for there could not be a conjuncture in which the superiority of his genius could not find some favorable opportunity of practising on the passions, and managing the hopes, and fears, and follies of men. So various were his stratagems of policy and of war, that the most penetrating of his cotemporaries professed themselves unable to form any probable conjecture concerning his designs. Something, however, of the vast and unbounded characterized his conduct, the ardor of his inventive genius, engaging him not unfrequently in projects beyond his utmost power to accomplish [1]. Nor were

[1] Vastus animus immoderata, incredibilia, nimis alta semper cupiebat. Sallust.

the powers of his capacious mind wholly abforbed
in fchemes of ambition. Whatever was elegant
or great touched his foul, and he was prone to the
pleafures of fociety and love. He was a friend to
men of letters, a patron of all the arts, an enthu-
fiaftic admirer and bountiful rewarder of merit of
every kind. And the greatnefs of his mind was
fo happily tempered with benignity and grace,
that the engaging affability of his noble deportment alleviated in the breafts of his fubjects the
hardfhips which they fuffered through his reftlefs
ambition. On the whole, it is difficult to conceive that qualities fo oppofite fhould co-exift in
the fame perfon: fo great boldnefs with fuch deep
defign; fuch loftinefs of fpirit, with fuch fweet-
nefs of demeanour; fuch ardor of mind with fo
much fubtilty, and fuch profound diffimulation [*].

This prince, who had opened his mind to the
greateft defigns, and whofe natural ambition had
been encouraged and fortified by confidence in
Henry, did not abandon them after he was deprived
by death of fo great an ally. His penetrating eye
had difcovered the languid ftate of the Spanifh
monarchy, and he entertained a contempt for the

---

[*] In this fingular character there is not a trait unfup-
ported by the teftimony of contemporary hiftorians, who, all of
them, mention this prince with an admiration which could
not have been excited but by the moft amazing talents. See
Bellum Sabaudicum, &c. Alfonfo Lofcai; Battifta Nani, Siri
Memorie recondite; Le Mercure François, Hiftoire de la Regence de Marie de Medicis, &c. &c.

BOOK V.
1610.

Charles Emanuel endeavours to revive the league against the house of Austria.

counsels by which it was now governed [9]. He did not, therefore, yet despair of being able to extend his dominion over that fair territory which had awakened his ambition. Should he be able to reunite the scattered forces of the league, success would be certain: even if France should remain neutral, he hoped to maintain a contest with the Catholic king, both with glory and with advantage. He, therefore, endeavoured to revive a powerful combination against the house of Austria, whose power he represented as excessive and dangerous. He attempted to establish an alliance with France, by obtaining from the new regency a confirmation of the promise that had been made by Henry of giving his eldest daughter in marriage to the prince of Piedmont. But, after the death of the French monarch, all the maxims of his policy were subverted, and the schemes he had projected abandoned. The parliament of Paris, intimidated by the menaces of the duke of Epernon, who commanded the regiment of guards, committed an involuntary act of usurpation [10], by declaring Mary de Medicis sole regent of France during the minority of her son, an infant only in the ninth year of his age. This queen, uniting in her character the refinement of an Italian, with the feebleness of a woman, and the superstition of a good Catholic, was governed by

Character of Mary de Medicis, queen regent of France.

[9] Batt. Nani, lib. i. Siri, Memorie recondite, tom. iii. p. 242.

[10] The right of electing a regent had hitherto belonged to the general estates of the kingdom.

maxims directly contrary to those which had been adopted by the manly and liberal genius of Henry. She sought to establish her authority, by exciting jealousies among those who wished to subvert it; and armed her enemies against herself by concessions intended to conciliate their favor. She had obtained the regency without opposition, but not without envy. The princes of the blood, highly offended at the advancement of a stranger, though a queen of France, to a dignity to which they themselves made pretensions, retired from court, and were followed by their numerous adherents. It was the policy of Mary to raise up in opposition to her domestic enemies a faction among the rest of the nobility, and to acquire friends by a profusion of pensions, offices, and governments. The treasures which the late king had amassed in order to overawe his enemies, she employed in soothing resentment, and allaying discontent. All the assiduities, and entreaties, and remonstrances of Charles Emanuel to a princess, whose conduct was directed by these principles, were fruitless. Far from joining a confederacy against the house of Austria, she hearkened with pleasure to a proposal, that had been rejected by the late king, of a double marriage between the dauphin of France and the eldest infanta, and of the prince of Spain with Elizabeth, the eldest daughter of France. This project was first suggested to the court of Madrid by the Pope, who believed that by means of these intermarriages the house of Austria would acquire such an influence in the

BOOK V. councils of France, as would in the end exterminate that herefy which had fo obftinately refifted all other efforts.

Immediately after the death of Henry, the court of Madrid, having firft difcharged the duties of decorum by going into mourning, and by the ftrongeft profeffions of condolence, renewed to the regent queen the propofition of that double alliance, which had met with her fondeft approbation before that tragical event which led to the power with which fhe was now invefted. That event did not produce any change in the inclinations of Mary towards an union with Spain; on the contrary, if that union appeared formerly defirable, it now feemed neceffary, in order to fupport her authority, in fo much danger of being overturned by the turbulence of faction.

1611.
Project of intermarriages between the royal families of France and Spain.

In the month of April, 1611, the king of Spain and the queen regent of France formally expreffed their confent to the intermarriage of their fons and daughters by their refpective ambaffadors. On this occafion they alfo entered into a defenfive league, engaging to give each other mutual aid in cafe of either inteftine commotions or foreign invafion. The Spaniards endeavoured to improve and confolidate this union, by engaging the French in a league, offenfive as well as defenfive; but to this the queen, whofe utmoft ambition was to maintain, not to extend her power, refufed, in pofitive terms, to confent ".

" Siri, Mem. recond. tom. ii. p. 524. Mémoires de la Regence de Marie de Medicis. Hiftoire des derniers Troubles en France. Malingre.

Thus not only was the house of Austria delivered from the attacks of that confederacy which had been formed against her, but she acquired an accession of strength by an ascendant in the counsels of that kingdom which so lately appeared her most formidable enemy. In vain did Charles Emanuel, seconded by the importunities of the Pope [12], solicit the Venetians to join in an offensive and defensive league against the ambitious Spaniards. The conduct of France determined that of Venice. The senate, having learned the designs of Mary de Medicis, replied to the duke of Savoy, that it was indeed the interest of all the sovereign powers of Italy to maintain a good correspondence among themselves, and to provide for the common safety; but it was to be feared, they added, that such a league as had been proposed by his highness would serve only to excite the jealousy of Spain, a nation which, of all others, had the strongest motives to cultivate peace with all her neighbours. To his holiness, whom they suspected of a versatility of character, which might soon lead him to relapse into the views of that court, against which he now declaimed, they answered, that they could not be persuaded that his apprehensions concerning the views of Spain were well founded. But Charles Emanuel, not discouraged by the defection of both France and Venice, pursued a thousand schemes, and extended his intrigues all over Europe. He held a close correspondence with the discontented lords in France. He

---

[12] Winwood's Memoirs, vol. iii.

BOOK V.
1611.

inflamed the jealousy and the resentment of the Protestant princes of Germany. He proposed to king James a marriage of the prince of Wales with the princess of Savoy, and of the prince of Piedmont with a daughter of England. The mysterious character of Charles, in the opinion of some writers, renders it doubtful whether he believed he should, or desired he might, succeed in this project; and whether it was not his only object, by exciting a jealousy among the great Catholic powers, of his connexion with a Protestant prince, to dissolve the treaty of the double alliance between France and Spain, and to obtain the eldest daughter of one of these crowns in marriage to the prince of Piedmont ". Whatever

---

" The conjectures of these writers, which mark so strongly the general opinion that was entertained of the duke of Savoy, appear rather refined. I find in Chamberlayne's Letters, among Dr. Birch's Collection in the British Museum, that the duke, on this occasion, showed every mark of sincerity and earnestness. To the English ambassador at Turin, he was highly munificent. He consulted the temper of the English monarch, by sending, as his ambassador to the court of London, a person who concealed the most profound penetration under the mask of dissipation, mirth, and pleasantry. "Fabricio, says Chamberlayne, in his Letters, anno 1612, spends his time merrily with the king, and is never from him." — "The Savoyard ambassador, says he again, gives himself buono tempo, notwithstanding that the match grows cold, and frequents good company." — King James, as is well known, had a passion for hunting, and delighted in a collection of wild beasts. The duke of Savoy, who knew this, as

were his views, they were fruſtrated by the mean vanity of the Engliſh monarch, who concealed not from the world his opinion that any alliance, below that of a great king, was entirely unworthy of the heir apparent to the crown of England.

In the mean time, the Spaniſh troops that were on foot in the Milaneſe, thoſe of Savoy in Piedmont, and the French army, under Lesdiguieres, in Dauphiny, were ſubjects of various jealouſies and apprehenſions. The Spaniards ſeemed ready to pour into Piedmont, and the Savoyards threatened an incurſion into Milan; while an army, commanded by a Proteſtant general, excited an uneaſineſs in the queen regent herſelf, as well as other Catholic princes.

In this ſituation of affairs, the Pope interceded with Mary de Medicis to diſband the troops in Dauphiny, and importuned the king of Spain and the duke of Savoy to diſmiſs thoſe troops which were a ſource of ſo much anxiety and dread to France as well as to Italy. The influence of his holineſs eaſily prevailed on the queen to diſband

a mark of attention to his majeſty, ſent him a preſent of an ounce and a leopard. The animals were fetched from London to Theobald's, where the king reſided. The leopard had almoſt committed an unpardonable fault, for he fixed on a red deer's calf, nurſed up at Theobald's by a woman entertained for that purpoſe, and much ado there was to ſave the poor ſuckling. Theſe circumſtances, however trifling, are proofs that the duke of Savoy had ſtudied the diſpoſition of James, and that he wiſhed to gain his affections.

BOOK
V.
1611.

an army, commanded by a general in whose fidelity she did not repose entire confidence, but did not operate so quickly on the minds of Philip and Charles Emanuel. The former insisted that the duke of Savoy should lay down his arms first, and make satisfaction for his engagement with the late king of France. The latter alledged, on the contrary, that the weaker party ought to stand upon his guard when he seemed to be threatened by a more powerful neighbour ".

The satisfaction which Philip demanded of the duke of Savoy was, that he should ask pardon for his secret treaty with France to the prejudice of the crown of Spain; and that he should send one of his sons to Madrid, to remain there as a pledge of his father's fidelity.

The duke of Savoy obliged to make submissions to the king of Spain.

Charles Emanuel, deserted by all the world, was under a necessity of complying with these mortifying conditions. Prince Philibert, of Savoy, set out from Turin to Madrid on horseback; and, while he pursued this long and tedious journey, he had a foretaste of those severe mortifications which he was to experience after it should be accomplished; for he received not, in any of the Spanish towns through which he passed, the least mark of attention or respect from the king his uncle. Philip, however, received his nephew, at the first interview, with a decent civility: not a word, indeed, was said of the duke, but the kindest inquiries were made concerning the princes and princesses of Savoy. But the second

" Siri, Memorie recondite, tom. ii. p. 335.

audience was not so agreeable to this stranger: he was now to make satisfaction to the king of Spain in name of the duke of Savoy. The prince, accordingly, had framed an address to his Catholic majesty, sufficient, as he imagined, to satisfy the pride of Spain on the one hand, but, on the other, such as was not unworthy the independent dignity of the duke his father. This address he delivered with a noble grace, and with all those demonstrations of respect which can have place in an intercourse between sovereign princes. With this appearance of his nephew, the mild temper of the king was inclined to be contented; but in the air and manner of Philibert, as well as in the sentiments he expressed, there appeared to the Spanish ministers something not sufficiently humble and submissive; wherefore they drew up a new form of submission, breathing the supplications of a subject prostrate before his offended sovereign. The prince, yielding to necessity, rehearsed these haughty dictates with indignant reluctance.

Philip now ordered his troops to withdraw from the Milanese; but Charles Emanuel, provoked even to madness at the indignities with which the court of Madrid had insulted him in the person of his son, refused to disband his army in Piedmont. He threatened to disavow the submission that had been made in his name to the king of Spain, against whom he declaimed with indignation and rage; and, by various movements, indicated an intention of revenging his

BOOK V.

1612.
Contract of marriage between Elizabeth of France and the prince of Spain.

cause either on that monarch, or his new ally, the queen regent of France. These confederates he attempted by various arts to divide; but all his efforts were fruitless; and the united authority of the Pope, Philip III. and Mary de Medicis, compelled him at last to lay down his arms [15].

The storm that threatened the house of Austria being thus finally dispelled by its authority rather than power, Spain, pursuing the same pacific system, studied to maintain her dignity by the arts of policy, not the terrors of war. In the month of August, 1612, the duke of Pastrana was sent to Paris to conclude and confirm a matrimonial contract between Elizabeth of France and the prince of Spain; and, about the same time, the duke of Mayenne arrived in Madrid, in order to settle and ratify a treaty of marriage between young Lewis and the infanta Anne. The two princesses renounced every right of succession to any of the states of their native kingdoms; and their dowries were equal, being each five hundred thousand crowns. But these contracts were not performed till an interval had elapsed of more than three years [16].

Cotemporary writers relate, with a minute circumstantiality, the festivity and magnificence that was displayed by the courts of France and Spain on occasion of these intermarriages, and describe,

[15] History of the Reign of Lewis XIII. by Levassor, vol. i. anno 1611.
[16] Histoire de Louis XIII. durant la Regence de la Reine Marie de Medicis. Malingre.

PHILIP III. KING OF SPAIN.

with equal exactnefs, the ceremonies that conftituted and accompanied them. They obferve, with a fort of fatisfaction, that the year 1612, in which the parties were mutually betrothed, was juftly ftyled the year of magnificence. For this year, alfo, Matthias II. being raifed to the imperial throne in the ftead of his deceafed brother, Rhodolphus, all Germany, as well as France and Spain, refounded with the voice of gladnefs and exultation [17]. So naturally do men fympathize with the great, and fo fincere is their joy at their profperity! This difpofition fufficiently accounts for thofe copious details of anecdotes, circumftances, and facts, which we find in the journalifts of thofe times; but would not apologize for a recital of them in a narrative addreffed to another age. Such particulars, however, as ferve to paint characters and manners are interefting at all times, and, therefore, ought not to be wholly omitted.

When the duke of Mayenne took leave of the court of Madrid, before his return to Paris, he entreated the infanta to honor him with fome commiffion to the king his mafter. " Tell him, faid the infanta, that I am very impatient to fee him." This anfwer of the princefs overwhelmed her governefs, the countefs of Altamira, with fhame and confufion. " Ah, madam, cried this

---

[17] Hift. du Regne de Louis XIII. et des principaux Evenemens arrivés pendant ce Regne dans tous les Pays du Monde. Hiftoria de Don Felippe IV. por Don Gonçalo de Cefpedes, libro. i. capitulo 2. Memoires de la Regence de Marie de Medicis. Mercure François, 1612.

BOOK V.

1615.

lady, what will the king of France think when the duke shall report to him that you have so great a passion for marriage?" "You have taught me, replied the infanta, with great liveliness, that one must always speak the truth." After this frank declaration on the part of Anne, Lewis could do no less in return than express, in like manner, an impatience to see and to receive his bride. Accordingly, as soon as he was informed that the infanta had arrived in France [18], he sent a letter to her, by his favorite Luynes, fraught with expressions of respect and of love. The queen-regent also wrote an affectionate letter to her daughter-in-law. Anne replied to the young monarch's address, in a manner that could not offend the delicacy of even the countess of Altamira. Having first expressed great satisfaction in the accounts she had received of his majesty's health, she professed a desire of arriving at a place where she might have an opportunity of serving the queen, her mother, and where she would be freed from the languor of her present solitude [19].

---

[18] This did not come to pass until the month of November, 1615.

[19] Hist. du Regne de Louis XIII.

"Sennor,

"Mucho me he holgado con Luynes con las buenas nuevas, que me ha dado de la salud de V. M. yo vengo con ella, y muy deseosa de llegar donde pueda servir a mi madre. Y assi me doy mucha priessa a caminar por la solicitud que me have a bezar a V. M. la mano a quien Dios guarde como deseo. Bezo las manos a V. M. Anna."

The Arabian conquerors of Spain had introduced into that kingdom an hospitality, generosity, and refinement, unknown before in the West [10]. The court of Cordova was the most elegant and polite in the world; and thither generous spirits resorted from all parts of Europe. Together with the mechanical, the Saracens cultivated the liberal arts; and while an external magnificence appeared in their buildings, furniture, and dress, their poetry and music, confecrated to heroism and love, displayed an inward generosity and elegance of mind still more noble and affecting. Hence the Spanish nation possessed a taste for grandeur, a generosity of disposition, and a delicacy of sentiment, which in the period under review were unequalled, and which have not yet been exceeded in any other nation. Accordingly in that competition of courtesy and gallantry, which arose, on occasion of the intermarriages, the Spaniards far outshone the French. Not only did they exhibit greater splendor in their equipages, processions, and shows, but a more delicate taste, and a higher style appeared in their manners. The munificence of the grandees to the princess of Spain and the ladies of her court, to the young queen of France and her attendants, and also to the queen-regent, was unbounded. The French ambassador, in his way to Madrid,

BOOK V.
1612—15.
The gallantry and honor of the Spanish nation accounted for.

[10] A very amusing as well as philosophical account of the causes that formed this national character, is given by Mr. Richardson in his Dissertation on the Languages, Literature, and Manners of Eastern Nations.

received a sumptuous entertainment at the mansion of the prime minister of Spain. This entertainment was so contrived that it appeared to have been given, not by the duke, but at the expense of the inhabitants of the town of Lerma, transported with joy at the presence of a stranger so honorably distinguished. In Burgos, Segovia, Madrid, and other towns of Spain, in which the prince had occasion to appear, the citizens celebrated his nuptials with fireworks, illuminations, triumphal arches, balls, masquerades, musical and dramatical performances, and other ingenious diversions[21].

At this time, there did not appear in the Spanish dominions any symptoms of declining trade, or exhausted wealth. The face of the whole empire was gay and magnificent. But so expensive a display of loyalty was not approved by the duke of Ossuna, viceroy of Naples, a man of wit, whim, and fancy, and in every respect himself the most extravagant person subject to the crown of Spain. The men of rank in Sicily[22], with a strange mixture of obsequiousness and vanity, presented a petition to Ossuna, humbly praying that they might be permitted to solemnize the publication of the double marriage as well as the other subjects of the empire. They proposed, at the same time, to levy a tax upon themselves for this purpose. The duke greatly applauded

---

[21] Mercure François, 1612. Historia de Don Felippe IV. por Don Gonçalo de Cespedes, libro i. capitulo 2.
[22] The Titolati. Winwood's Memoirs, vol. iii. p. 377.

this design, which he encouraged, by contributing himself to its execution with equal frankness and liberality; but, after the money of the Sicilians was all put into one bank, the viceroy, in the plenitude of his transcendant power, gave orders that not one maravedi should be wasted in idle pomp and show; but that it should be distributed among certain poor virgins of honorable descent; adding withal, that, in his opinion, the money would be better employed in the multiplication, than in the solemnization of marriages. The subsequent conduct of this singular person will recal this anecdote to the mind of the reader, and incline him, perhaps, to conjecture that this judicious disposal of the Sicilian treasure, did not originate either in a disapprobation of waste, or in mere regard to the Sicilian damsels.

The Spaniards had now leisure to breathe after the toils of war; and the authority of the Spanish name being in some measure restored by the submission of the duke of Savoy, and an advantageous connexion with France, they endeavoured, for the present [11], to maintain it by policy, rather than to extend it by a hazardous appeal to arms. But the ambitious spirit of Charles Emanuel, incapable of rest, and impatient of disgrace, soon obliged them to quit that shade of ancient authority and renown, under which they attempted

The political schemes of Spain disordered by the restless ambition of the duke of Savoy.

[11] There are writers who affirm that at this time the Spanish ministers were so elated at the alliance with France, that they considered it as the sure forerunner of the reduction of the revolted provinces.

BOOK V.
1613.

to conceal the real state of Spain, and to prove its strength or its weakness in the field of battle. The duke of Savoy, being descended from the imperial house of the Paleologi, possessed ancient pretensions to the sovereignty of Montferrat, which was also claimed and enjoyed by the family of Gonzaga. In order to compose the differences which frequently arose from this contested claim, a marriage was concluded between Francis, duke of Mantua, and Margaret of Savoy; Charles Emanuel, in favor of this alliance, having resigned to his daughter and her children his right of succession to the marquisate in question. Francis died in the month of December, 1612, leaving behind him an only child, a daughter, in the fourth year of her age. Ferdinand, cardinal of Gonzaga, brother to the late duke, was, beyond all doubt, heir to the dutchy of Mantua; but the sovereignty of Montferrat, *The duke of Savoy revives his pretensions to the sovereignty of Montferrat.* which was not a fief-male, descended upon his niece, the young princess Maria. In these circumstances the duke of Savoy conceived the design of reviving his pretensions to that state. His right to the marquisate he did not consider as diminished, but rather strengthened by that of his grandchild; and the guardianship of this infant would give him an entire power over that inheritance, which he claimed in her name, as well as his own. And, that the cardinal might not derive any advantage over him, in the contest that was likely to ensue, by immediate succession, he had recourse to one of those stratagems of which his genius was so singularly fruitful. His daughter Margaret, the widow of the deceased duke of Mantua, as well as all his other children, returned the fondness of his parental affections with a tenderness and filial reverence that knew no bounds. This lady he easily persuaded to declare that she was pregnant; and soon after, he sent the prince Victor Amadeus to Mantua, on pretence of consoling his sister, but, in reality, in order to conduct her to Turin, if that could be accomplished, or to Milan, or to Montferrat. "It is not fit, said the prince of Piedmont to the court of Mantua, that a mournful widow should pass her days in a place where every thing around her renews her grief, by recalling to her imagination the object of her sorrow, nor is it decent that she should remain longer under the eye of a person jealous of the succession to Mantua. And whithersoever my sister goes, continued the prince, thither it is reasonable that the young princess should accompany her. Nature herself recommends children to the care of their parents: and, what nature unites by the dearest ties of affection, it would be impiety to separate." But the cardinal, well knowing the end of this discourse, replied, that it would be improper to remove the dutchess from Mantua, while she carried in her womb the important pledge of the happiness of the Mantuan state. "If the sight, said he, of my deceased brother's palace be afflicting to his widow, others are not wanting, whither she may retire with safety and, and where she may live with comfort."

In the mean time Charles Emanuel, the better to effect his designs, endeavoured to engage in his cause the influence and authority of the crown of Spain. The Spanish governor of Milan at this time was John Mendoza, marquis of Inoiosa, who had formerly signalized his valor in the military service of the duke of Savoy, and who had been rewarded with the marquisate of St. German. By this substantial mark of favor, and perhaps not less by those honors and assiduities with which he cultivated the friendship of Mendoza, Charles Emanuel had acquired an ascendant over his mind that seemed almost the effect of superior and invisible power. This man he persuaded to send the prince of Ascoli, accompanied by a numerous retinue, to Mantua, to demand the persons of the dutchess and her daughter in the name of the king of Spain; not doubting that, if they should once be brought to Milan, he would afterwards be able to find means of conducting them to Turin. But the cardinal refused to let the princesses go; a resolution in which he was confirmed and supported by the emperor, the queen-regent of France, and the republic of Venice[24]. At length, after an interval of three months, the dutchess Margaret, having declared that she was not pregnant, was allowed to return to her father's house; but all her tears could not obtain permission to take along with her her infant daughter. Ferdinand, having assumed the title

---

[24] Batt. Nani, lib. i. 1613. Siri, Mem. recond. tom. iii. Winwood's Memoirs, vol. iii.

and power of duke of Mantua, sent the bishop of Diocesarea to Milan to apologize for his disobedience to the orders of Spain, from a regard to the decree of the emperor, who had adjudged to him the tutelage of his niece; farther enjoining the prelate to pass on to Vercelli, to console Margaret who lived there, and at the same time to infinuate a proposal of a marriage between that princess and the cardinal duke, as the only means of quenching the flames of discord, and uniting the houses of Savoy and Gonzaga both by blood and affection.

The bishop, discharging his trust with fidelity and zeal, pressed the duke of Savoy to consent to an accommodation of differences. The duke discovered a readiness to converse on that subject, which inclined the Mantuan envoy at first to conclude that his embassy would not be fruitless. But Charles, still rising in his demands, in proportion to the importunity of the bishop, had nothing else in view than, by amusing this ecclesiastic with frequent conferences, to gain time for ripening a project as bold as any that had ever been conceived by any politician or hero. Before his eyes there lay the state of Montferrat, to which he had ancient pretensions, and which intersected and broke the strength of Piedmont, on one side extending itself even to the Alps, and on another stretching well nigh to Turin. This state, defended only by the lamentations and complaints of its present possessor, lay naked and exposed to the sudden attack of any hostile invader. The princes of Italy, enervated by luxury, would not eafily be awaked from that profound fleep into which they had been lulled by long habits of indolence, fubordination, and peace. The emperor, on that fide of the Alps, fcarcely poffeffed the fhadow of power. The kingdom of France was torn in pieces by inteftine difcord; and the power of Spain, though formidable, was diftant. The Milanefe, lately difarmed, was deftitute of military ftores and provifions; and, what was a great encouragement to Charles Emanuel, it was governed by his confident Mendoza, whofe mind he might regulate with his ufual addrefs; or, if he fhould prove unmanageable, which poffeffed not thofe mafterly powers which are requifite to act a fuccefsful part in new and difficult fituations. The deliberative genius of Spain would not act with an unufual celerity on an occafion, when a fear of drawing the French into Italy, would naturally recommend cautious circumfpection: or, if the perfonal hatred of the duke of Lerma fhould prevail in the breaft of that favorite, over reafons of ftate, before the hands of Inoiofa could be ftrengthened by a reinforcement from Spain, the power of Savoy might be eftablifhed in Montferrat. Of all confiderations, that which gave the duke of Savoy moft uneafinefs, was the vigilance of the Venetian fenate, to whom no revolution in their neighbourhood ever appeared an object of indifference. But he hoped that however they might interpofe their counfels, they would not haftily exchange the bleffings of peace for the calamities of war. On the whole, while diftant ftates were ignorant of his fchemes, and before the princes of Italy, involved in clouds of mutual jealoufy, diffidence, and doubt, would unite either in power or defign to oppofe him, he refolved to carry into Montferrat the thunder of his arms, and to anticipate refiftance by decifive conqueft and firm poffeffion.

Having fecretly affembled his troops, while the bifhop of Diocefarea yet waited for a definitive anfwer to the propofals he had made for reconciliation and peace, Charles Emanuel iffued forth from Vercelli in the filence of the night that followed the 22d day of April; and diftributing his army in three divifions, poured into Montferrat the terror and devaftation of war. There was not any thing in that marquifate capable of fuftaining his impetuous force; Cafal, the capital, in which the duke Vincenzo had planted a ftrong fortrefs, only excepted. And this alfo would have quickly fallen into his hands, if Gonzaga, duke of Nevers, who happened at that time to be in Italy, had not fuddenly thrown himfelf into it, with a fmall force which he haftily raifed on the coaft of Genoa. By garrifoning and fortifying fuch of the towns he had taken, as were moft important for their fituation and ftrength, he formed a chain of pofts which opened a communication between thofe rich and fertile countries that are extended along the courfes of the Tanarus and the Po: and in thefe he

BOOK V.
1613.

The duke of Savoy invades Montferrat.

hoped to maintain his army by contributions and plunder[25].

It was now the duke of Savoy's object to secure his conquests, and, for this purpose, he endeavoured either to appease those powers whom he well knew the violence of his conduct had offended, by submissive professions of respect, and insidious concessions; or, to divert their attacks from himself, by making them objects of jealousy to one another. The queen regent of France, being informed of the irruption of the Savoyards into Montferrat, was not untouched by the situation of her nephew the duke of Mantua. In the first fervor of passion she declared her resolution to support the house of Gonzaga, both with her influence and arms. Accordingly she immediately sent the dutchess of Nevers to Grenoble, to engage the marefchal Lefdiguieres, who commanded the troops on the confines of Savoy, speedily to march with a powerful army to check the progress of that prince in Montferrat, and to chastise his presumption. But Charles Emanuel wrote a letter full of respect to the Queen, and, in order to sooth the first transports of her resentment, offered to submit his pretensions to her arbitration, and to resign into her hands, in the mean time, the places he had taken in Montferrat, as a pledge of his deference to her authority and her justice. At the same time he instructed his partisans at the court of Paris, where he had

---

[25] Mercure François, 1613. Batt. Nan. Hist. lib. i. 1613. Hist. du Regne de Louis XIII.

found means of conciliating the good-will of the favorites, the marefchal and marchionefs D'Ancre, to reprefent to the queen the impolicy of trufting a great army in the hands of a Proteftant general; and the defperate imprudence of roufing the jealoufy, and inviting the refiftance of the king of Spain. The nuncio too, and the Spanifh ambaffador having, from obvious motives, urged the fame arguments, the queen determined to countermand the orders fhe had fent, or rather the application fhe had made to Lefdiguieres, and to employ in behalf of her nephew only her good offices at the court of Madrid ²⁴.

In order to divert the refentment of Spain, or to fufpend its effects, Charles Emanuel employed greater art than that which had managed the court of France, but with lefs fuccefs. He difpatched his confeffor to the governor of Milan, humbly to apologize for his invafion of Montferrat, without the knowledge and confent of the king of Spain. This meffenger was, foon after, followed by the prince of Piedmont, and the prince of Piedmont by multitudes of other ambaffadors in rapid fucceffion. Thefe were all of them charged with offers fo various and incompatible, that the mind of Inoiofa, diftracted and confounded amidft fo great a variety of views, knew not which to purfue, and remained in a ftate of inactivity and irrefolution. Thus the

²⁴ Batt. Nani, Hift. lib. i. 1613. Hiftoire du Connétable de Lefdiguieres, lib. viii. ch. 4 & 5. Siri, Memorie recondite, tom. iii. p. 92, 93.

BOOK V.
1613.

duke endeavoured to prevent a contest with his friend Mendoza in arms, by storming as it were the seat of his affections and passions, whence alone flow all the operations of war and of peace; and by making, in the language of the celebrated Nani, a war of wit upon his mind. But the ingenious subtilty of Charles Emanuel, not satisfied with preventing Inoiosa from acting at all, attempted to make him act in such a manner, as to advance the interests of Savoy in Italy, and wholly to ruin those of Spain. The stratagem by which he hoped to effect this bold design was specious. He proposed that the governor, in the name of the king of Spain, should, with his assistance take possession of the metropolis, the only place of considerable strength in Montferrat, but that every other part of that marquisate should be annexed to his own dominions. At the same time, that the authority of the Spanish monarch might be paramount over the whole province, he proposed farther, that the towns which he had taken, being garrisoned by Savoyards, should have the arms of Spain affixed to all their gates. But Mendoza, who wanted decision rather than penetration, was not ensnared by this insidious proposal. For he was aware, that should the Spaniards seize a part of Montferrat, while the pageantry of their name blazed over the whole, a jealousy would be excited among all the neighbouring powers, which the policy of Charles Emanuel, at a time when the Milanese were almost wholly disarmed, would use as an engine to subvert the Spanish power in Italy.

The deep alarm which the invasion of Montferrat spread throughout all the Italian states, was a severe mortification to the lofty spirit of Spain, as it implied a suspicion, that the power of that kingdom might not be sufficient to control the ambitious designs of the duke of Savoy. The Catholic king, reluctant to enter on war, endeavoured at first to subdue the turbulence of that prince with menaces and frowns; and, by the mere authority of Spain, to quiet the fears and restore the peace of Italy. The secretary Vargas was dispatched from Madrid to Milan, with orders to the governor to announce to Charles Emanuel, that it was the will of Philip that he should withdraw all his troops from Montferrat, and to threaten force in case of disobedience.

BOOK V.
1613.
The duke of Savoy's conduct a subject of mortification to Spain.

The Spanish ministers in Italy, in like manner, labored to maintain the authority of their nation by raising their language to the most majestic tone. The marquis of Inojosa encouraged the Italian princes to trust in the protection of the king of Spain, rejected with disdain the idea of admitting any associate with that monarch in composing the differences of Italy, and attempted by various artifices to prevent Cosmo, duke of Tuscany, from sending assistance to his relation the duke of Mantua. Don Alphonso de la Queva, the Spanish ambassador at Venice, assured the senate, "that, without any noise or trouble, Charles Emanuel should be punished, and Ferdinand restored to his rightful inheritance; that there was no reason to be fearful of any event, or

BOOK V.
1613.

Artifices of the duke of Savoy.

to dread the turbulent ambition of any prince, while the undiminished goodness and power of the great potentate whom he served, would not suffer any innovation in Italy, nor any disturbance of that peace which was so happily enjoyed under his authority [27]."

But, although he was thus threatened by Spain, although the emperor denounced the imperial ban, and his adversary was directed and supported by the counsels and wealth of Florence and of Venice; yet the duke of Savoy remained undaunted, and steadily pursued his object by policy and arms. In order to alarm the jealousy of Spain, he threatened to call to his aid the troops of France. When the Pope exhorted him to peace, he protested that he would overwhelm Italy with an inundation of heretics. He dismissed the Venetian ambassador with orders to inform the senate, that if they should persist in affording succour to the duke of Mantua, he would cover the Adriatic with Turkish pirates. But while he thus studied to work on the fears of his adversaries, he neglected not to use any means by which he might conciliate their favor. He offered to deposite in the hands of the Spaniards his rights to Montferrat, and the places he possessed in that province, on condition that the princess Mary should be brought to Milan, and remain there along with her mother, a proposition by which he intended at once to show his own deference to the king of Spain, and to sow the seeds of

[27] Batt. Nani, Hist. lib. i. 1613.

jealoufy between that monarch and the duke of Mantua. Nor was his defign difappointed; for to the meafure which he had propofed the governor of Milan cordially agreed. But Ferdinand utterly rejected it, with bitter complaints againſt Inoiofa, who prefumed, without his knowledge, to difpofe of the blood of Gonzaga.

Charles Emanuel, having thus thrown the blame of difobedience to the will of Spain on Ferdinand endeavoured to improve the advantage he had gained by fending Victor Amadeus to reprefent to the court of Madrid, how much the duke, his father, inclined to do what fhould be agreeable to their defire. Of this, he faid, he had given a fignal proof, by committing into their hands the heir of his dominions as a pledge of the obedience of his whole houfe.

On the ftrength of all this merit with the court of Spain, the duke, having haftily thrown a garrifon of four hundred men into Ponteftura, under the colors of Spain, marched onward with his army to Nizza de la Paglia, and began to batter it from three different places. This town, which was but weakly fortified, was, however, effectually defended by the fidelity and valor of its governor, Manfrino Caftiglione, who, by rigorous difcipline, and by frequent fallies, gained time for its relief.

The governor of Milan, who had by this time reinforced his army, roufed by a general clamor, and conftrained by the orders of Spain, refolved effectually to curb the troublefome ambition of

The governor of Milan checks the ambition of the duke of Savoy.

his friend, the duke of Savoy. He sent the prince of Afcoli with five thoufand men to join the prince Vincenzo, who waited their arrival with three thoufand more in the fervice of the duke of Mantua. The flownefs of Afcoli's march feemed to indicate an intention to hearken to a propofition that had been made for a fufpenfion of arms; but the Mantuans urging him to advance without delay, the united army at laft approached to Nice. The Savoyards, no longer doubting the intention of Inoiofa to raife the fiege, on pretence of refpect to the enfigns of Spain, retreated in good order without being purfued. The duke of Savoy now offered to furrender all that he poffeffed in Montferrat, and peace was made on this condition. But this pacification did not remove the apprehenfions of the princes of Italy; for the duke of Savoy had uniformly contended for an act of oblivion in favor of count St. George, and other fubjects of Mantua, who had taken up arms to fupport his claim to Montferrat; and the duke of Mantua, on the other hand, had as conftantly infifted on their punifhment, and alfo on reparation of damages.

Thefe mutual pretenfions appeared to the fagacity of the Italian ftates the embers of a war, ready to flame out with increafed fury. There was evidently a collufion, they thought, between Charles Emanuel and the marquis of Inoiofa, fome fecret defign which would foon tranfpire: for though the duke evacuated the towns he had taken, he did not difmifs, but, on the contrary, reinforced his troops; and the governor, though he seemed to have accomplished the design of his military preparations, remained still in arms. Their conjectures were not without foundation; for Ferdinand would not pardon the partisans of a competitor for the sovereignty of any part of his dominions, and still insisted on reparation of damages. And Charles published to the whole world, in writing as well as discourse, that the governor promised him that no farther mention should be made of damages, and that the exiles of Montferrat should be restored to their estates, and all the privileges of other subjects; a condition from which he was determined never to depart.

In this contest the marquis of Inoiosa took a decided part in favor of Savoy, and in the most haughty strain threatened Ferdinand with all the rage of war, if he should refuse to agree to the terms which he had prescribed. He instantly dispatched Antonio Pimentelli, general of the Milanese light-horse, to bring the young princess from Mantua to Milan. This, Pimentelli would have done, even by force, if, having been conducted into the apartments of the child, he had not been convinced, that, from illness, she was not in a condition in which she could be removed. Upon this the duke of Mantua sent an envoy to Madrid with his excuse for not giving up the princess, and another to France to solicit the good offices of the queen-regent with the Spanish monarch, which she readily granted. The ministers

BOOK V.
1613.

The award of Spain respecting the dispute concerning Montferrat.

BOOK
V.
1613.

of Spain at laſt declared the will of Philip to be, " That the differences between the dukes of Savoy and Mantua concerning reparation of damages, and the pardon of the rebels, ſhould be referred to the arbitration of the pope, the emperor, and himſelf; that the princeſs Mary ſhould be brought to Milan; that the dutcheſs Margaret ſhould marry Ferdinand; and that both dukes ſhould diſarm their forces, thoſe of the king being ſufficient to execute whatever ſhould be neceſſary for relieving the oppreſſed, and ſubduing the obſtinate."

The marquis of Inoioſa, at the ſame time that he ſent Pimentelli to Mantua, in order to preſerve the appearance of impartiality, diſpatched Sancho de Luna, governor of the caſtle of Milan, to Turin, to ſignify to the duke of Savoy that he muſt lay down his arms. Charles was now ſenſible that his conteſt with Ferdinand had no other tendency than to reduce himſelf, as well as that prince, under the dominion of Spain: unwilling, therefore, to diſband his army, the only pledge of his ſovereign independency, he immediately ſet about framing excuſes, and inventing ſtratagems. He repreſented to the Spaniſh miniſters at Milan, that in the province of Dauphiny there was an army, commanded by the mareſchal Leſdiguieres, which waited only the queen-regent's orders to pour into Piedmont; it was, therefore, neceſſary for him to ſtand on his guard. Inſtead of diſbanding, he inſiſted on leave to reinforce his army; and, as a pledge of his fidelity

to

to the king, and his difpofition towards peace, he defired that fome Spanifh regiments might be quartered in Piedmont. This, he faid, would be doing him an effential fervice; becaufe, his country being defended by the arms of Spain, he would be at liberty to march whitherfoever the neceffity of his affairs fhould call him. But the Spaniards were by this time too well acquainted with the artifices of Charles to fall eafily into his fnares. They perceived that it was his aim to excite the jealoufy of France, and to produce a rupture between that kingdom and Spain. He doubted not, that if he could draw the Spanifh troops into Piedmont, he would eafily prevail on the marefchal Lefdiguieres to crofs the Alps in order to expel them. Hoftilities, once begun, would not ceafe with the retreat of the Spaniards into their own dominions; and, amidft the contentions of his enemies, he might find fome means of his own aggrandizement. Such was the refined project of the duke of Savoy!

About this time, the fecretary Vargas, in his return to Spain, paffing by Turin, demanded of the duke a categorical anfwer to the queftion, whether he would difband his troops or no? Charles hefitated not a moment to fhow his refpect to the Catholic king by anfwering in the affirmative. He immediately made a fhow of difbanding his army in the prefence of the Spanifh minifter; but he took care to keep on foot his foreign troops, having difmiffed only his militia, which might be quickly re-affembled.

BOOK V.
1614.
Effect of the award of Spain on the minds of the dukes of Savoy and Mantua.

The determination of the Catholic king, and his peremptory tone respecting Montferrat, filled Ferdinand with resentment, and Charles with indignation. Nevertheless, Ferdinand declared that he was willing to accept all the other terms prescribed by the court of Madrid, provided they would not insist that the young princess should be carried to Mantua; a condition to which they agreed without difficulty. But Charles Emanuel, to all the foreign ministers residing at his court, poured forth the bitterest invectives against the pride of Spain, which he represented as a just ground of general apprehension. " If the Spanish monarch, said he, shall be suffered to impose his imperious commands upon me; the princes of Italy, deluded by treaties, or subdued by arms, will thenceforth lie at his feet, fearing punishment and asking pardon. If the present juncture shall prove the servility of our dispositions, we shall quickly be stripped of the shadow of that power of which we wanted wisdom to preserve the reality."

Reception of the prince of Piedmont at the court of Madrid.

The indignation of the duke was still more inflamed when the prince of Piedmont gave him an account of his treatment at Madrid. He had no sooner arrived in Catalonia than he received an order to remain in that province, until it should be known whether his father would yield obedience to the orders of the king; and, if he was at last received at court, it was with coldness and with scorn. The prime minister spoke of the duke of Savoy with disdain and with hatred, and threatened the severest chastisement if he should not submit, without reserve to the authority of his Catholic majesty.

This narrative of his son fixed the resolution of Charles. He instantly declared his firm purpose to maintain his independence with his sword, or to perish in the attempt. Accordingly he levied fresh troops, and exerted every nerve again to form a confederacy against that imperious race, whose incurable ambition still aimed at the sovereignty of Europe [18]. He still kept up a close correspondence with the prince of Condé and the discontented lords in France, hoping to find employment for the arms of Philip in supporting the authority of Mary de Medicis. And in spite of the positive orders of the queen-regent, Lesdiguieres found means to pass several thousands of French soldiers from Dauphiny into Piedmont, who greatly reinforced the Savoyard army [19].

Charles also insinuated himself, on this occasion, into the confidence of Maurice, prince of Orange, and engaged in his service some troops under count John of Nassau. But, what encouraged him most, was the hope of assistance from the republic of Venice, which, he doubted not, would readily unite their arms with his for the purpose of removing from their confines, or at least of humbling the power of an imperious

BOOK V.
1614.

Courageous resolution of Charles Emanuel duke of Savoy.

---

[18] Mercure François, 1614. Siri, Memor. recon. tom. iii. p. 222. Mémoires de la Régence de Marie de Medicis. Batr. Nan. lib. i. 1614.

[19] Histoire du Connétable de Lesdiguieres, lib. viii.

neighbour. He therefore difpatched to Venice John James Pifcina, a man of diftinguifhed abilities and powerful eloquence, to propofe to the fenate a league, defenfive and offenfive, for the prefervation, or rather, the recovery of the liberties of Italy. Pifcina painted, in glowing colors, the dependent condition of the Italian princes, and the inordinate ambition of the court of Spain. He offered to refer to their arbitration the difference between the houfes of Savoy and Gonzaga; implored their aid and their advice; declaring, at the fame time, that whatever counfels other ftates fhould follow, the duke of Savoy was determined to die with his fword in his hand, rather than to live in fubjection to the tyranny of any power on earth.

The Venetians admired the noble fpirit of the duke, and found the higheft fatisfaction in reflecting that the natural guardian of Italy [10] poffeffed all that courage and forefight which that important character required. Neverthelefs, being unwilling to involve themfelves in war, while there was a ray of hope that the liberty of Italy might be united with its peace, they declined to interfere in the difpute concerning Montferrat, as that matter, they faid, had already been referred to the arbitration of the emperor and the king of Spain. They advifed Charles to accommodate all differences with the duke of Mantua, and to yield to the

---

[10] "Al cui Senno, al cui Petto, alla cui Deftra
Commife il Ciel la Cura
Delle Italiche Mura."

superior power of Spain whatever satisfaction might not be unbecoming the dignity of a sovereign prince. At the same time they assured him of their affection and good offices, and that they would not remain idle spectators of injustice and oppression.

Faithful to their promise, the Venetian senate exerted their influence in all the courts of Europe in favor of the duke of Savoy. To the Spanish ministers, particularly, both at Madrid and Milan, they represented the calamities and the dangers of war, and expatiated on the advantages of concord and peace. But the deep wound which the boldness of the duke of Savoy had given to the pride of Spain was fomented by lenitives, and to be cured only by the sharp remedies of fire and sword. The Spaniards provoked, not pacified, by the intercession of the Venetians in behalf of Charles Emanuel, proudly rejected every condition that might wear the complexion of treating that prince on a footing of equality, or even of honoring him with a capitulation.

Inoiosa, although his own inclinations were wholly towards peace, in obedience to the positive and reiterated commands of the court of Madrid, sent an ambassador to Turin with orders to Charles to lay down his arms; to require a promise, in writing, that he would not molest the territories of the duke of Mantua; and to inform the duke, at the same time, that the king of Spain would not be bound by any conditions but such

The duke of Savoy favored by the Venetian senate.

BOOK V.
1614.

as should be dictated by his own moderation. The duke of Savoy listened to this message with a serene countenance, and without making any reply; but he ordered the ambassador instantly to leave his dominions; and, tearing from his neck the ensign of the Golden Fleece, he returned it into the hands of that minister, desiring him to deliver it to the king, and to tell him that he scorned to wear a badge of honor conferred by a prince who threatened him with chains. The duke hastened to Asti to collect his forces[11].

The governor of Milan takes the field against the duke of Savoy.

Inoiosa, whose army, lately reinforced with troops from Spain, consisted of thirty thousand foot and three thousand horse, crossed the Sesia, and took up his quarters at Caresana, not far from Vercelli, in the hope that Charles would humble himself before so great a military force, and yield to the renown of the Spanish arms. But the duke, with an army in numbers greatly inferior to that of Inoiosa, passing over to the other side of the Sesia, let loose on the Milanese all the rage of war; and, having surprised and burned several towns and villages, returned within his own confines with prisoners, plunder, and troops inspirited by success. The Spaniards seeing the Milanese thus invaded, and knowing that it was naked and exposed to the frequent attacks of their vigilant and enterprising enemy, having set fire to Caresana and La Motta, abandoned

[11] Mercure François, 1614. Batt. Nan. lib. i. 1614.

their pofts in Piedmont, and retired within their own territories.

The governor of Milan, in order to make up, in fome meafure, the lofs and difadvantage he had fuffered in this conteft with the duke of Savoy, encamped near Vercelli to cover the building of a fortrefs within the Spanifh bounds, but fo advantageoufly fituated as to protect the Milanefe by fhutting up a paffage through which it was open to hoftile invafion, and at the fame time to curb the power of the Savoyards in the adjacent quarter of Piedmont. This fortrefs was a mile in circuit, and, in honor of the duke of Lerma, called Fort Sandoval. The Spaniards had long meditated this defign, but hitherto deferred its execution, being unwilling to excite any jealoufies in the princes and ftates of Italy. In this undertaking feveral weeks were fpent; mean while the feafon elapfed that was fitteft for action.

The rage of the Spaniards againft the duke of Savoy.

When the news of the ravages committed by the duke of Savoy in the Milanefe reached Madrid, the Spanifh minifters were aftonifhed at his boldnefs, and being unaccuftomed to refiftance in Italy, were inflamed with the higheft degree of refentment. They vowed his deftruction, execrated his name, and reproaching the governor of Milan with ignorance, or want of fpirit, excited him to revenge the difhonor that had been done to the territories of Spain, and to the royal ftandard. The refentment of Spain was farther vented in a manifefto, devolving to king Philip all the eftates of Charles Emanuel which were fiefs of

Milan; and the imperial ambaffador [12] denounced againft Charles the ban of the empire, if he fhould not inftantly difband his army [13].

Againft thofe attacks of the pen, Charles Emanuel defended himfelf with the fame weapon. That none of his eftates were fiefs of Milan, he proved from the records of hiftory. To his imperial majefty he wrote a refpectful letter, giving an elaborate and circumftantial detail of the reafons he had to be diffatisfied with the conduct of Spain, of the ravages of the Spanifh troops, and the neceffity he was under of keeping up a force to oppofe them. In conclufion, he entreated the emperor to revoke the interdict he had iffued againft him; and farther, that he would employ his influence with the king of Spain, in order to engage him to difband his troops [14]. The other Spanifh minifters in Italy, perceiving that the lofty fpirit of Charles Emanuel was ftill unbroken, complained of the remiffnefs of Inoiofa, and expreffed to that commander a fufpicion that the Spanifh arms had loft their character of invincible [15]. In order to retrieve their reputation, they fent a powerful naval force, part of a fleet which had been fitted out to watch the motions of the Turks, to make a defcent on the coaft of Piedmont.

[12] At Milan.   [13] Batt. Nan. Hift. lib. i. 1614.
[14] Hiftoire du Regne de Louis XIII. Roy de France, et des principaux Evenemens arrivés pendant ce Regne dans tous les Pays du Monde. Merc. François.
[15] Batt. Nan. lib. i. 1614.

The marquis de Croix, who commanded this armament, finding that he had not a force sufficient to take Nice, turned his arms against Oneglia, a maritime town of Savoy, environed by the confines of Genoa, except where it is separated from Piedmont by the Appennine mountains. Disembarking his troops on the territories of the Genoese, he placed within their bounds his battering cannon, which played upon Oneglia with success. To this place Charles Emanuel could not send any succours, without the consent of Genoa, which was refused. This act of hostility he revenged by reducing Zuccarello, a fief of the empire, under the protection of that republic. Oneglia was defended five days, by the valor of the marquis of Dogliani. Having surrendered this town on honorable terms, this commander brought a part of the garrison into Marro, a castle situated on a rock, a little more inland, and which commands some vallies full of villages. This fortress was also soon after reduced by the Spanish forces, increased to the number of five thousand, by the arrival of several gallies from Sicily.

The governor of Milan, urged by the reproaches and importunities of his countrymen, in order to support this naval expedition, put his army in motion, though weakened by sickness, and afflicted in their march, by those excessive rains which at that season overflowed all the country. Having crossed the river Tanarus, not without a gallant opposition from the duke of Savoy, he found himself in a situation full of embarrassment

marginal note: BOOK V. 1614. Oneglia taken by the Spaniards.

BOOK V.
1614.

for the advanced feafon did not admit of the fiege of Afti, and to canton his troops in the open country, would expofe them a prey to the vigilance and rapid movements of Charles Emanuel. He, therefore, judged it prudent to retire to the country about Alexandria.

Treaty of peace between the Spaniards and duke of Savoy.

In the fpring following, the hoftile armies were reinforced, and on both fides great preparations made for war. But in the city of Afti, and prefence of Charles Emanuel, a treaty was framed by Julius Savelli, nuncio at Milan, and the marquis of Rambouillet, ambaffador extraordinary in Italy from France, the chief articles of which were, that the duke of Savoy fhould difband his troops, keeping on foot only his ufual garrifons; that within fifteen or twenty days after, Inoiofa fhould alfo difband his army, and give his word to the pope and the king of France, that he would not commit any act of hoftility againft the duke of Savoy; that the prifoners and places taken on either fide fhould be mutually reftored; that the jewels and dowry of Margaret fhould be returned; and that an act of indemnity and oblivion fhould he paffed in favor of fuch fubjects of Montferrat, as had taken up arms in oppofition to the duke of Mantua. Thefe conditions were not altogether fatisfactory to Charles Emanuel; neverthelefs, having in vain endeavoured to roufe other powers to arms againft Spain, and being defirous of conciliating the favor of the pope and France, who offered to guarantee the treaty they propofed, he declared his readinefs to accept them. It is alledged by some writers, that this prince would not have agreed to this treaty, while he had no other enemy to contend with than Inoiosa, if he had not imagined that it would be rejected by the Spanish ministers. If this was his conjecture, he was not deceived; for when Rambouillet and Savelli presented it to the governor of Milan, in full confidence that he would sign it, he told them that he was deprived of all power of making peace with the duke of Savoy, by a late order from Madrid.

The resolution of the Spaniards to maintain the predominancy of their power over the princes of Italy was heightened and confirmed by the success of their arms in Germany.

Prince Maurice, assisted by troops from France and England, on the first of September 1610, made himself master of Juliers, which, with all its dependencies, immediately submitted to the marquis of Brandenburgh, and the count Palatine of Neuburgh, known at that time by the title of the princes in possession. These princes lived upwards of two years in the same castle, and governed the states of Cleves and Juliers by their joint authority. But having quarelled at last, as might have been expected, they broke through the agreement that every thing should be done in concert, and issued edicts, not conjointly, but separately. Their mutual friends, in order to heal this rupture, advised them to cement a friendship by marriage [u]. But this advice, widened

[u] Intérêts des Princes, par Monsieur de Rohan, part. i. disc. iv.

the difference it was designed to compose. For the prince of Neuburgh, having, in consequence of this counsel, gone to demand the daughter of Brandenburgh in marriage, at a feast, when his blood was warm, and his spirits high with wine, let fall some expressions, which so exasperated the elector that he gave him a box on the ear. This effectually cured the young suitor's passion for his daughter. Henceforth the princes in possession became avowed enemies, and thought of nothing but fortifying themselves against each other by strong-holds, troops, and allies. The count Palatine, by various acts of obedience, courted the favor of the emperor; and, in order to conciliate that of the Catholic league, the prince of Neuburgh married the sister of the duke of Bavaria, and the elector of Cologne. The marquis of Brandenburgh, on the other hand, called to his aid the military power of the states general of the United Provinces. It is probable, that when this infant republic consented to employ its arms in defence of Brandenburgh, it apprehended not any opposition from those of Spain. That monarchy, about five years before, had betrayed its inability to prosecute war, by its eagerness for peace. Since that time, it had exhibited a striking token of improvidence and languor, when it beheld without concern, at least without any exertion, the mighty preparations of Henry the Great; and the duke of Savoy had insulted it in Italy, as yet with impunity. Prince Maurice, therefore, without any apprehension of resistance from the

Spaniards, on pretence of carrying relief to the marquis of Brandenburgh, prepared to extend the boundaries of the United Provinces by new conquests in the dutchies of Cleves and Juliers. Having gained the governor of the castle of Juliers, he poured into that fortress a strong Dutch garrison, without opposition. He afterwards came to fort Schenck with an army of eighteen thousand men; and penetrating into Germany, took Emmerick on the Rhine, where he placed a garrison, and many other places in the dutchy of Cleves, and the county of La Marck.

The accession of the states of Cleves and Juliers, to those of the United Provinces, would, in the issue, have extended the dominion of that republic over all the Austrian Netherlands, had not the rapidity of prince Maurice's conquests received a check from the judicious and rapid movements of the marquis of Spinola. This penetrating genius, who had strenuously supported the pacific counsels of Prince Albert at the court of Madrid, now perceived the necessity of having recourse to arms. He convinced the archduke Albert, and also the ministers of Spain, that the present was the proper time to oppose the views of that youthful state, whose successful struggle with the power of Spain had inspired ideas of ambition and new conquests. It was better, he said, at this juncture, to commit their cause to the fortune of war, and to contend for what remained of their sovereignty in arms, than to remain inactive until the power of the revolted

BOOK V.
1614.
Ambition of the United States.

Prince Maurice opposed by the Marquis of Spinola.

BOOK V.
1614.

Provinces, in the Low Countries, fhould be irrefiftible. On pretence of reftoring the fupremacy of the emperor and the pope over the Proteftants of Aix la Chapelle, who had depofed the Catholic magiftrates of that city, and banifhed the Jefuits and Romifh priefts, Spinola, affembled an army of thirty thoufand men, and provided a great train of artillery. By fecrecy and celerity he furprifed Aix la Chapelle, where he re-eftablifhed the papal jurifdiction and imperial power. Thence he bent his courfe to the north-eaft, and by this movement feemed to indicate an intention of laying fiege to Juliers. But, wheeling fuddenly about, he croffed the Rhine two leagues below Cologne, and, joining the troops of Neuburgh, entered Molfheim, fell down the Rhine, reduced Orfoy, and proceeded onward to Wefel, which he invefted with part of his forces. The inhabitants of this place, by a conftant and heavy fire, repulfed the affailants with great flaughter. But Spinola, having brought up his whole army, formed his intrenchments with fo much judgment, that his troops, covered from the fire of the enemy, made their approaches with celerity and with fafety. And, having planted three batteries of eight cannons, he kept up fo hot a fire, that within lefs than two hours, one of the city-gates, and all that could oppofe an entrance by that way, was reduced to afhes. The befieged, underftanding that prince, Maurice and the marquis of Brandenburgh were coming to their relief, determined to make a vigorous refiftance. But the women mounting the walls with their children in their arms, with tears

Siege of Wefel.

and cries entreated them to furrender. The men, melted by the fuppliant voices of their wives and fcreaming infants, fent deputies to Spinola to afk a favorable capitulation. This was readily granted: it was ftipulated on the one fide, that no change fhould be introduced in the religion or government of the city; that the military officers of Brandenburgh fhould march out of the city with their baggage, arms, and warlike ftores; and that the citizens fhould have liberty to retire and fettle wherever they pleafed. On the other hand, Spinola only demanded that he fhould be allowed to introduce into Wefel a garrifon of a thoufand men, there to remain until the Dutch garrifon fhould be withdrawn from Juliers. As foon as he entered this place he began to ftrengthen its fortifications, and by all means to fecure its poffeffion. He built three hundred barracks near the walls, and obliged the inhabitants to furnifh beds and other neceffary furniture. He alfo increafed the garrifon of Wefel with two thoufand foot, and three hundred horfe, under the command of Velafco. The inhabitants in a ftrong remonftrance reprefented to Spinola, that, according to the terms of capitulation, he was to introduce a garrifon of one thoufand men. Spinola fternly replied, that it was indeed agreed that he fhould bring into Wefel one thoufand men; but that he had never promifed that he would at no time increafe their number [17]. Having obliged the

[17] Intérêts des Princes par M. de Rohan, partie ii. difcours v. Hiftoire du Règne de Louis XIII, et des principaux événemens, &c.

BOOK V.
1614.

inhabitants of Duyſburgh, a city between Weſel and Duſſeldorp, to admit a ſtrong garriſon, he paſſed the Rhine, and approached ſo near the camp of Maurice that the centinels of the oppoſite armies frequently converſed, and ſometimes drank together. The prince of Orange ſent a meſſenger to Spinola, to know in what prince's name he entered the States of Cleves and Juliers. Spinola anſwered, by putting a ſimilar queſtion to the prince.

Theſe illuſtrious antagoniſts lay near to one another for a conſiderable time; but neither found an opportunity of attacking the other with advantage. And, without breaking the truce, or incurring the uſual calamities of war, they had fallen on a very convenient method of making conqueſts, by a kind of tacit compact, to divide between them the ſtates they pretended to protect. The United Provinces, alarmed at the ſucceſs, and apprehenſive of the future enterpriſes of Spinola, at laſt engaged France, England, and certain Proteſtant princes in Germany to mediate a reconciliation between the princes in poſſeſſion. A conference was held for this purpoſe at Santhen, a town which in this quarrel had remained neutral, but without effect. The articles of agreement propoſed by the mediators of peace, though they would in all probability have been accepted by Brandenburgh and Neuburgh, were only a ſubject of cavil to both Maurice and Spinola, who ſought not to compoſe the differences of theſe princes, but to fix themſelves in the places they had taken. Thus ended the ſingular campaign, which

Convenient method of making conqueſts.

PHILIP III. KING OF SPAIN.

which is not diftinguifhed by bloody battles and splendid victories; but whofe origin and iffue convey important political inftruction. For thence it appears that conceffions to a hoftile people naturally invite them to repeat their attacks; that the only proper time for a nation to make peace, is when the enemy defires it; and that no ftate can admit within its bounds the arms of a fuperior power, without endangering its own independence.

A little good fortune is fufficient to revive the projects of mortified ambition. The court of Madrid elated by the fuccefsful career of Spinola in Germany, felt their refentment more and more inflamed againft that daring prince who firft expofed the Spanifh weaknefs in Italy; and not lefs againft his feeble opponent the marquis of Inoiofa. A letter was intercepted from the king of Spain to the governor of Milan, in which he upbraided him with the remiffnefs of his former conduct, and gave orders from that inftant to make an irruption into Piedmont, before the duke of Savoy, or any others of the enemies of the monarchy, could collect their forces, difperfed in winter-quarters, to oppofe him. The governor, who had received repeated orders to the fame purpofe, as foon as the feafon of action arrived, took the field at the head of an army of thirty thoufand men. To this formidable body of veteran Spaniards the duke of Savoy oppofed an army of feventeen thoufand men, French, Swifs, and Savoyards, and thofe noble efforts of courage

The fuccefs of the Spaniards in Germany inflames their refentment and ambition.

Duke of Savoy takes the field againft the governor of Milan.

and conduct with which he was wont to encounter danger, and to raife himfelf above misfortune. The conteft which enfued proved how much the fuccefs of an army depends on the genius of one man ; and how vain are the greateft military preparations , if they are committed to the conduct of an unfkilful commander.

The firft movements of the Spaniards, in the prefent campaign, indicated an intention of furprifing Cortemiglia, the poffeffion of which would lay open to their incurfions the ftates of Piedmont on the fide of Afti, Seve, and Canelli. Into this place, therefore, Charles Emanuel immediately threw three regiments of French, and eight hundred Swifs, under the command of the count of St. George. The duke himfelf, haftening from Turin with feven thoufand men, came up with the marquis of Mantua, in his route to Cortemiglia, at the head of five or fix thoufand, at Biftagno, a fortrefs of Montferrat, fituated upon a height, commanding a highway from the fea to the confines of Milan. The thick and folid walls of Biftagno, and the frequent and bold fallies of the garrifon, rendered all the efforts of the duke of Savoy to reduce it under his power fruitlefs. In the hurry of his march he had not been able to bring up to this place more than two fmall cannons. He attempted therefore to fcale the walls, and attack the garrifon fword in hand. He was perfevering in this defperate and mad attempt, when he was informed that Inoiofa was on his march for the relief of Biftagno.

at the head of a powerful army. He therefore immediately raised the siege, retreated in good order to Canelli[18], and thence to Asti, having perceived that thither the Spaniards bent their course. This place, before the arrival of the duke, was garrisoned with four thousand foot, and a considerable number of cavalry, under the command of prince Thomas. Here the whole forces of Charles Emanuel were now collected; and the issue of the siege of Asti, was likely to decide the fate of the house of Savoy. But the city being of large extent, and the walls in many places infirm, the duke determined to meet the enemy at the river Versa, on the banks of which Inoiosa appeared with an army of twenty-four thousand men. The rest of his forces he had thrown into St. Damiano and Ulpiano[19], towns of Montferrat, the first not far from Asti, and the second on the verge of Turin. The duke of Savoy, with fifteen thousand foot, and fifteen hundred horse, opposed the passage of the Spaniards over the Versa in vain. And Inoiosa, having crossed this river with his whole army, endeavoured to gain the heights of a hilly tract which stretched in a winding course to Asti. This station he hastened to occupy, that he might thence be enabled not only to cut off the duke's retreat to that city, but to drive him out of the adjacent plain. But Charles, having penetrated his design, immediately fell back to two posts in that strong ground,

[18] Hist. du Regne de Louis XIII.
[19] Batt. Nan. Hist. della Republica Veneta, lib. i. 1615.

BOOK V.
1615.

Engagement between the duke of Savoy and the Spaniards under the marquis of Spinola.

which he had already slightly fenced by small trenches. These posts he committed to his French and Swiss troops, forming together about two-thirds of his army, with some pieces of cannon. The Savoyard infantry he reserved to act as necessity might require, and with the cavalry he flanked his two posts in a plain immediately below them. The firm order, and deliberate valor of the Spanish troops sustaining the furious assaults of the Savoyard cavalry, and pressing up the hill which was occupied by the French, gained at last an eminence, the possession of which decided the contest. For two pieces of cannon played from thence on the enemy with such effect, that they retreated, with such confusion and trepidation to the second post, as struck a panic into the Swiss, and threw them also into a disorder that was soon after followed by a precipitate flight. The duke of Savoy, on this important day, which seemed pregnant with the fortune of his house, appeared resolute to maintain his sovereign power, or at least to prove that he deserved it. Performing the duty both of an able commander and gallant soldier, he directed the fight, brought relief to the oppressed, animated the weary, rallied the faint-hearted, and poured on those that fled the bitterest reproaches. But the terror that had seized multitudes being more contagious than the courage of an individual, though a general and sovereign prince, every effort of Charles to withstand the steady valor of the Spaniards was ineffectual. At last, yielding to adverse fortune, but not despairing of better, by the most extraordinary exertions off courage and of art, he carried off from the scene of action five field-pieces, and part of that baggage which had been left by the Swifs.

Nothing was now wanting to make Italy tremble, but either the duke of Savoy at the head of the Spanish army; or the Spanish army under the colors of the duke of Savoy. The governor of Milan knew indeed how to fight; but not how to direct a campaign, or to improve a victory. He suffered the enemy to march unmolested to Asti. And, instead of laying siege to that city, fortified himself against the attacks of his antagonist, by the most extensive lines of circumvallation, and every possible method of defence. The distant and ineffectual bombardments of Inoiosa, the skirmishes which followed between the Savoyards and Spaniards, and the desperate but unsuccessful assault that was made by the former on the camp of the latter, might demand a particular description, were it necessary farther to illustrate the courage which was exhibited this campaign by the duke of Savoy, or that incapacity which disgraced the conduct of the governor of Milan. The Spanish troops lay for six weeks in the open air, on the hills near Asti; and the excessive heat, the unripe fruits, and the impurities of the camp, producing diseases, there ensued a great mortality both of men and cattle. Although the army had been reinforced with the troops at Sandoval, and others that arrived by sea, it was not half so strong as when it sat down before Asti. Charles, on the other hand, though he enjoyed more commodious quarters, experienced such frequent mutinies among his foreign troops, that it was difficult for him to determine whether they were of greater service or disadvantage. Thus both parties were in situations which inclined them to hearken to terms of peace. A capitulation was drawn up by the marquis of Rambouillet, and effectually recommended to the acceptance of the governor and the duke, by the Venetian and English ambassadors. This was not materially different from the treaty which had been framed by the pope's nuncio and the French ambassador, in the name of their respective courts, towards the end of the preceding year, in the city of Asti. Only, it gave greater security to the duke against the attacks of Spain. For it was guaranteed by the republic of Venice; and, in case of its being violated by the Spaniards, a power was consigned to the duke of Savoy, of summoning to his assistance, in the name of the king of France, the mareschal Lesdiguieres, and all the governors of provinces bordering on his dominions. The French ambassador, thinking he had now accomplished the object of his embassy, returned to Paris. But no sooner had he left Piedmont than Ferdinand, whose thirst of vengeance was in proportion to the narrowness of his capacity, began to let loose all the fury of his resentment on his revolted subjects. And Charles, on the other

hand, only made a show of disbanding his
troops [10], being justly apprehensive, that the late
agreement between him and the governor of Milan would be disavowed by the court of Madrid. The treaty of Asti was equally violated on both sides.

When the court of Madrid was informed that Inoiosa had concluded a disgraceful war by a dishonorable peace, they were moved with great indignation. But the man whose wrath on this occasion blazed forth with the greatest fury, was Don Pedro de Toledo, marquis of Villa Franca, distinguished even in Spain by a haughty boldness, and a zeal for the glory of the monarchy. His temper was vehement, yet his understanding was at once subtle and solid, and his courage both exalted and constant. Such a character would have appeared a fit instrument for inflicting the vengeance of Spain on the duke of Savoy; although he had not been allied by blood to the house of Mantua. This man, therefore was chosen by Philip to succeed the marquis of Inoiosa in the government of Milan, and the consenting voice of the Spanish nation applauded his choice [11].

1615.
Inoiosa superseded in the government of Milan by the marquis of Villa Franca.

[10] He very formally disbanded his French troops, but took care that they should be all of them incorporated into his Savoyard companies. As to the Swiss they could not be discharged without payment, concerning which there arose innumerable delays and difficulties.

[11] A famous Italian historian (Bat. Nani), and others in deference to his authority, suppose that Inoiosa would have

BOOK V.
1616.

The duke of Savoy, dissembling his suspicions of the hostile designs of Spain, sent a gentleman of his bed chamber with two letters to Toledo, in one of which he congratulated him, according to the custom of Italian princes, on his safe arrival at Milan, and in the other he described, in a pleasing manner, the mutual advantages of faithfully fulfilling the treaty of Asti. To the first of these letters the governor, with becoming politeness, replied, by returning his most humble thanks to the duke for the honor he had done him, and declaring that he would not fail to acquaint the court of Madrid with the respect and affection his highness had expressed for the Catho-

been recalled sooner, had not the duke of Lerma been afraid, by too great military successes in Italy, to defeat the project of the double marriages, which were not consummated (as has already been observed) till the end of the year 1615. But when we reflect on the great military force committed to Inoiosa, which was nearly double that of Charles; on the repeated orders he received from his court to act with expedition and with vigor; and on the attempts he made in consequence of these orders; that conjecture appears rather refined than solid. The regency of France wished for the final accomplishment of the double marriages as ardently as the court of Spain: and if they had been averse to that measure, an unsuccessful struggle on the part of Spain with the duke of Savoy would not have been the means of reconciling them to it. The appointment of the marquis of Villa Franca, at this time, to the government of Milan, seems to have been the natural result of the feelings of the Spanish ministry, on an occasion that wounded their pride, and excited their resentment.

lic king. To the other he anfwered, "that the true way to regain the favor of Philip, and to preferve lafting concord, was, not to think any longer on what was to be done, when both parties had their fwords in their hands ".." This anfwer, had it needed any comment; would have been fufficiently explained by the governor's common difcourfe, and ftill more by his actions. It was his common talk that the peace of Afti was a mere collufion between his predeceffor and the duke of Savoy, and that a powerful king could not be tied down to the obfervance of a treaty with an inferior prince, by any other bands than thofe of his own moderation. In the mean time he did not leave Charles in any uncertainty concerning what he had to expect from his Catholic majefty's moderation; for he every day made new levies, and reinforced his army with a great number of Swifs, Germans, and Italians.

The menaces of Don Pedro did not efcape from that wary politician through any intemperance of difcourfe. They were intended to bend the lofty fpirit of Charles to a humble fubmiffion to the crown of Spain, and to prepare his mind to catch at the bait by which he hoped to govern his ambition. He infinuated to his envoy at Milan, that if the duke his mafter would afk pardon of Philip, and fubmit his pretenfions wholly to his arbitration, that monarch would add to

"¹ Siri, Mem. recond. tom. iii. p. 409, 410.

BOOK V.
1616.

the dominions of Savoy the city of Geneva. But Charles Emanuel was not unacquainted with the artifices of the Spanish court. It was but lately that they had attempted to incite the prince of Piedmont to rife in rebellion againſt his father, and that Toledo himself had entered into a treaty with the governor of Zuccarello to deliver that place into the hands of the Spaniards. The duke, provoked equally at the pride and infidious policy of Spain, rejected with indignation the offer of Toledo, and prepared to maintain his independency and honor by force of arms. He repreſented to the guarantees of the treaty of Aſti the conduct and the deſigns of Toledo, and immediately ſummoned to his aid the mareſchal de Lefdiguieres, in virtue of that authority with which for this purpoſe he had been inveſted by the king of France. Toledo, on the other hand, inveighed againſt the obſtinacy of the duke, and ſolicited Lewis to compel him to diſband his troops, and to deliver the places and priſoners he had taken, into the hands of the king of Spain, promiſing that this monarch ſhould afterwards take every ſtep, not inconſiſtent with the dignity of his crown, to remove all jealouſy of his arms. Lewis had already ſent the count de Bethune, a man of capacity and ſingular addreſs, into Italy, in order to accommodate thoſe differences which diſturbed the repoſe of that country. He now ſent the mareſchal Lefdiguieres to join his influence to that of Bethune, hoping, that Toledo would yield to the preſence, and reputation, and power

The king of France reſolves to maintain the treaty of Aſti.

of the marefchal, what he might otherwife find means to evade. Lefdiguieres without delay went to Turin, where, in conjunction with Bethune, he framed a treaty of accommodation, which being propofed to the confideration of the governor and the duke, both parties agreed to a ceffation of arms. The marefchal, having affured the duke of Savoy of his warmeft fupport, if it fhould be found neceffary, departed from Turin, and returned to Dauphiny ".

Mean while the duke of Monteleon, the Spanifh ambaffador in France, affured the court of Paris, that the views of Philip in Italy were not thofe of ambition, but of juftice and peace. And this affurance being accompanied by arguments that fpoke directly home to the wants of fome courtiers, and the avarice of others, effectually changed thofe refolutions which had been taken in favor of Charles Emanuel. The ftricteft orders were iffued that no troops fhould be levied in France, without the exprefs commiffion of the king. The defign of thefe orders was, either to oblige the duke of Savoy to give his confent to an accommodation, on terms dictated by Spain, or to render him unable to carry on a war with that nation, fhould he refufe it.

But the duke found firmer fupport in the wifdom and fortitude of the Venetian fenate, than was to be expected from the feeble and fluctuating counfels of France. That republic levied for his fervice a confiderable body of French troops, and

" Hift. du Connét, de Lefdiguieres.

BOOK V.
1616.

contributed befides, a fupply of feventy-two thoufand ducats a month, for the purpofe of maintaining his army in Piedmont. The orders of the young king of France were in vain oppofed to the gold of Venice, the authority of Lefdiguieres, the duke of Mayenne, and other chiefs who encouraged all foldiers of fortune to crofs the mountains, and to join the ftandard of the duke of Savoy. But above all Charles was encouraged by the profpect of the duke of Nemours pouring down into the plains of Milan from the mountains of Savoy, at the head of an army of fix thoufand men. He was ignorant that the military preparations of this duke, was that which chiefly nourifhed the hope of victory in the breaft of Toledo.

The duke of Nemours joins the Spaniards againft the duke of Savoy.

Henry, duke of Nemours, chief of a branch of the houfe of Savoy, eftablifhed in France, had been amufed by Charles Emanuel with the hope of marrying a princefs of his family, for not a lefs fpace of time than fix or feven years. The difappointment made a deep impreffion on his mind, and filled him with refentment. Don Pedro, having learnt thefe circumftances, conceived the project of fixing Nemours in the interefts of Spain, by operating at once on his ambition, and that fpirit of revenge which was then his domineering paffion. He infinuated to his rankling mind, through the dukes of Guife and Monteleon, that on condition of his taking up arms on the fide of Spain againft his relation Charles Emanuel, the Spanifh monarch would reward his fervices with the inveftiture of the dutchy of Savoy. The duke of Nemours did not hesitate to close with these terms. Counterfeiting an ardent desire to maintain the independency of that sovereign family whence he derived his origin, he raised a force of seven thousand men [*], which he was about to lead into the heart of Savoy, while Toledo with a powerful army was ready to penetrate into Piedmont. But Charles Emanuel, having discovered the designs of Nemours, instantly sent orders to the governor of Savoy to secure those places which had been destined for the reception of the troops of Nemours. And the prince of Piedmont hastening to the northern passes of the Alps, seized the posts on the route which a body of troops was to take, that had been levied by the Spaniards in Franche Comté and Burgundy.

In the mean time the duke of Nemours had taken the field, and penetrated through lofty mountains, by rugged and difficult ways, into the valley of Sizeri. This small district yielded to the superiority of his power, without much resistance. He was preparing to improve the advantage he had gained, and to press forward upon the other territories of Savoy, when part of his troops deserted him, carrying along with them the greater part of both the provisions and ammunition. The troops that remained, being few in number, and weakened exceedingly by hunger and thirst, served as pastime to the shepherds of the mountains, who harrassed and hunted them from one place to another. In this extremity the duke of Nemours implored

[*] Batt. Nani, lib. ii. anno 1616.

BOOK V.
1616.

Operations of the new governor of Milan.

the succour of Spain, that he might be enabled to save the remains of his army from inevitable ruin by crossing the Rhone; but the Spaniards were deaf to his prayers. They even refused to send him a supply of bread and ammunition, and debarred him from the liberty of lodging his troops in Franche Comté, a province which in those days belonged to the crown of Spain. In this desperate situation he found relief in the generosity of Charles Emanuel. That magnanimous prince, at the intercession of Lesdiguieres, and other chiefs of France, pardoned his revolt, and, on the disbanding of his troops, restored him to the possession of his estates in Savoy [45].

The governor of Milan, in expectation that the irruption of the duke of Nemours into the dominions of Charles would distract his mind, and divert his arms, drew near with thirty thousand men to the frontiers of Piedmont. And, having thrown bridges over the Tanarus and the Sesia, and fortified and garrisoned them at either end, he waited for a favorable opportunity of entering that country, his head-quarters being fixed at Candia and Villata. The duke of Savoy, on the other hand, lodged in Caresana and la Motta, in the province of Vercelli, with an army not exceeding twenty thousand. After various skirmishes with the troops of Savoy with various success, Toledo, having separated his army into two divisions, ordered one of these to pass the Sesia at

[45] Mercure François, 1616. Hist. du Regne de Louis XIII.

Gattinara, and to join the other, which he was to conduct himfelf, near Crefcentino, a town on the Po, on the confines of the principality of Vercelli and Montferrat. It was Don Pedro's defign, by this movement, to inclofe his enemy by the Sefia with fortified bridges and fort Sandoval on the eaft, by the Po with Crefcentino on the fouth, and by taking and garrifoning St. Germano, a fortrefs equidiftant from both thefe rivers. Charles was now pofted in Sigliano, a place environed with lakes and moraffes, and acceffible only by one narrow entrance. This ftation the duke had chofen, as being very convenient for the relief of Vercelli, the reduction of which feemed the object to which all the fteps of his adverfary ultimately tended. As foon as he perceived that Toledo directed his courfe to Crefcentino, he mounted two thoufand mufqueteers behind an equal number of cavalry, and paffing by the Spaniards with great fpeed, threw fuccours into that town fufficient for its protection. The Spanifh general in revenge ravaged the villages of Piedmont, and Charles, from a like motive, thofe of Montferrat.

The autumnal rains now overflowed the country on all fides, and the hoftile armies lay for fome days inactive, the Savoyards in Crefcentino, the Spaniards in Livorno and Bianze, towns of Montferrat. The waters having fubfided, Toledo, aided by the treachery or cowardice of the governor, made himfelf mafter of St. Germano, the poffeffion of which was a confiderable ftep

BOOK V.
1616.

towards the reduction of Vercelli. This important place was still his aim, though, in order to obtain it, he made a feint of marching to Crescentino. The duke constantly harrassed his troops in flank, that by interrupting the march of his enemy, he might be enabled himself to pre-occupy the plain of Apertole, where he might make such arrangements as would put it in his power either to give battle, or to stand upon the defensive. The subtilty of the Spanish commander, on this occasion, practised a successful stratagem against the artful Charles Emanuel. Toledo made such a disposition of his troops as seemed to indicate an intention of obstructing the march of the Savoyards, even at the expense of a battle. Upon this the duke brought forward the flower of his army into the van, expecting every moment to be attacked in front by the enemy. But the Spaniards, with ten thousand foot and some cavalry, suddenly made an attack on his rear, consisting of four thousand French infantry and some cavalry, when they were filing through a wood. The Savoyards, struck with surprise and terror, began to retreat in the greatest confusion; but the duke saved his dismayed forces, if not from the disgrace, yet from the slaughter that commonly pursues a flying army. He dispatched the intrepid count of St. George to check the pursuit of the victorious enemy, with a select band of five hundred musketeers. The brave resistance of the count, and the quick approach of night, enabled the French troops

troops in the fervice of Savoy to retreat with fafety to the main body of the army.

The duke, whofe fanguine temper contemplated the bright fide of every object, comforted himfelf under this misfortune, by reflecting, that it would revive the ancient animofities between the Spaniards and the French, and that this laft nation, enraged at their late difcomfiture, would retrieve at once his lofs and their own honor. With thefe fentiments he retired to Crefcentino. The feafon was now far advanced; and Toledo, having in vain attempted to furprife Crefcentino, and finding that keeping the field ferved only to diminifh the number and impair the health of his troops, abandoned the pofts he poffeffed in Piedmont and Montferrat, having left garrifons only in Trino, St. Germano, and Gattinara. This laft was a town which commanded a paffage over the Sefia, and which had been reduced under the power of the Spaniards by Don Sancho de Luna, governor of the caftle of Milan ".

The duke of Savoy, through exceffive fatigue and agitation of mind, about this time contracted an illnefs, which, concurring with the rigor of the advanced feafe, feemed to promife on his part a refpite from all hoftilities. He could not take the field in perfon, and was even unable to walk abroad. In this irkfome confinement the activity of his mind amufed the tedious hours by forming various projects and ftratagems of war. And,

" Batt. Nani, lib. ii. 1616. Levaffor. tom. iii. Merc. Franç. 1616.

BOOK V.
1567.

Movements of the prince of Piedmont.

under his prefent infirmities, he felt a fenfible confolation in the capacity, bravery, and filial affection of four illuftrious fons, who were ready to execute with fidelity and alacrity whatever he fhould command them to perform. The duke of Nemours having been conftrained to lay down his arms, the prince of Piedmont repaffed the mountains by the valley of Aofta, and conducted his troops to Ivrea. Here he received orders to lead them againft Gattinara, in which was a Spanifh garrifon of four thoufand men. The prince did not hefitate to carry the orders of the duke his father into execution. But yielding to the remonftrances of his moft experienced officers, he exchanged an enterprife which appeared to be impracticable, for another which might be accomplifhed without difficulty, and which was not of lefs importance.

The principality of Mafferano is bounded on the eaft by the river Sefia, and in every other quarter by the territories of the duke of Savoy; a circumftance which naturally placed it under the protection of Spain. Toledo, with a view to ftrenghten that chain by which he defigned to inveft and ftraiten Vercelli, had made an offer to the prince of Mafferano to garrifon his capital, and alfo the fortrefs of Crevalcor with Spanifh forces. The prince, aware of the danger of fuch a meafure, chofe rather to undergo the hazard of an irruption from Piedmont than to refign the finews of his power into the hands of Toledo. He returned the governor thanks for his proffered aid, but expressed a hope that it would not be necessary. Toledo had in the mean time marched his troops to the banks of the Sesia, and seemed ready to pour into the territories of Masserano. In this situation of affairs the prince of Piedmont, by a concealed and forced march, surprised and invested the capital of that small state, which opened its gates without resistance. He now marched against Crevalcor, with eight thousand foot and four hundred horse. He appeared before the walls of that place on the 27th of January, and having seized all the avenues by which it might receive relief, he soon made a breach in the walls, and took the town by assault. The terrified inhabitants fled before the slaughtering sword, directing their trembling steps towards the castle. Multitudes were trodden to death in this scene of confusion and horror, and eager in the contest to enter through that narrow gate which was the only avenue of life. A very few made their way into the castle. The rest were either taken prisoners or slain by the sword.

The prince of Masserano, as soon as he learnt the hostile designs of Victor Amadeus, had implored that aid which he had formerly rejected. And the governor of Milan had immediately dispatched to his relief Don Sancho de Luna, with two thousand foot and three hundred horse; but in the mean time the castle capitulated. And, in too late an attempt to relieve it, Don Sancho, with many officers and private men, lost his life [47].

[47] Batt. Nani, lib. ii. 1616. Merc. Franç. 1617.

BOOK V.
1617.

Thus the duke of Savoy contended with the power and the art of the marquis of Villa Franca not without advantage. It is however probable that all the efforts of Charles Emanuel would have been repelled in the end, by the valor, difcipline, and ancient renown of the Spanifh arms, directed by the genius of Toledo, if they had not been fupported by the magnanimous refolution of the marefchal Lefdiguieres equally to confult his own and the glory of France, in fpite of all the allurements and the threats of the mifled princes, by whom it was at that time governed.

Character of the marefchal Lefdiguieres.

Although fortune fometimes raifes the worthlefs and the weak to the higheft offices, yet it muft have been fingular merit that, in times productive of great characters, could exalt a private gentleman of a very narrow fortune, to the firft dignity of a great kingdom that can be enjoyed by a fubject. Francis de Bonne, with a patrimony of fifty crowns a year, rofe to the ftation of conftable of France, in oppofition to many rivals of noble birth and great power. He was of an agreeable afpect, a mild temper, and eafy manners; qualities which were not indeed very fhining in themfelves, but which contributed not a little to raife the marefchal Lefdiguieres to fituations in which he had opportunities of difplaying the greateft talents and virtues ". His underftanding was manly and folid; he poffeffed in an eminent degree the virtues of political and martial courage; and though he was fufceptible both of friendfhip and

" Amelot de la Houffaie.

love, his ruling paffion was ambition. The duke of Savoy cultivated the friendfhip of this man with uncommon attention, and practifed with unwearied diligence all his addrefs in order to gain fo important an acquifition. To the marefchal Lefdiguieres he fhowed all the refpect due to a crowned head. If he received him at Turin it was with the utmoft pomp and magnificence. If he addreffed him in writing, he beftowed on him the endearing and flattering appellations of " good neighbour, and faithful friend. " He confulted him on every occafion: and the marefchal returned his confidence and affiduities with the finccreft fidelity and affection. The attachment of Lefdiguieres to Charles Emanuel was well known to the court of Spain, and they endeavoured to counteract its effects by operating on his natural ambition. The king and queen of France, at the inftigation of the Spanifh ambaffador, attempted to feduce him from the interefts of Savoy, by calling him to court in order to be invefted with the privileges and rank of a duke and peer. And, that he might be enabled to fupport the magnificence of that character, the king of Spain offered him any fum of money he fhould be pleafed to demand, to be paid in any part of Europe. Thefe allurements failing of fuccefs, a fupply of money was offered fufficient to raife and maintain for a year, an army of forty thoufand men, with a fuitable train of artillery, to be employed in making himfelf mafter of Savoy. Of this dutchy the duke of Monteleon, in name

BOOK V.
1617.

BOOK V.
1616.

Magnanimous resolution of Lesdiguieres.

of the Spanish monarch, offered him the investiture, on condition of his assisting the Spaniards to conquer Piedmont. This temptation having been also resisted, Monteleon engaged Louis to transmit to the mareschal the most peremptory orders to abstain from levying troops, and on no pretext whatever to move to the assistance of the duke of Savoy. These orders were in vain reiterated and enforced, at the desire of the feeble court of Paris, by the authority of the parliament of Grenoble. Lesdiguieres, in a letter to the king, represented to his majesty, in a firm though respectful tone, that his duty called him to restore the dignity of France in Italy, by fulfilling the engagements of that kingdom to the duke of Savoy, and chastising the perfidy and insolence of Spain. And he added, that, however treacherous counsels might beguile the good intentions of his majesty for a time, he did not despair of his present conduct meeting one day with the approbation of his sovereign [d].

On the nineteenth day of December 1616, the mareschal Lesdiguieres, exhibiting a signal proof of the greatness of his own mind, and the weakness of the crown of France, set out from Grenoble, at the head of an army of seven thousand foot and five hundred horse, raised in Dauphiny by his own authority, and at the expense of the republic of Venice. Having crossed the Alps in the midst of winter, he arrived at Turin on the third day of January. Reinforced by so considerable

[d] Hist. du Connétable de Lesdiguieres, lib. ix.

a body of gallant troops, and encouraged by the presence, reputation, and aid of a great commander, whose natural abilities were matured by long experience in the military art, the duke of Savoy was elated with the hope of vindicating his own independence, and inflicting severe vengeance on that haughty court which threatened him with subjection. The united forces of Lesdiguieres and the duke were irresistible. St. Damiano, Alba, and Montiglio, with other places of inferior importance, reduced under the power of Charles, with a rapidity corresponding to the ardor of his mind, nourished his hopes of making other conquests still more important. The reduction of Montiglio is eminently distinguished, not by any noble display of generosity or courage, but by an incident extremely humiliating to man, as it reminds him how much he partakes of the nature of those ferocious and noxious animals which are the constant objects of his hostility and abhorrence. A contest having arisen concerning the garrisoning of that fortress between the French and the Savoyards, the fierce disputants, enflamed by their engagement with the common enemy, directed their unsettled fury and reeking swords against each other. Upwards of a hundred had fallen on either side, before the authority of the general, the count of St. George, was able to prevent a mutual and complete massacre. The savage thirst of blood being now excited, and incapable of being suddenly quenched, loudly demanded an inhuman gratification, and found it

Reduction of Montiglio, and a memorable incident that happened on that occasion.

in the slaughter of the garrison that had capitulated on favorable terms [10].

The discontents in France had now drawn to a crisis which threatened the crown with all the violence of civil war. These discontents Charles Emanuel, as above related, had assiduously nourished with his usual dexterity and address. But the most enlightened genius sees not far into futurity, and often the most sagacious ambition blindly labors for its own destruction. The intestine discords and commotions of France obliged the king to recal Lesdiguieres; and instantly the marquis of Villa Franca, who yielding to a torrent which could not be resisted, had resolved to confine his troops within narrow limits, and to act wholly on the defensive, renewed his attacks on the duke of Savoy, commencing his operations with the siege of Vercelli. He sat down before this important place towards the end of May, with a strong army and a very great train of artillery. When Charles was informed that the governor of Milan had begun to put his troops in motion, he was not at a loss to discover his intention; and, with a view to disappoint it, having speedily increased the garrison of Vercelli to the number of four thousand, he determined to march his army from Gabbiana, and, by reducing the fortress of Pontestura, to oppose, with advantage, the progress of the Spanish army. But, while he meditated this scheme, he discovered that other dangers threatened him than the siege of Vercelli.

[10] Batt. Nani, Hist. lib. iii. 1517.

Don Pedro, conftrained to relinquifh for a time all open attacks on the ftates of Charles Emanuel, had employed the natural fubtilty of his active mind in laying plots againft that prince's perfon and family. Different perfons were fuborned to cut off the duke by affaffination or by poifon; and a confpiracy was formed by certain French officers of the garrifon of St. Ja to feize the prince of Piedmont, who commanded that fortrefs; and to deliver him into the hands of the Spaniards. The difcovery of thefe ignominious plots " diverted the defign of the duke

" It is remarkable, that, although there never was a people more diftinguifhed than the Spaniards for honor and fidelity, yet there is not any period in the hiftory of any nation more difgraced by plots and confpiracies than that which forms the fubject of this narrative. When refentment, ambition, or other paffions, cannot find gratification openly, and in the direct road of fuperior force, they have recourfe to ftratagem, as fully appears from the hiftory of nations as well as individuals. Perhaps, too, ideas of fuperior dignity have a tendency to blunt the fenfe of injuftice committed againft inferiors. The different prices or compenfations for wounds, and even for murders, that took place about eight hundred years ago in fo many nations of Europe, is a ftriking proof how much this iniquitous fentiment naturally prevails in the human mind. There is as great injuftice in wantonly maiming, or otherwife torturing, or putting to death a dog, a horfe, or other animal, as there would be in wounding or deftroying a man; yet there are but few whofe confciences would be ftung with remorfe at the commiffion of fuch crimes; a matter which is to be accounted for only from that immeafurable diftance which our fancy, ftill more than

BOOK V.
1617.

against Ponteſtura, by ſummoning his attention to cares more immediate and urgent. The conviction and puniſhment of conſpirators and aſſaſſins employed that critical time which would otherwiſe have been occupied in preventing the ſiege of Vercelli, or, by plentiful ſtores of proviſions and ammunition, to prepare it for a vigorous reſiſtance.

The ſiege had not been continued above fixteen days, when the Savoyards were reduced to the neceſſity of ſupplying the place of iron balls and lead with tin and ſtones. The quantity of

nature interpoſes between men and the inferior animals, and which precludes all ſympathy. A nation accuſtomed to think itſelf vaſtly ſuperior in dignity to all others, and to arrogate to itſelf an excluſive privilege of dominion, fancies it has a right of aſſerting that privilege by all means, however inconſiſtent with juſtice. The inhabitants of Calais were ſaved from the furious reſentment of Edward III. of England by the tranſcending virtue of ſix of their fellow-citizens, who devoted themſelves to certain deſtruction for the ſake of their relations, friends and companions: the condition required by that haughty and cruel conqueror. Theſe ſix heroic burgeſſes were ſaved from death, not by the generoſity of Edward, but by the importunity and tears of his queen. Yet this prince was profuſe enough in his civilities to the French officers, who, about the ſame time, had fallen into his hands, although their bravery was not to be compared with that of the burgeſſes. Had ſix knights appeared before him in the guiſe of malefactors, inſtead of ſix citizens, he would have been ſhocked at the idea of ordering them to be led to execution, and have been full in his praiſes of their ſignal patriotiſm and reſolution.

their powder alfo was infufficient; nor could all the efforts of Charles encourage the gallantry of the befieged by a frefh fupply. Two hundred and fifty cavalry, with facks of powder of twenty-five pounds each, were waylaid in their concealed march to Vercelli, through the vigilance of Toledo; and the fire of the Spaniards having been communicated to fuch inflammable materials, only thirty of that number made their way into the place of their deftination. Two hundred and twenty horfes, with their riders, miferably perifhed in one fudden conflagration; yet the befieged made a gallant defence, and repulfed the Spaniards, in different fallies, with great flaughter. The affailants made a furious effort to carry the place by a general affault; but, 'if the valor of the Spaniards was animated by the love of glory and the hope of plunder, the Savoyards, anticipating in their imaginations the calamities and horrors that awaited themfelves, and objects ftill dearer to them than life, in cafe of defeat, were roufed with the fury of defpair. The fteady bravery of the befiegers gave way on this occafion to the rage which impelled the befieged; and, in the firft moment of their retreat, a hundred cuiraffiers, falling with their fwords in their hands into the ditch, made a dreadful carnage. Fifteen hundred men perifhed on the fide of Spain; on that of Savoy not a hundred. The duke of Savoy, being informed of the defperate intrepidity of his faithful garrifon, was filled with all thofe emotions which the fidelity, bravery, and danger of men suffering in his cause, were naturally fitted to produce in his generous mind. He attempted, a second time, secretly to convey ammunition and provision into Vercelli; but lost by that fruitless effort four hundred men. At last, exasperated by repeated disappointment, he drew near to the Spanish camp by night, by storming, or even making a faint of storming which, he hoped to be able to succour Vercelli. Having ranged his troops along the banks of the Sesia, he sent a strong detachment over that river, in separate parties, under the marquis d'Urfe, who was repulsed by a body of Spanish horse with the loss of six hundred men. This bold measure of the duke was not wholly without success; for while the Spaniards hastened to oppose the Savoyards in that quarter where d'Urfe directed his attack, a thousand men, loaded with ammunition, made their way into Vercelli by another. But this scanty supply was far from being sufficient; and, besides this circumstance, the garrison was now greatly diminished by the accidents of war and the fatigues of duty. In this situation were the besieged, when Toledo, on the 5th of July, which, being the festival of St. James, was deemed fortunate for Spain, made a general assault, and effected a lodgment in a bastion, against which, from the commencement of the siege, he had principally directed the fury of his artillery. The garrison, at that instant, demanded and obtained honorable terms of capitulation; their baggage, and arms, and all the honors of war. Toledo, having garrisoned Vercelli, and levied very high contributions on the inhabitants, marching his army along the course of the Tanarus, reduced, under the power of Spain, Soleri, Felician, and Anona, with other places, the possession of which he hoped would pave the way to the execution of an enterprise he meditated against the important city of Asti [1].

An unexpected and tragical event in France interrupted the career of Toledo in Italy. Concino Concini and Eleanor Galigai, afterwards the mareschal and the lady mareschal d'Ancre, made their first appearance at the court of Paris in the train of Mary de Medicis, on her first arrival in that city from Florence. Their abilities and address, aided by that sympathy which men feel for their compatriots, however humble their rank of life, when in the course of Providence they accompany or meet each other in foreign lands, so gained on the favor of the indulgent queen, that she raised them to a degree of power intolerable to the nobles, and odious to the people. Depending on the queen-regent, they depended also on Spain, the great prop of her power, and were naturally devoted to the interests of a crown, which, by supporting Mary's, supported also their authority. In order to prolong the period of their borrowed power, they diverted the thoughts of Lewis, now of age, from matters of state, by encouraging him in the pursuit of those youthful

---

[1] Bat. Nan. lib. iii. Hist. du regne de Louis XIII.

BOOK V.
1617.

Albert de Luines becomes the favorite of the king of France.

amufements which had hitherto occupied all his time, and engroffed all his attention. The more effectually to fix his mind in an indifference towards all political objects, they provided him with companions of his own age, whofe fociety, they imagined, would amufe his leifure, and heighten, by fympathy, his relifh for thofe pleafures to which he was addicted. Among thefe, Charles Albert de Luines, a young gentleman of Avignon, was diftinguifhed for the handfomenefs of his perfon, the gracefulnefs of his air, and the obliging politenefs of his behaviour. He gained by degrees the affection and confidence of his young fovereign, and was indulged, at all times, with familiar accefs to his perfon. Concini perceived the afcendant this young favorite had acquired over the king; and, in order to attach him to himfelf, preferred him to the government of Amboife. But Luines, prompted by his own ambition, and encouraged by the murmurs and difcontents that pervaded the kingdom, gave fuch an account of the conduct and defigns of his benefactor, as filled the inexperienced mind of his prince with horror, and perfuaded him that the prefervation of his own life, as well as his power, depended on the death of the marefchal d'Ancre. Vitri, captain of the guards, undertook and accomplifhed the bloody purpofe of facrificing the life of the marefchal to the fufpicions of the king. On the 20th of April the unfortunate Florentine careleffly entered within the gate of the royal palace of the Louvre, which was inftantly fhut behind him, and was walking towards the apartments of the queen-regent, reading a letter as he went, when the captain of the guard arrefted him, in the name of the king, and beckoned to his accomplices, who ftood by him in anxious expectation of that fignal. Three affaffins, at that inftant, poured the contents of their fire-arms into his body, which, after he had fallen dead on the ground, they fpurned, and cut in different parts with their fwords; but the populace, greedy of every opportunity of giving went to the animal ferocity of their nature, and zealous of all occafions to avenge on the powerful and great the unequal diftributions of fortune, dug up the mangled corpfe of Concini, which had been ignominioufly buried, and dragged it in horrid triumph along the ftreets of Paris. They afterwards, having cut it in fmall pieces, roafted and inhumanly devoured it; and happy was the man who could obtain the fmalleft morfel of the favage facrifice ".

The wretched Galigai was condemned to death, on pretence of forcery. She exerted on her trial, and in her laft moments, a conftancy and ftrength of mind, which the melting fpectators compared with the fortitude of Socrates, and contrafted with thofe tears which, not many years before, difgraced the exit of the intrepid duke of Biron.

" Bernard, Hiftoire de Louis XIII. Siri, Mem. recon. tom. iv. Relation de la mort du maréchal d'Ancre. Journal de Baffompierre. Mémoires d'Amelot de la Houffaie.

BOOK V.
1617.

The authority of the queen-regent was annihilated by the stroke which cut off the mareschal d'Ancre; and Luines, who succeeded to all the power of that stranger, agreeably to the common conduct of new ministers in all nations; departed at first from the maxims, and vehemently arraigned the conduct of his predecessor. He particularly exclaimed against that uniform deference which had been shown by the former administration to the counsels of Rome and Madrid[18]. In this temper was the court of France when news arrived of the surrender of Vercelli. Immediately it was resolved to succour the duke of Savoy. Lesdiguieres once more crossed the mountains with twelve thousand foot, and two thousand horse. In this train were many lords and gentlemen of France, volunteers, among whom was the great duke of Rohan, at the head of three squadrons of cavalry. The orders of the mareschal were strenuously to aid the duke of Savoy in his efforts to recover his own dominions, but not to involve the court of France in a war with Spain, by insulting either the territories of Milan or Mantua. But Lesdiguieres had grander objects in view than to expel Don Pedro from the coasts of Savoy. The military reputation of the Spanish commander, instead of repressing the courage of the mareschal, filled him with an ardent desire to take the field against an antagonist whose genius and vigor would give full exercise

Lesdiguieres marches to the assistance of the duke of Savoy.

[18] Siri, Mem. recond. tom. iv. p. 68. Relation de la mort du maréchal d'Ancre. Mémoires de Rohan, lib. i.

to all his abilities and experience, and over whom a victory would be truly glorious. However, making a show of respect to his majesty's command, he ordered his troops to lay aside, for a while, the colors of France, and to wear those of Savoy.

Don Pedro de Toledo, after the reduction of Vercelli, had distributed his army, for the purpose of refreshment, in different towns and villages of Montferrat, but chiefly in those of the province of Alexandria. In the midst of all his quarters lay the village of Feliziano, which was slightly barricadoed, and defended by two thousand men. The experienced eye of Lesdiguieres quickly perceived, that by surprising this centrical station, he would deprive the Spaniards of the most proper place of rendezvous in their possession, and prevent a junction of their divided forces. He communicated these ideas to Charles Emanuel. The duke was at first struck with the danger of attempting an enterprise against a place surrounded by the posts of the enemy; but Lesdiguieres insisted that by a nocturnal, rapid, and unexpected march, it would not be difficult, but, on the contrary, a very easy matter to make the duke master of Feliziano; from which centre he might turn his successful arms against the other quarters of the Spaniards with great glory and advantage. Charles acquiescing in the reasoning, or yielding to the authority of the mareschal, an expedition was concerted against Feliziano. Thither the combined army began to march, as

BOOK V.
1617.

soon as the darkness of the night favored the enterprise, in three divisions. The van was led by the marefchal Lefdiguieres, the main body by the duke of Savoy, and Shomberg, marefchal of the camp, brought up the rear with the artillery. But Charles Emanuel, taught by the reduction of Vercelli to refpect the valor of the Spaniards, and the abilities of the marquis of Villa Franca, bethought himself, after the troops under Lefdiguieres had moved, that the fituation and motions of the Spaniards rendered the expedition on which he had entered extremely dangerous; he therefore fent a courier to the marefchal, advifing him to return on his fteps. The marefchal, who, in an advanced age, poffeffed all the fire of youth, replied to the meffenger with much emotion, "I have followed the profeffion of arms above fifty years without having ever turned my back on the enemy: an honor of which I am determined my conduct on this day fhall not deprive me. There is more fhame in retreating than danger in going on." Having faid this, he jumped out of the litter in which he had hitherto been borne; and, notwithftanding fome feverifh fymptoms that were about him, mounted on horfeback, placed himfelf at the head of his troops, and continued his march[55]. He arrived at Feliziano about the dawning of the day; and the duke of Savoy having joined him foon after with the main body of the army, which he conducted

[55] Hift. du Regne de Louis XIII. et des Evenements principaux, &c.

by a private way with astonishing celerity, the place was immediately invested, and taken by assault. All the common soldiers, and many of the inhabitants, were put to the sword. The officers were made prisoners. Not a man of Feliziano escaped with his liberty and his life ". Quatordeci, Renfracora, Anona, Rocca, and Nice, were also quickly subdued by the united arms of Charles Emanuel and Lesdiguieres, the rapidity of whose conquests, in the space of a week, weakened the Spanish army by a loss of more than five thousand men. Don Pedro now abandoned his design of besieging Asti, and retreated from Soleri into the Milanese; all his force, vigilance, and art, being necessary to put that country in a posture of defence against the threatened irruptions of the duke of Savoy. But the duke of Monteleon having assured the king of France that Vercelli should be restored, and the treaty of Asti executed with fidelity and promptitude on the part of Spain, Lesdiguieres was recalled in the full career of victory. The marechal, having in vain remonstrated that the present juncture presented a glorious opportunity for recovering the Milanese to the crown of France, yielded obedience to the reiterated commands of his sovereign. Toledo agreed to a cessation of arms, and promised to use his utmost endeavours to effectuate an entire accommodation, and, particularly, came under an engagement to Bethune, at Pavia, the 9th of October, that, on condition

" Batt. Nan. lib. iii. 1617. Mém. de Rohan. liv. i.

the places he had taken in the courfe of the current month, he on his part would give up Vercelli with the other places he had feized, and difarm his troops, in November. This agreement being made, the marefchal marched back to Grenoble [57]. But the minifters of Spain, not fatisfied with the return of the French troops into Dauphiny, remonftrated to the court of France, that the keeping on foot fo great a force, fo near the confines of Savoy, would be an infraction of the treaty of Afti. They declared that Vercelli would not be delivered up to Charles Emanuel, while the Swifs troops hovered in the county of Vaux; and his friend, Lefdiguieres, was ready, on the fhorteft notice, to march to his aid at the head of an army. Lewis, who was willing to maintain the independency of Savoy, but averfe to any violent rupture with the Catholic king, not only difbanded his own troops in Dauphiny, but alfo urged Charles to preclude Toledo from every pretext of war, by laying down in good earneft his arms; affuring him of his warmeft fupport and protection, in cafe the Spaniards fhould attempt, either by open force or fecret artifice, to elude the execution of the treaties of Pavia and Afti. The promife of the king having been warranted, at his majefty's defire, by the fuperior authority and credit of the marefchal Lefdiguierer, Charles Emanuel difbanded his army. Upon this the French ambaffadors, Modene and Bethune, went from Turin to the governor of

[57] Hift. du Connétable de Lefdiguieres, liv. ix.

of the duke's disbanding his army, and restoring
Milan to assure him of this fact, and to engage
him to imitate the duke's pacific example. They
soon perceived, from his affected difficulties and
evasions, not only that he had no mind to restore
Vercelli, but that it was his intention to make
fresh attacks on the duke of Savoy.

Lewis, who, in the solitude of rural scenes and
amusements, had hitherto concealed an elevated
courage, was moved with equal indignation and
surprise at the treacherous conduct of Toledo.
"I am not at a loss, said he to the Spanish ambassador, to conjecture the cause to which I ought
to ascribe the delays of Spain to give satisfaction
to the duke of Savoy. The king, your master,
thinks I dare not go out of my kingdom without leaving it full of distractions; but I wish him
to know, that it is not altogether in so bad a
condition as he imagines it to be; and, if my
kingdom should be ruined, and my sovereignty
annihilated by my absence, I am determined to
cross the mountains, and, at the hazard of my
life and of my crown, to fulfil my promise to the
duke of Savoy, and to oblige the king of Spain
to make good his word to me." The voice, the
looks, and gestures of the young king, made
an impression on the mind of Monteleon, which
he communicated to the court of Madrid. Orders were forthwith dispatched from thence to the
government of Milan, to execute with promptitude
and good faith all the articles of the treaties of

BOOK V.
1618.

Afti and Pavia [18]. But the court of Spain found that it was as hard a tafk to incline the marquis of Villa Franca to peace, as it had been to roufe Inoiofa to arms. His firft excufe for not difbanding his troops was, that the Swifs regiments, lately in Piedmont, had not returned to their own country, but halted in the country of Vaux, ready to obey the nod of the duke of Savoy, from whom they ftill drew their ufual pay. Bethune protefted, in writing, that the troops of the duke were difbanded, and charged Toledo with all the calamities that might arife from his difbelief of a matter of fact, of which he might eafily obtain the moft undoubted evidence. The governor, driven from this ground, privately offered the duke of Savoy the greateft advantages, if he would abandon his connexions with Venice and France, and unite his interefts with thofe of Spain. Provided that Vercelli fhould remain in the hands of the Spaniards, and that Cafal fhould alfo be added to the ftate of Milan, he promifed to extend the dominion of Charles over all the reft of Montferrat. This artifice having failed of fuccefs, he endeavoured to perfuade the duke of Mantua to infift on a compenfation for damages, and on, what he had always fo much at heart, the liberty of punifhing fuch of the fubjects of Montferrat as had efpoufed the caufe of his adverfary. But neither did this ftratagem fucceed. He next had recourfe to a contrivance which he deemed infallible. He attempted to excite the

[18] Difcours de ce qui s'eft paffé dans le Piedmont et l'Etat de Milan, &c. Apud Hift. du Regne de Louis XIII.

jealoufy of the duke of Savoy by circulating whifpers, that, when Ferdinand fhould be reftored to the fovereignty of Montferrat, the houfe of Gonzaga would give it up to Spain, in exchange for other poffeffions. But Charles having difregarded thefe falfe reports, Don Pedro devifed yet another expedient, which might fubdue the wary but fpirited duke, by provoking his indignation. His fecretary, Carone, who was then at Milan along with the French ambaffadors, Toledo haughtily ordered inftantly to leave the territories of Spain, and to go about his bufinefs. By this artifice he furprifed the mind of Charles, and gained an advantage over his underftanding through the agency of his paffions. The high-fpirited duke, not adverting that Toledo was now practifing fuch ingenious ftratagems on his own mind, as he himfelf had employed when he carried on a war of wit on that of Inoiofa, inftantly fufpended the evacuation of the places he had taken, and fent advice to Modene and Bethune to return from Milan. The fubtilty of the Spaniard (fuch is the advantage of making an attack!) would have triumphed over that of the Savoyard, which was equal, if not fuperior, had not the French ambaffadors conjured the latter not to make fport to the former, who fought for nothing elfe than a pretext for reviving hoftilities. The duke, admonifhed by the prudence of thefe minifters, reftored, on the 6th of April, all the places he poffeffed in Montferrat: he alfo evacuated Zucarello, Anona, and Mafferano, and every other fief he had feized of the empire. His prifoners he delivered into the hands of the French ambaſſadors. News having arrived of all thefe things at Milan, the governor, equally furprifed and chagrined, exclaimed, "It appears that the treaty of Afti muft at laft be executed, fince heaven and earth will have it fo [1]." He releafed his prifoners, and evacuated St. Germano, but ftill held faft poffeffion of Vercelli.

The court of Madrid, in the mean time, had fent repeated and pofitive orders to fulfil all the conditions, without exception, of the treaty of Afti; and, in order to give the world a ftriking proof how much they difapproved the conduct of Don Pedro, they determined to recal him, and to appoint the duke of Feria his fucceffor in the government of Milan. This intention was not kept a fecret from Don Pedro, yet he perfevered in the invention of new evafions. "It is not confiftent, faid he, with the honor of the monarchy to reftore Vercelli, while the French ambaffadors remain at Milan. The reftitution of that place muft not feem to be extorted by the threatenings of France, but to be, as it in reality is, a voluntary deed on the part of Spain." This pretext was removed by the immediate departure of Modene and Bethune. "Before I give up Vercelli, faid Don Pedro, once more, I infift that Garefio, (a town of Montferrat, belonging to the count de St. George, but now garrifoned by the troops of Savoy) fhall be reftored to its right

---

[1] Bat. Nan. Hift. lib. iii. anno 1618.

owner." Garcsio was restored, and Toledo, all his artifices being now exhausted, began, with proud reluctance and by slow degrees, to carry away from Vercelli the ammunition and the arms. But, after this operation was begun, he bethought him of yet another pretext for gaining time. He required a new promise from Charles Emanuel, that he would not give any occasion of offence to the duke of Mantua; but the ministers of Ferdinand, impatient of these multiplied delays, and more suspicious of Toledo himself than of any of the princes of Italy, declared in writing, to the great vexation of Toledo, that they required not any other assurances of the pacific intentions of the duke of Savoy, than those they had already obtained.

BOOK V.
1618.

Men's astonishment at the public conduct of the marquis of Villa Franca was heightened when they remarked its coincidence with that of the duke of Ossuna.

Don Pedro Giron, knight of the Golden Fleece, and a grandee of the first class of Spain, inherited from a long line of ancestors the pride of noble birth, and the command of a princely fortune: circumstances which are sometimes indeed found in conjunction with meanness of sentiment, but which fostered that natural sublimity of imagination that carried Ossuna to pursue grand designs by extraordinary means. His temper was uncommonly fervent, and his fancy lively even to extravagance. Hence, though his understanding was quick and penetrating, his con-

Character of the duke of Ossuna.

BOOK V.
1618.

duct was neither regulated by the common maxims of policy and prudence, nor his demeanour, in the intercourses of life, by the rules of propriety and decorum. In the presence of his sovereign, he would talk with a gaiety and boldness unknown in the courts of kings, and which appeared to the sage gravity of his compatriots to border upon madness. But his conversation in all companies, and on all occasions, was adorned with a brilliancy of wit, which, in the eyes of most men, would more than compensate many levities and indiscretions. This duke is justly censured by grave historians for his gallantries, which were not veiled or palliated by delicacy of sentiment; but, on the contrary, sensual, open, and licentious. Yet that grosser species of love was attended with this advantage, that it left his mind free and disengaged, and did not interfere in any respect with his projects of ambition ⁶⁰. He had served in the army in the war with the United Provinces, in a high rank, and with great glory; and his merit, as a soldier, was either the cause, or; as oftener happens in courts, the pretext for his preferment to the important station of viceroy of Naples. In this station he amazed the world with the singularity of his character, and disturbed its repose by the boldness of his ambition ⁶¹.

⁶⁰ What was said of Sylla is applicable to Ossuna. Voluptatum cupidus, gloriæ cupidior, otio luxuriofo esse, tamen a negotiis nunquam voluptas remorata.

⁶¹ Batt. Nan. Hist. della Republica Veneta, lib. iv. 1620. Historia de Don Felippe IV. Rey de las Espannas por Don Gonç. de Cespedes. Lib. segundo, capitulo seg.

When the race of Ottoman extended their conquests from the Black Sea to the gulf of Venice, a number of the ancient inhabitants fled from the terror of their irresistible arms, to the forests and mountains on the frontiers of the countries now known by the name of Turkey in Europe. And, having acquired, from their wandering and unsettled manner of life, a ferocity of character, they gradually became careless of their herds and flocks, and subsisted chiefly by hunting and by rapine. The Uscocchi, for that is the name by which those fugitives were distinguished, were no longer that effeminate race which yielded without resistance their fertile possessions to the invasions of their enemies. Impelled by the hardships and the courage of barbarians, they made frequent inroads into the settlements of their conquerors, and satisfied their wants by plunder, while they gratified their revenge by devastation. In this vagabond state they lived for many years, wandering from place to place, still directing their course to those wild and rugged abodes which prosperous nations avoid, but which the unfortunate count as the seats of freedom. The Austrian coasts on the confines of Istria, broken by the operations of the elements into a thousand rocks and creeks, and small islands of difficult access, appeared a fit habitation to the Uscocchi: and the emperor, Ferdinand, desirous by all means, to form a barrier against the irruptions of the Turks into Hungary, bestowed on this fierce and warlike people, the strong town of Segna, which

BOOK V.
1615.

became their capital. In the neighbourhood of these fugitives lay the territories of a people similar in their origin, but more prosperous in their fortune[¹], whose wealth both on sea and land, invited the rapacity of men who had no other profession than that of robbers and pirates. The Uscocchi, instead of punishment for these offences, received protection from Ferdinand, archduke of Gratz, within whose government Segna was situated. This produced a war between the Austrians and the Venetians. The menaces of the Turks[²], and the prospect of an expensive election to the crown of Bohemia, soon inclined Ferdinand to hearken to terms of accommodation with the republic, whose army, powerfully reinforced by soldiers of fortune from Holland, had invested the capital of Goritia, and reduced it to the greatest extremity of distress. The Spaniards would have willingly furnished the means of carrying on a war against a people that on every occasion strenuously opposed their domineering schemes in Italy. But their contest with Charles Emanuel fully employed all their resources, and prevented a disjunction of their forces. Yet, whatever could be done in favor of Ferdinand and the Uscocchi, was performed by the duke of Ossuna and the marquis of Villa Franca. Amidst

War between the Austrians and Venetians.

[¹] The Venetians found an asylum from the fury of Attila, in the insignificancy still more than the natural strength of their fens and morasses.

[²] Winwood's Memoirs, vol. iit. A letter from Sir Dudley Carleton, dated Venice, 27th February, 1612.

the heat of the campaign in Piedmont, Toledo kept up a confiderable military force near the Venetian borders, and made other preparations which feemed to threaten a diverfion in favor of the Auftrians. This, the truce with the duke of Savoy brought about by the marefchal Lefdiguiers, enabled him afterwards to accomplifh. While Don Pedro, by his menaces, and by his attacks on the Venetians by land, endeavoured to relieve the Auftrians; Offuna, by various operations at fea, and with great fuccefs, labored for the fame end. By his orders, a Spanifh fleet cruifed in the Mediterranean, in order to intercept any fuccours that might be fent to the republic by that channel; while another interrupted the fources of their wealth and power, by feizing their merchant fhips in the Adriatic. Thefe were brought in triumph into the port of Naples, which became the rendezvous of corfairs and pirates. Here, fuch of the Ufcocchi as had been driven from their ftrong holds on the Auftrian coaft, found freedom of trade and perfonal protection. The profufe genius of Offuna did not afford fhelter to the Ufcocchi and other pirates that he might fhare in their plunder, but that he might collect a fufficient number of defperate men for the execution of any daring enterprife. In the mean time, the Neapolitan merchants found means of reprefenting to the court of Madrid, that the piratical trade which was now carried on at Naples, had ruined fair commerce, and of courfe diminifhed the royal revenues. Happily for the Neapolitans, their complaints coincided both in time and intention, with the remonſtrances of France. An order was diſpatched to all the Spaniſh miniſters in Italy to ſuſpend hoſtilities, as a negociation was now on foot for a general peace between Savoy and Spain, and the Venetians and Ferdinand of Auſtria.

The marquis of Bedmar ſoon after paid his compliments to the Venetian ſenate on its happy concluſion [a]; and Toledo withdrew the troops he had ſent into the ſtates of the republic, into the territories of Milan. But Oſſuna, enraged at the very name of peace, ſent a fleet into the Adriatic, under the command of the famous admiral Rivera, and denounced immediate death againſt the man who ſhould dare to complain to the court of Madrid of the interruption of commerce. Both this fleet and that which was ſent to oppoſe it from Venice, after a ſlight encounter, were diſperſed by a ſtorm. The Spaniards took ſhelter in Brundiſium, the Venetians in St. Croce, a port which they had occupied for ſome time, with a view to prevent Oſſuna from fortifying, as he threatened, ſeveral rocks on the confines

---

[a] It was agreed that the Venetians ſhould reſtore their conqueſts without reſerve: and on the part of the Auſtrians, that they ſhould reſtrain the piracies of the Uſcocchi; baniſh their ringleaders, and alſo the banditti of the republic that lived among that people; that they ſhould change the governor of Segna, and bridle that place by a German garriſon; and finally, that they ſhould give up all the captures of Oſſuna.

of Ragufa, a small republic protected by the Turks. The Ragufans, a commercial people, were naturally difpofed to give every encouragement to a power that difputed the empire of the Adriatic with a nation whom they had long confidered as their oppreffors: accordingly, they had received, at different times, Offuna's fleets into their harbours, and both refrefhed them with provifions, and recruited them with failors. The Venetians now chaftifed this avowed partiality for their enemies; and the Ragufians complained of their conduct, and reprefented their defigns as dangerous to the Ottoman port. A military force was immediately ftationed along the coafts of Dalmatia and Albany; and Offuna, taking advantage of this circumftance, endeavoured to fpread, throughout all the Italian ftates, the terror of a Turkifh invafion. The beft poffible expedient on this alarming occafion, he faid, would be to ftrengthen his hands with fuch a naval force as might be fufficient to defend the liberties of Europe, and raife, among the Infidels, the name of Chriftians. But the vigilance of the Venetian fenate, difcovered that at this very time Offuna was practifing on all the paffions which ufually determine the public conduct of the Porte, in order to draw the fury of their arms upon the ifland of Candia, at that time fubject to the dominion of the republic. This fact, announced to all the courts of Europe, confounded the fubtilty of Offuna, and left him, for a fhort time, without the refource of a fingle

BOOK V.
1618.

stratagem. The Spanish fleet in the mean time, and numbers of privateers, continued to plunder the ships, and to ravage the coasts of Venice. The pope, and the ambassadors of France, interposed their good offices with Ossuna, in behalf of the republic, in vain. Philip himself, by letters written with his own hand, commanded him to abstain from all hostilities, and to restore all that he had taken from Venice. His Catholic majesty had not better success than his holiness and the count de Bethune. Ossuna offered, indeed, in consequence of the orders of the king, to restore the empty vessels, but declined to give back their valuable freights. He continued his piracies and depredations, deigning, however, to cover his disobedience to the commands of the king, by those excuses which the various course and accidents of war readily suggest to the imagination of an ingenious commander. " It is not fit, he would say, at one time, that I should sit still, while the Venetians are fortifying the harbour of St. Croce." " I will persist, he would exclaim with vehemence at another, in my present conduct so long as the Venetians shall retain in their pay the most inveterate enemies of the king my master." When he was ordered to deliver an account of the merchandize he had seized, he seemed to sport with the orders of Philip, by giving an inventory so imperfect as the Venetian ambassador refused to accept, and even complained of the mockery. The Venetians, thus plundered, and insulted, equipped a fleet, which

retaliated

retaliated on the Spaniards all the piracies and depredations of the viceroy of Naples: but, at the same time, the senate regretted the necessity they were under of defending themselves by making such reprisals. To the marquis of Bedmar, the Spanish ambassador, they complained of the never-ceasing hostilities of Ossuna, and professed themselves at a loss to reconcile the actions of the viceroy of Naples, with the declarations of the court of Spain. The ambassador, in reply, touched with an imposing delicacy on the irregularity of Ossuna's disposition, and insinuated that the conduct of that duke was neither under the control of the king, his master, nor of any fixed principles or regular system of action. In reality, the behaviour of Ossuna seemed to furnish matter for such an apology, while he directed the Spanish arms, in spite of repeated orders from his sovereign, against a state with whom he had not declared war; and constantly meditated hostile designs, of which he talked without reserve to all around him, although, from their nature, the utmost secrecy was necessary to their execution. His conversation turned wholly upon surprising the Venetian ports in Istria, plundering their islands, and even making a descent on Venice. He had himself carefully studied the plan of that city, and he now described it with infinite accuracy to all who possessed his confidence. He contrived flat-bottomed boats, with machines to facilitate their motion, and made daily experiments of the weights which the several depths of

BOOK V.
1618.

water were capable of bearing, according to the different conftructions and dimenfions of veffels. To the Venetians, tranfactions fo open and avowed, were a fubject of laughter, and gave weight to the defence which had been made for the viceroy by the marquis of Bedmar. They were ignorant that the hoftilities, of which they complained, proceeded from the fecret machinations of this minifter himfelf, which were more effectually concealed by the extravagance and apparent folly of the duke, than they could have been by the moft ftudied fecrecy and circumfpection ⁵¹.

Ferquency of plots and affaffinations accounted for.

The princes and ftates of Italy, enervated by luxury, or employed in commerce, committed themfelves to the protection of mercenaries ⁵⁵. diftinguifhed by the name of Leaders of Bands ⁵⁷. The tranfition was not unnatural from mercenary foldiers to private affaffins. The military and generous fpirit of ancient Rome was fubdued by defpotifm and by luxury; and throughout the whole of Italy, broken into innumerable principalities by the diffolution of the Roman empire, the petty fovereigns had recourfe on all occafions to ftratagems and plots, not the valor of arms. And, as cuftoms and manners always defcend from the higher to the lower ranks of men, plots and affaffinations became common among the

⁵¹ Batt. Nan. lib. iii. 1617. Conjuration des Efpagnols, etc. par M. L'Abbé St. Real.
⁵⁵ Nicol. Machiavelli, Storia Fiorentina, lib. i.
⁵⁷ Condottieri.

people as well as their princes. Conspiracies, together with other practices and arts, were diffused from Italy over other parts of Europe; and especially over those countries between which and Italy there was a close intercourse and connexion ⁰⁰. It is the nature of every passion to tend as directly as possible towards its object ⁰⁰. The love of power, and the desire of revenge, wait not the slow process of conspiracies, nor trust to their uncertain issue, when they can gain their end by the plain and direct road of superior force. It was a proof of the decline of Spain, that she adopted a practice, founded in fear and weakness. But

Spanish conspiracy against Venice.

⁰⁰ It is confessed, that plots and assassinations are to be found in the history of all nations: yet it will readily be allowed, that these are more frequent in that of modern Italy than in the accounts we have of any other country, if the reign of Philip III. of Spain does not form an exception to this position. As writers commonly chuse for the subjects of their productions, things not wholly unknown, but which they suppose to need new proofs and illustrations, so the famous Machiavel did not interweave into his political system, those dishonorable artifices which set all justice and fidelity at defiance, from a mischievous originality in his own mind. He laid down rules for conspiracies, because conspiracies were in every body's mouth, and every where practised. To plan and accomplish an ingenious plot, formed, in his time, a branch of political education. Archbishop Spotswood, in his History, relates, that when he visited the earl of Gowrie, who formed a conspiracy against James VI. king of Scotland, he found him reading a Latin book de Conjurationibus. The earl had been a professor of philosophy in Italy, from whence he had just returned.

⁰⁰ Unde feritur eo tendit gestitque coire. Lucret.

BOOK V.
1618.

of all the conspiracies or plots which were formed or connived at by the Spanish ministers, in this or any other period, that which was framed against the republic of Venice, by Don Alphonso de la Cueva, marquis of Bedmar, was the most remarkable, and the most important, whether we have respect to its end, or to that complicated machinery by which it was to be accomplished. That the marquis was a person of very extraordinary abilities sufficiently appears from this circumstance, that, at a time when the cabinet of Madrid had an option of distinguished abilities, he was appointed ambassador in ordinary at Venice, of all the courts of Europe the most refined in its politics and determined in its counsels. From an intimate acquaintance with ancient as well as modern history, which he read with the eyes of a philosopher and statesman, and much observation on the scene of human life, in which he was at once an important actor and judicious spectator, he acquired a sagacity to which the council of Spain looked up with an almost superstitious veneration. To a deep insight into the nature of political affairs, he added those qualities that are so requisite in a practical politician; a facility of speaking and writing with inexpressible grace; a quick discernment of characters; an air and manner always frank and unreserved; and at the same time such force of mind, that under the most trying feelings of the heart, and the severest agitations of the passions, he betrayed not the smallest symptom of perturbation,

Character of the marquis of Bedmar.

PHILIP III. KING OF SPAIN.

but on the contrary retained the moſt unequivocal appearance of perfect ſerenity [70]. With theſe qualities, which diſtinguiſhed his character, he poſſeſſed in an eminent degree another, which is common to all Spaniards; a zeal for the glory of the monarchy and the honor of the Spaniſh name. This had of late undergone an eclipſe, and the marquis was willing to revive its luſtre by the total ruin of a power that had contributed ſo greatly to its decay, the republic of Venice. He was invited to attack this ſtate by various circumſtances; the war with the Auſtrians had drained Venice both of arms and men; the fleet was confined to Iſtria, the ſeat of the war; the land army was equally diſtant; the exigencies of war had occaſioned the moſt oppreſſive taxes, which, as the people ſuſpected, were not wholly applied to the public uſe: the marquis, therefore, perſuaded himſelf that the revolution he had planned would not only be practicable, but to the generality of the people, acceptable; nay, of the nobility, not a few were diſcontented with the government, and rejoiced in all the misfortunes of the ſtate, as the effects of meaſures which they had diſapproved. The more neceſſitous of that order, the marquis knew by experience, might be prevailed on, if not to act a part in the tragedy, yet to give ſuch intelligence as might in reality promote the cataſtrophe of Venice. Another ground of encouragement was, that the flower of the Venetian army conſiſted of

[70] Conjuration des Eſpagnols, etc. St. Real.

BOOK V.
1618.

Hollanders and Walloons, mercenaries, whose officers he trusted might be seduced by the powerful allurements of gold, to betray the cause of Venice, and to espouse that of Spain. The fleet of the republic was indeed formidable, but there too he hoped to make dreadful havoc with the same weapons he proposed to employ in weakening the Venetian army. It only remained, that he should attach to his person, and to the terrible object he had in view, a sufficient number of determined confidents, by means of whom he might combine the efforts of thousands in a scheme, with the nature of which they were not to be intrusted until the moment of execution. He imparted his project to the marquis of Villa Franca, and the duke of Ossuna. These ministers were delighted with the novelty and the boldness of his ideas, and without hesitation promised to contribute all in their power towards its accomplishment. It does not appear that he communicated his design to the court of Madrid; but he was sufficiently acquainted with the ideas of ambition that still reigned in the council of Spain, to know, that if the project should be carried happily into execution, of which he did not entertain any doubt, it would meet with their hearty applause and admiration. But while this project was ripening by degrees, the court of Spain was obliged, by the vigor of the young king of France, to make gradual advances towards a general peace in Italy. This would have disarmed the troops of Spain, and deprived the conspirators of those instruments with which they hoped to subject to the monarchy the states of Venice. Hence the various artifices of Toledo and Ossuna to prolong the war, and to prevent a final accommodation of differences. The marquis had by this time entered into the most intimate correspondence and confidence with a number of men, who, confiding in the transcendent powers of his mind, and contemplating the mighty rewards that were exhibited to their view, were ready to execute his orders with promptitude and alacrity. These men were highly distinguished from the multitude, by constancy in the most trying situations, by unshaken fidelity to their engagements, and by a bold and daring courage. Nothing was wanting to entitle them to the highest degree of praise, but the exertion of these virtues in a worthy cause.

The principal arrangements in this conspiracy were these: fifteen hundred veteran troops, chosen from the Spanish army in Milan, by Don Pedro himself, were to be introduced into the city of Venice, not in a body, but a few at a time, and unarmed. They were to receive arms from the marquis of Bedmar. But lest any unforeseen accident should mar the intentions of Toledo, five thousand Hollanders, who lay at the Lazaretto, not above two miles distant from the city, were ready to be introduced, man by man, at first, and afterwards, in the tumult and confusion that was expected to ensue, in a body. Brigantines and barks were to be sent from Naples into the channels and ports of Venice, having on board fix thoufand men. A number of large fhips were afterwards to caft anchor on the fhores of Friuli. Under the countenance of the latter, and amidft the confufion and horrors to be excited by the former, the confpirators were to act their feveral parts in the intended tragedy: one was to fet fire to the arfenal, others to different parts of the city; fome were to take poffeffion of the mint; fome to feize the principal places of ftrength; and the part allotted to many, was, to annihilate the conftitution of Venice by murdering the fenators. Artillery was to be drawn up to the higheft eminences, for the purpofe of laying the city in ruins, in cafe the inhabitants fhould attempt refiftance. Field-pieces were to be difpofed in different quarters of the city, pointing into the principal ftreets. And as it was neceffary to be in poffeffion of fome inland town in the territories of the republic, which might ferve as a barrier againft the return of the Venetian land-army, if called to Venice to oppofe the confpirators, and as a magazine for the Spanifh army, Don Pedro held a clofe correfpondence with certain officers of the garrifon of Crema, who were to betray that town into the hands of the Spaniards. Another plot was yet neceffary to give full effect to the grand confpiracy. A port was to be occupied in the Venetian gulf, which might receive the Spanifh fleet, if, by any accident, it fhould be obliged to feek a retreat, when employed in that fea. There is a place of confiderable ftrength, called Marano, in an island bordering upon Istria, with a harbour capable of receiving a large fleet. The officer second in command in the garrison of Marano engaged to assassinate the governor, whenever he should receive orders from Toledo, and to hold the town in the name of the Spaniards [71].

Such was the complicated scheme formed for the destruction of the renowned city and republic of Venice: a scheme which involved in its nature whatever human ingenuity could plan, or the courage of man dare to execute, but which failed of success from some of those unforeseen accidents that so often happen to intimidate the hearts of assassins, and to disconcert the projects of conspirators [72].

A conspiracy so important in its end, and at the same time so various in its means, does not occur in history. That of Catiline against the Roman republic, pointed to equal horrors, and to a still greater revolution; but the means by which he hoped to accomplish it were more simple, and consequently less absurd than those employed by

[71] Conjuration des Espagnols, &c. St. Real. Conspiration & Trahison admirable des Espagnols, &c. en 1618. Histoire du Connet. de Lesdiguieres, liv. ix. But. Nani, Historia della Republica Veneta, lib. iii. 1618.

[72] The abbé St. Real says, that the conspiracy was discovered by one of the conspirators, who was struck with horror and remorse at the intended ruin and bloodshed: Battista Nani, that it was discovered by two French gentlemen, who had come to the knowledge of it, relations of marechal Lesdiguieres.

BOOK V.
1618.

the bold imagination, rather than the solid judgement of the marquis of Bedmar. It was probably in imitation of that circumstantial and interesting narrative which the Roman historian has given of the Catilinarian conspiracy, that the eloquent and profound Saint Real composed his beautiful account of the Spanish conspiracy against Venice. This copious narrative, though heightened in some instances by the colorings of poetry, and the circumstantiality of fiction, is yet true in the most material particulars, and serves, in the words of the author to display the "power of prudence over human affairs, and the dominion of fortune; the extent of the limits of the human mind, its greatest strength, and its secret frailties; the numberless considerations to which the politician must attend, who aspires to govern his fellow men; and the difference between true and false refinement." It is this last reflection which perpetually recurs to the reader, and strikes him with peculiar force. Nothing but the extravagance of hope, and the blindness of passion, could have seduced the judgment of Don Alphonso de la Cueva, to believe that he should be able, by any efforts of genius, to combine into one harmonious machine, so many and such various springs. The various ideas and corresponding emotions and passions which rise in the mind on different occasions, and in different circumstances, render the views and designs of men fluctuating and uncertain. The smallest incident in health or fortune is sufficient to shake a refolution big with danger and death. The minds of men are fo delicate, refined, and variable inftruments, that a thoufand accidents difturb their operation. The moft fortunate adventurers in life, are thofe who do not pretend to form, but who have vigilance and fagacity to improve conjunctures. Political revolutions are not to be effected by the fubtilties and refinements of a genius profound and metaphyfical; but by the boldnefs and dexterity of a Cæfar or a Cromwell, who know to feize the important moment of decifive execution.

But if fo vaft a project as the confpiracy againft the city and republic of Venice, had not been altogether beyond the reach of human abilities, it might poffibly have been accomplifhed by the united efforts of Toledo, Offuna, and the marquis of Bedmar. Though the revenues of Spain were greatly diminifhed, and a manifeft languor and irrefolution appeared in her counfels, her military genius was yet entire and unbroken; nor in the hiftory of any people is there to be found a greater compafs of political ability and art than at this time diftinguifhed the Spanifh nation. While the minifters of Spain in Italy, by the moft extraordinary efforts to fupport or retrieve the glory of the monarchy, fignalized at leaft their own ingenuity and courage, the abilities of her ambaffadors generally managed the courts at which they refided with equal dexterity and fuccefs. The ties of intereft and blood, which united the two

BOOK V.
1618.

branches of the houfe of Auſtria, obſcure the praiſes that are due to the abilities of the Spaniſh miniſters at the courts of Ferdinand and Matthias. But in France, Monteleone knew how to adapt his tone to the timidity of Mary, the high ſpirit of Lewis, and the different paſſions and views of their reſpective favorites. And in England, Gondomar gained mightily on the favor of the pedantic, ſocial, and impolitic king, by talking falſe Latin [73], with other facetious humors, and by amuſing him with the hope of a marriage between the prince of Wales and the ſecond infanta [74].

---

[73] Mr. Arthur Wilſon, in his Life of King James, informs us, among other curious anecdotes of that good-natured monarch, that "Gondomar in his merry fits would tell the king that his majeſty ſpoke Latin like a Pedant, but that he himſelf ſpoke it like a gentleman." The king, we may preſume, accepted this as a high encomium. There was nothing in which James exulted ſo much, as in that ſuperiority which he undoubtedly poſſeſſed over moſt of his courtiers, in literature. "Sir Edward Conway, ſays Mr. Wilſon, governor of the Brille, one of the cautionary towns, was made by king James, ſecretary of ſtate: a rough unpoliſhed piece for ſuch an employment! But the king, who wanted not his abilities, would often make himſelf merry with his imperfect ſcrawls in writing, and hacking expreſſions in reading, ſo that he would break into laughter, and ſay, had ever man ſuch a ſecretary, that can neither read nor write?" Gondomar had perfectly underſtood the character of the king: and he practiſed on his weakneſſes with infinite dexterity.

[74] Franklin, p. 71.

A war with the Saracens, prolonged, with few intervals, for eight hundred years, nourished in the Spaniards a vigor of character, a love of their country, and a passion for glory. The necessity of continually engaging, formed as many heroes as there were men in each city: military renown was the great object of their vows; and the tombs of the deceased were adorned with a number of obelisks equal to that of the enemy they had slain in battle [75]. While they lived exposed to continual dangers they acquired that gravity of deportment, that deliberate valor, that perseverance and vigilance which still distinguish the Spanish nation. Before the ambitious and warlike reigns of Ferdinand, the emperor, and Philip II. the sagacity and vigilance of the Spaniards appeared formidable to the other nations of Europe [76]. These reigns continued to call forth and exercise the spirit of the nation, and to support, if not to heighten, that national character which had been formed by the wars with the Moors. And this national character still shone forth with undiminished lustre after the imprudence

---

[75] Johannes Genesius Sepulveda de Rebus Gestis, Caroli V. lib. i.

[76] Machiavel says, in his Account of the State of France, that the French were afraid of the Spaniards on account of their sagacity and vigilance. It is true, that this account was written after Ferdinand had begun to reign: but it was before the exertions of that prince could have stamped on the minds of his subjects, a national character.

BOOK V.
1618.

of the court, and exhausted resources, had undermined the foundations of the grandeur of the empire. As prosperous war rouses the genius of a nation, the glory of letters would have corresponded to that of the Spanish arms, had not the progress of taste and knowledge been checked by the tyranny of the inquisition, and that despotism which was introduced into the government. But although these circumstances have prevented among the Spaniards the growth of sound philosophy, in their poetry, history, romances, and even their commentaries on the sacred scriptures, as well as on Aristotle, whose metaphysical notions were deemed so orthodox by the Catholic church, we recognise that boldness and invention, that subtilty and refinement which were conspicuous for ages in the military and political conduct of Spain.

Thus, that power of genius and valor among his subjects, which at once adorned and disgraced the feeble reign of Philip III. seems deducible from a train of moral causes, as obvious in their existence as powerful in their nature. But when the reader revolves what is left on record concerning ancient Spain, he will be inclined perhaps to subscribe to the opinion of an ingenious writer, that the characters of nations as well as families, are influenced by accidents antecedent to birth [77], and particularly by climate, acting either immediately with powerful energy on the fabric of

---

[77] Essays on the History of Mankind, &c. by Dr. Dunbar.

their being, or as a local circumftance leading to a variety of action in the economy of civil life. At all times, valor and genius have ennobled the character of the Spaniards. Not the robuft German, impelled by the fury of a favage religion, difplayed fuch enthufiafm in arms and contempt of death, as fhone forth in the invincible refolution of the inhabitants of Numantia, Aftapa, and Saguntum. A greater hero than Viriatus is not to be found in the hiftory of ancient Rome "[78]. Between the times of the Scipios and thofe of Auguftus, there intervened a period of two hundred years. During this long fpace, Spain maintained a conteft with the policy and difciplined valor of Rome: and it feemed uncertain which mafters the world was to obey, the Spaniards or the Romans. The deftiny of Rome to give law to the nations finally fubdued all refiftance, and Spain had the glory of being the laft that yielded to the Roman yoke. But it was the fortune of the vanquifhed to receive literature and refinement from the conquerors of the world: and in return, Trajan added luftre to the Roman purple; and the names of Quintilian, Martial, Mela, Seneca, Lucan, and Florus, appeared in the lift of Latin authors.

---

[78] This man, who had refifted the Roman arms for twenty years, and who was deemed invincible, was at laft infidioufly cut off by the Romans, who bribed his bodyguards.

BOOK V.
1618.
The duke of Savoy and the Venetians maintain their independence.

All the valor and artifices of Spain were found unable to subdue the independence of the duke of Savoy and the Venetian republic. And the discovery of Bedmar's conspiracy was quickly followed by the restoration of Vercelli to the duke, and that of their ships and merchandize to the Venetians. The court of Madrid at the desire of the senate, recalled de la Cueva; but a commission to act as first minister in the Netherlands, a department which the situation of affairs in Germany rendered equally difficult and important, proved how much they approved his designs, as well as confided in his abilities.

THE HISTORY

OF THE REIGN OF

PHILIP THE THIRD,

KING OF SPAIN.

BOOK VI.

THE astonishing efforts of that extraordinary triumvirate Bedmar, Ossuna, and Villa Franca, to restore the predominancy of Spain in Italy, was an eruption of that ardent spirit which had been bred in times of national enterprise and prosperity. The monarchy, drained of its blood and spirits by emigrations, and by war, was in a state of languor which naturally sought for repose. To maintain the dignity of the Spanish nation in that languishing state, was the arduous task devolved by the feeble hands of Philip on the duke of Lerma. That pacific and prudent minister, unwilling to expose the weakness of the empire, avoided as much as possible all appeals to arms, and it was not without reluctance that he drew the sword which he had sheathed at Antwerp, in the dispute concerning the succession to Juliers, and in the contest with the duke of Savoy. It was his chief study to support the authority of Spain by intrigue, and by external magnificence and profusion. The court of Madrid was the moſt brilliant in Europe: and a veil of pomp and ſplendor thrown around all the departments of government concealed from the vulgar eye the ſymptoms of its decay [1]. The duke alſo made ſome attempts to recruit the vigor of the ſtate, as well as to hide its infirmities, by reviving agriculture, and protecting commerce.

The frequent examples of immenſe and rapid fortunes, made in the Indies, inſpired a contempt of tillage, the profits of which, though certain, were both ſlow and inconſiderable. Until the fatal year 1609, Spain poſſeſſed a remedy againſt this evil. The Moreſcoes, excluded by the laws from America, and from the profeſſion of arms, were not only expert manufacturers, but ſkilful and induſtrious huſbandmen; but their expulſion was followed by a ſtill more general neglect of agriculture, and a ſcarcity of the neceſſaries of life puniſhed the people for the bigotry of the court, and their own indolence. The duke of Lerma, in order to repair the loſs of the induſtrious Saracens, iſſued an edict, offering an order of nobility [2] to every man who ſhould give proofs of induſtry and ſkill in agriculture. It is remarkable that this meaſure, the propriety of which ſeemed to be founded in the national paſſion for lofty titles, was altogether fruitleſs. An exemption from all military ſervice was then

[1] See Appendix C.
[2] The title and rank of Eſquire. Les Délices d'Eſpagne & de Portugal.

promised to all industrious men; but neither had this proffered indulgence any considerable effect. A great part of the land still lay waste, and in the succeeding reign, strangers were invited to cultivate the fields of Spain, with several advantages of great importance.

The commerce of the Spaniards in the Mediterranean having been disturbed by the corsairs of Barbary, Don Lewis de Faxarado received orders to build a strong fort on the gulf of Marmora. This was happily effected in the month of August 1613, and contributed not a little to scour the sea from pirates[1]. But commerce still languished as well as manufactures and agriculture, and the exactions of a government profusely expensive, were severely felt by the oppressed people. Nor were the exigencies of the public the only source of those taxes which afflicted the nation. The minister amassed an immense fortune from the spoils of the people. From the island of Sicily alone he drew an annual revenue of as much wheat as, being converted into money, amounted to seventy-two thousand ducats. This he obtained from his easy master, in the name of a reward for his important services. Even the good qualities of the duke multiplied the oppressions of his administration. His love of splendor and magnificence, his liberalities to his servants, his dependants, and to all men who had recourse to his bounty, rendered his paternal inheritance wholly inadequate to

[1] Summarium de Rebus Hispaniæ. Mariana.

BOOK VI.
1618.

his constant profusion, which he supported at the expense of the public. The great offices of state too, he either seized himself or bestowed on particular favorites. And although caution and prudence are qualities generally and justly ascribed to the duke of Lerma, in the distribution of offices he was not always governed by motives of policy, but sometimes those of personal attachment. But of all his favorites the chief was the famous Don Roderigo de Calderona, whose singular fortune and fate demand particular attention. He was the son of a poor soldier of Valladolid, and Mary Sandelen, a native of Flanders. He possessed fine talents, and there was something highly interesting and engaging in his manner. He entered on the career of ambition in the character of a menial servant to the duke of Lerma, then marquis of Denia, and gained over the mind of his master such an ascendant as that favorite possessed over the mind of the king. Having risen through all the principal offices in the household of the duke, he was advanced by the unbounded favor of his patron to places of great power and trust in the state, created first count of Oliva, then marquis of Siete Iglesias, and acquired an estate of a hundred thousand crowns a year. Agreeably to the natural progress of human wishes, Calderona considered all the favors of fortune only as so many steps to farther preferment. He openly aspired not only to a vice-royalty, but to the rank of a grandee of Spain. He was at first ashamed of

Don Roderigo de Calderona.

the meanness of his descent, and affected to conceal it: a frailty to which he afterwards showed himself far superior, by receiving his father into his family, procuring for the old soldier offices of emolument as well as honor, and treating him throughout life with the greatest tenderness and respect. Though he had risen from the lowest rank of life, there was nothing in his behaviour unworthy of the highest birth. The dignity both of his sentiments and manners was such as might beseem a prince. The vanity of Calderona which had made him ashamed of his father, was now converted by an excess of prosperity into a haughty boldness and overbearing pride. His temper, naturally violent and impetuous, was unrestrained by any of those condescensions and regards, which were so necessary in his situation, to sooth jealousy and disarm the rancor of envy. He mingled in all the intrigues at court; he delighted in the exercise of power; his favor was the surest road to preferment, and this he distributed, for the most part, according to his own fancy and caprice, and without any regard either to merit or natural pretensions. He had audiences as if he had been a sovereign prince, held frequent consultations, and shared in one word, the administration of public affairs with the duke of Lerma. The haughtiness and impetuosity of Don Roderigo was contrasted by that decent moderation which appeared in the whole conduct and deportment of his father. This man frequently told his son, that his bark, which had so little ballast, if he should continue to crowd sail, would infallibly be overset in a storm: a prediction which was afterwards fatally verified [*].

The nobles of Spain, whose power and influence had been reduced in the two preceding reigns, from the highest to the lowest pitch, were called to the court of Philip III. and many of them enjoyed important political stations. But during those reigns the order of nobility, if it was depressed by the vigor and the tyranny of the court, had not the mortification to see any subject exalted so far above them in the royal favor as to possess in reality the power of the sovereign. To the grandees of Spain, a favorite was a hateful novelty, and the immoderate aggrandizement of Calderona seemed a studied insult on nobility of blood. Nor was the present administration distinguished by any prosperous events which might drown the general murmurs of discontent in the voice of applause and acclamation. The prime minister was accordingly a general subject of satire and invective, both in discourse and in writing. The complaints of the nation served as an engine in the hands of his enemies to effect his downfal, which was embittered by this cruel circumstance, that his power was subverted by those very men who were the most bound, by the ties of blood, or of gratitude, to support it.

[*] Gonç. de Cespedes, lib. i. capitulo vii. Amelot de la Houssaie, Discours historique, p. 142. Las Memorias, &c. con Escolios de Don Juan Vitrian, 11. 13.

Having risen to the highest power attainable by a subject, and having no farther object of ambition, the duke of Lerma only labored to establish the authority he possessed in the councils of Spain, on the firmest foundations, and to perpetuate it, if possible, in his family. With this view he introduced his son, the duke of Uzeda, at proper times, into the presence of the king, and used every art to recommend him with effect to the royal favor. And, well knowing that the influence he possessed on the mind of Philip might be either strenghtened or overcome by any argument that should make its appearance in the guise of religion, he brought Lewis Aliaga, a monk, from his convent to court, and advanced him to the office of confessor to the king. Aliaga was a man of a narrow capacity, and the duke entertained a high opinion of his probity. From a character of this kind he imagined he had nothing to apprehend. And, as the monk owed every thing to his favor, he trusted that he would be entirely devoted to his interest. Uzeda was one of those insignificant characters, whose understandings are below mediocrity, and who are neither remarkable for vice nor virtue. But he possessed in an eminent degree the polished manners of a court, and by his constant assiduities to please, soon obtained as high a place in the affections of the king as Lerma still maintained in his esteem. The bewitching smiles of sovereignty, equally dissolving filial reverence and paternal tenderness, occasioned a rivality between

BOOK VI.
1618.
Fall of Lerma.

BOOK VI.
1618.

the father and the son, which terminated in an animosity that promixity of blood seemed only to irritate. Aliaga perceived the power which this diffension placed in his hands, and deliberated whether he should cast the balance in favor of Lerma or Uzeda. The alternative he embraced is worthy of attention, not only on account of its political consequences, but as it seems to prove that there is in the mind of man a disposition to expect, in his own behalf, a higher degree of virtue from others than he is conscious of possessing himself. Friar Aliaga, equally unmindful of that creative bounty which the generosity of a patron so readily extends to the person whom he has already obliged, and of the treachery and ingratitude of his own heart, determined to abandon his benefactor, and to unite his interest with that of Uzeda, imagining that he had more to expect from a minister on whom he had conferred, than from one to whom he owed the greatest obligations. The duke of Lerma endeavoured to counterbalance the growing influence of his son, by raising up a rival to him in the affections of the king. For this purpose he now labored to insinuate into the royal favor his sister's son, the count of Lemos, a nobleman of high spirit and sublime genius. He hoped to excite such movements of jealousy and envy between the count and Uzeda, as that he himself should be equally necessary to both, and be able to hold in his own hands the balance of power between the contending rivals. But the pliant mind, and gentle manners of Uzeda, were more congenial to the nature of Philip than the erect and independent spirit of Lemos. The king was constantly attended by his new favorite and his confessor, and surrounded with numbers of discontented nobles, with whom these men kept up a close correspondence.

In the midst of these intrigues the duke of Lerma solicits and obtains the rank of a cardinal, hoping that this religious dignity would prove the means of prolonging his power over the mind of the pious king, or at least, that it would place him above the malice of his enemies and the inquiries of justice. But it was the fortune of this duke to undermine his own power by those very measures which were intended to support it The indolent Philip was displeased to be under the necessity of exchanging the ease of former familiarity for those ceremonies of respect which were due to the purple. The regard that had been every where shown to the duke of Lerma was well pleasing to the king, so long as all that he enjoyed was derived from his own bounty. The respect that was paid to the creature of his power he considered as an homage done to himself. But all his affections for the duke ceased the moment he attained to an equality with kings, and derived the splendor of his character from another source than the grace of his sovereign. The presence of the cardinal was uneasy to him, and if he received him with formality, he received him also with coldness.

BOOK VI.
1618.

The estrangement of the king from his old minister was not unobserved by the eager eyes of the courtiers. The enemies of the cardinal duke, who had hitherto conducted their attacks by regular and slow approaches, now resolved to carry that fortress, which had so long defended him, and in which he still fondly confided, by assault. Upon the plausible pretext of zeal for the service of the king, and affection for his person, they represented the nation as one scene of oppression, disorder, and discontent, and threw the blame of the whole on the duke of Lerma. That minister, they affirmed, bestowed the most important offices on persons who possessed not any other merit than that of being agreeable to his fancy, and the creatures of his power. And as the appointment to offices was a matter that depended solely on his favor, so the exercise of the power he bestowed was determined by his will: for he over-ruled the freedom of deliberation in the different councils established for the conduct of public affairs, and assumed the prerogative of dictating on every subject. The judges, in all cases where he chose to interfere, being obliged to give sentence according to his orders, the very tribunals of justice were organs of his pleasure. On the distresses of the people they insisted with peculiar zeal, lamenting, that the poor of a whole nation should be despoiled of the few things they possessed, and even deprived of the necessaries of life, for the purpose of supporting the magnificence and mad extravagance of one man: a man who by various impolitic meafures, and particularly by the circulation of brafs-money; had contributed fo fatally to the decline of manufactures, the ruin of commerce, the depopulation and impoverifhment of the kingdom. Paffing beyond the limits of Spain, they reviewed the conduct of the duke in the dependencies of the monarchy. The revenues of Sicily he had converted into a private eftate. The war in Piedmont, fo unavoidable in its progrefs, and in its iffue fo difhonorable to the Spanifh name, might have been crufhed in its beginning by force of arms, or prevented by a timely attention to the fituation and defigns of foreign ftates. As in war an able commander makes it his chief ftudy to divide the forces of his enemy, fo the art of government confifts not in refifting, but in preventing confederacies. Wars which, even if fuccefsful, cannot be advantageous, ought never to be undertaken. The lion, faid they, in the proverbial manner of Spain, is not honored by a victory over the lamb. A fuperior power, if not greatly dificient in forefight, can never be at a lofs to reftrain the turbulence of an inferior, without coming to an open rupture, and refting its authority on the doubtful events of war. From Italy they turned the eyes of the king to the feven United Provinces, once a part of that fair inheritance to which he had fo juft a claim as the heir of the duke of Burgundy. The truce with Holland; the formalities and folemnities with which that treaty had been ratified, and particu-

lastly the pompous title that had been given in that contract to the rebels, they mentioned with particular marks of indignation. They contrasted the virtue and the ability of the pensionary Barnevelt, with the incapacity of the duke of Lerma, and his indifference to the prosperity and glory of the nation. Unable to conduct the war, the Spanish minister, they said, sought to establish his own power in peace; a peace that was disgraceful in its nature, and which involved in its consequences a greater loss to the monarchy than it had incurred during a war of forty-five years that preceded it! While the war continued in the Netherlands, the main force of the rebels, concentrated in those provinces, acted only on the defensive. But the ignominious treaty of Antwerp had let loose that force on the widely scattered settlements of Spain in both the Indies, which were either torn from the monarchy, or demanded such additional garrisons for their protection, as might have been employed with greater honor, as well as advantage, in prosecuting the war on the theatre of rebellion. If the Spanish crown, in a glorious contest to maintain its just rights, should have proved unsuccessful, nothing more disastrous could have ensued than what had actually happened: while, on the other hand, to have continued the struggle, would have supported the honor of the nation among foreign powers, and, in the end, might possibly have derived some advantage from the chance of war, or that change which is incident to the policy and the views of states and princes. These and many other charges against the duke of Lerma, were constantly sounded in the ears of the king, by his confessor and his favorite, and confirmed by the testimony or the authority of all whom they permitted to have access to his person.

Though sovereign princes, from the supereminence of their stations, be naturally capricious, and fickle in their attachments [s], it would be unreasonable, after these remonstrances, to ascribe the fall of Lerma to any inconstancy in his sovereign. There never was a prince, however despotic, so secure against the resentment, so insensible to the applause, or so unconcerned for the prosperity of the public, as to oppose, for the sake of a favorite, the general voice of his people. The constant appointment to offices, in contradiction to the recommendation of Lerma, fully illustrated the nature of that reserve, which had given that minister so much pain, and was an unequivocal proof that he had wholly lost the royal favor. In this extremity he labored to acquire the good graces of the prince of Spain, fondly hoping that the rays of the rising would brighten up the gloom that attended the setting sun. The count de Lemos, and Don Ferdinand de Borgia, a man of sound understanding, and possessed of talents for business, both lords of

---

[s] Go, says Agamemnon to Achilles, if you have a mind; there are not wanting others who will show me honor. First Iliad.

BOOK VI.
1618.

the bedchamber to the prince, had been raifed to that dignity by the duke their uncle. Betrayed and injured by the cunning of Aliaga and Uzeda, the duke of Lerma had recourfe to the friendfhip of his nephews; he met with virtue and honor where one would wifh to find them, and where in reality they are oftenest to be found, in conjunction with vigor of underftanding, and fublimity of genius. The count of Lemos and Don Ferdinand de Borgia were united by the ties of blood, of friendfhip, and gratitude to their uncle. They readily undertook to ufe their good offices with the prince in behalf of their beloved relation; they reprefented to his highnefs the weak capacity of Uzeda; and expatiated on the talents, virtues, and political experience of the duke his father. And their authority and addrefs prevailing over the fubtilties and affiduities of the conde duke of Olivarez, confoled Lerma with the hope of living in the favor of the heir apparent to the Spanifh empire. But this intrigue was not long concealed from the king, and, like all the other efforts of the minifter to prolong his power, ferved only to precipitate his fall. The image of death which was held up to the imagination of the king by the court that was paid to his fucceffor, converted his indifference to Lerma into averfion. The count de Lemos had gained fo much on the favor of the prince, that he was in the practice of converfing with him fometimes for hours after he went to bed. Orders were now fent to the count to forbear this practice in future; but to these he did not yield a ready obedience. The king therefore difmiffed from the fervice of his highnefs * four officers of his bedchamber, who were in the confidence of Lemos, and appointed his coufin and faithful friend, Don Ferdinand de Borgia, viceroy of Arragon. The high-fpirited count, deeming the difgrace of the officers, and the exile of his friend from court, an affront and injury to himfelf, had the boldnefs to afk the king his reafons for removing Don Ferdinand from the fervice of the prince, adding, that if Ferdinand fhould be banifhed from the court, he would accompany him to the place of his retirement. The king replied in an angry tone, that it was his pleafure to treat Don Ferdinand as he had done; and that the count, if he were fo minded, might accompany him in his exile. Lemos was mortified by fo fevere a reply; yet he made another effort to keep Borgia at court, and that almoft in fpite of the king. He engaged the council for Italian affairs, of which Borgia was prefident, to remonftrate againft the removal of a minifter, who, of all men in the world, was the beft informed with regard to the affairs of Italy. The king anfwered, that he would appoint as fucceffor to Don Ferdinand the count of Benevento, whofe knowledge of Italian affairs was unqueftionable. Upon this the count de Lemos retired from court, confoling himfelf with the reflection that he had made no mean compliances to gain the royal favor, but had per-

* Su Altezza, fo the prince was diftinguifhed.

formed the duties of friendship, and in the whole of his deportment maintained the noblest propriety and dignity of character.

The magnanimity of the count seemed to arraign the conduct of the duke of Lerma, who, even after the disgrace of his friends, lingered about the Escurial, and manifested the most eager desire still to hold his office. The king, finding that no marks of his disgust, however striking, were able to induce his old minister to prevent the disgrace of a formal dismission, in a billet written with his own hand, ordered him in express terms to withdraw himself from Madrid; but permitted him to retire to whatever place he should chuse, and enjoy in peace the effects of his former bounty. In these circumstances the duke condescended to appear as a suppliant at the feet of the treacherous Aliaga. He entreated the monk to intercede in his behalf with the king. It is superfluous to inform the reader that this humble application was wholly fruitless. He then sent a message to his brother, the archbishop of Toledo, whom he had raised to the high dignity and opulence he enjoyed, and who at that time resided at Madrid, earnestly soliciting him to come to the Escurial, and to support him with his countenance, his advice, and his influence with the king. The archbishop excused himself from undertaking that ungracious office, by alledging that he was in a bad state of health; but he sent to the assistance of his brother father

Jerome

Jerome, of Florence, a Jesuit, a preacher for whom the king entertained a particular respect. Father Jerome, in his private discourse with the king, endeavoured with great address to revive in his mind sentiments of favor and regard to the duke of Lerma. But Philip did not receive his favorite preacher with his usual affability, nor listen to his instructions with wonted attention. The Jesuit, perceiving this alteration in the deportment of the king, did not persevere in his commendations of Lerma, and only pleaded, in favor of that minister, for a short respite, which was refused in positive terms.

The duke of Lerma now summoned up all his fortitude, and by the propriety and dignity of his deportment atoned for the meanness of his former solicitations. On the 4th day of October 1618, being still in his apartments in the palace, he was ready to take his journey to his paternal estate, with a train of attendants suitable to his high rank, when the prince of Spain, who happened to take a walk in the garden, came up to the door of his chamber, and calling him aside, conversed with him a considerable length in the language of tenderness and complacency. The duke then went to take leave of his sister, the countess of Lemos, first lady of the bed-chamber to the princess of Spain. Having bowed to that lady five times, with great respect, he went into his chariot, and repaired for the last time to the mansion of the king. On his approach, he alighted from his carriage, and viewing the royal apartments with an eager eye, he ardently poured forth his blessing on them, and on the royal family. Having performed this duty, he remounted his chariot, and drove straight to Guadarrama, where he lodged all night. At this place he received a letter from the king, the contents of which were never revealed to the curious and speculating world, with a present of a stag, slain by his own hand that day in the chase. Thus both the king and the prince of Spain, with a generosity worthy of their exalted stations, mixed the bitter cup of Lerma with refreshing spices: and as no minister ever descended from a greater height of power, so none was ever laid more softly down [7], and few perhaps ever deserved a gentler fall.

The duke of Lerma was a personage of a noble mien, gentle manners, and a beneficent disposition. The natural benignity of his heart appeared in the mildness of his aspect, the tone of his voice, and innumerable acts of munificence and liberality. His promotions to public offices were chiefly determined by political motives and personal friendship. Yet, it may be safely affirmed, that during his administration, all the places of principal trust and importance were filled with men of extraordinary

---

[7] Historia de Don Felippe III. por Don Gon. de Cespedes, lib. i. cap. 3, 4. lib. ii. cap. 1. 17. Anecdotes du Ministere du Comte duc d'Olivarez. Las Memorias de Comines con Escolios proprios de Don Juan Vitrian. Amelot de la Houssaie, Disc. Histor. Addiciones à la Historia de Espanna, por Malvezzi.

abilities. The judgments of men are commonly influenced by their natural temper. Agreeably to the mildnefs of his own difpofition, and his love of magnificence, he was of opinion that the dignity of the Spanifh monarchy was beft maintained by peace, pomp, and parade [*]. And though he might, perhaps, have purfued this plan with greater economy, as it is certain that his profufion was not the main caufe, fo it is probable that all his favings, had he been ever fo much inclined to frugality, would not have been able to alleviate in any confiderable degree the diftreffes of the nation. Though his capacity was but moderate, his foul was elevated, and his mind was firm. If he defcended from his natural dignity to humble applications, in order to preferve the good graces of his prince, we ought not on that account too haftily to ftigmatize his memory with meannefs of fpirit. The greateft political and military courage has funk under the deprivation of royal favor. Neither the refolute Ximenes, nor the undaunted Albuquerque, was able to fupport the frowns of his fovereign. Notwithftanding the invectives

---

[*] He was very careful to exact every mark of refpect to the crown of Spain from neighbouring nations, and fometimes difcovered a jealoufy on this head which was unworthy of a great nation. I find in Chamberlayne's Letters MSS. anno 1616, in the Britifh Mufeum, the following paffage: "The Spanifh ambaffador complained to the king at Theobald's, that whereas we kept ambaffadors at Venice and in the Low Countries, an agent ferved the turn in Spain and with the archdukes.

BOOK VI.
1618.

of Lerma's enemies, the moſt reſpectable Spaniſh hiſtorians [9] not only celebrate the beneficence of his diſpoſition, but do juſtice to the moderation of his power, and the prudence of his public conduct. Theſe indeed, were afterwards confeſſed by the whole nation, when the vaſt ambition, and ſublime but irregular genius of Olivarez, by ſtretching the ſinews of the empire beyond their utmoſt tone, threw it into convulſions, and only rendered the diſſolution of its ſtrength more violent and painful.

The whole employments of the duke of Lerma devolved on his ſon Uzeda, except that of governor to the prince, which was conferred on Don Balthazar de Zuniga, a man of cultivated genius, and great experience in political affairs, particularly in embaſſies [10].

Tragical end of Don Roderigo de Calderona, count of Oliva.

Soon after the diſgrace of Lerma, the count of Oliva was arreſted by order of the king, and thrown into priſon, where he languiſhed for the ſpace of two years. His riſe from ſo low a ſtation to ſo great a height of power gave birth to an opinion that he was a ſorcerer, which his enemies were at great pains to propagate. He was charged with having poiſoned the queen, who died in 1612; a charge as improbable in itſelf, as it was found to be unſupported by any evidence; for Don Roderigo ſtood as high in the favor of that princeſs as the duke of Lerma did in the affections of the

[9] Gon. de Ceſpedes y Meneſes. Don. Juan de Vitrian, &c. [10] Gon. de Ceſpedes, lib. i. cap. 4.

king. Many other groundless accusations were brought against him: but at last he was found guilty of having been accessary to the murder of two Spanish gentlemen: a matter which, according to some historians, was never clearly proved; he was however condemned to death, and his estate was confiscated. The evidence on which he was convicted was not direct, but circumstantial; and if we may judge from some of the circumstances left on record, as the principal ground of his condemnation, we may infer, that the deficiency of the proof was supplied by the zeal of both his accusers and judges. The trial and confinement of Calderona were prolonged for two years and six months; a measure calculated to keep alive the general odium against his patron the duke of Lerma, and to prevent the return of that ancient favorite to court, of which the new ministry were not a little apprehensive. During all the time that Calderona lay in prison, there was not one among the multitudes he had obliged, except the cardinal Don Gabriel de Trejo, whose name deserves to be recorded, nephew to the countess his lady, who had the humanity and the courage to attempt his relief, or to afford him any comfort. The cardinal was no sooner informed of the imprisonment of Calderona, than, impelled by a generous gratitude, he set out from Rome to pay his respects to his patron in a dungeon, and determined to move every engine that his utmost efforts could command in order to release him. But the cardinal

BOOK VI.
1618.

was neither permitted to visit the court nor the prison. He lingered, however, a long time in Spain, in anxious hopes of finding some fortunate occasion of saving his friend; but, on the death of pope Paul V. which happened in February 1621, he returned, by order of the king, to Rome.

Don Roderigo bore confinement, solitude, and torture, with incredible patience. After his doom was fixed, he was visited, at his own earnest desire, by the ministers of religion. His great soul, which had braved all the rage of his enemies with such singular constancy, discovered, on the approach of death, a nobler heroism in the most perfect resignation to the will of God; and in the most candid confession, and sincerest contrition for the errors of his life. The ardor of his mind was now displayed in the severities of self-mortification. He was covered with hair-cloth: he watched and prayed night and day: he afflicted himself with fasting, and with stripes; and, had not his confessor interposed, he would, in all probability, have anticipated the stroke of the executioner, by an excess of voluntary pain. On the 19th day of October, 1621, the first year of the reign of Philip IV. he received intimation, that within two days he should die. He received the messenger of this welcome news with a chearful countenance, and tenderly embraced him. He now abstained from sleep and food, and spent his time in acts of devotion. About eleven of the clock on the 21st of October, he came to the door of the prison,

encompaſſed by the officers of juſtice. Afflicton
had ſoftened the natural dignity of his looks and
mien: and his grey hairs, his beard, and his dreſs,
ſuited to the preſent ſad occaſion, conſpired with
the expreſſion of his countenance to impreſs the
ſpectators with ſentiments of veneration and love.
He yet poſſeſſed ſufficient ſtrength to mount on a
mule that waited for him at the priſon. This he
did with great tranquillity, and paſſed through the
ſtreets to the place of execution, embracing and
adoring a crucifix which he held in his hands,
amidſt the tears and lamentations of the ſurrounding
multitude. The executioner held the reins of the
mule, and, as he went along, proclaimed aloud
the following words: " This is the judgment,
which, by the orders of our ſovereign lord the
king, is inflicted on this man for his having been
the inſtigator of an aſſaſſination; and acceſſary to
another murder; and divers other crimes which
appeared on his trial: for all of which he is to be
beheaded, as a puniſhment to him, and a warning
to others." Having arrived at the ſcaffold, the
reſigned ſufferer beheld with a ſerene countenance
the inſtruments of his approaching death; the chair,
the ſword, and the man whoſe office it was to
uſe it. He converſed, for ſome time, with his
confeſſor and other divines. And, having been
received into the boſom of the church, he took
leave of his attendants, and ſat down on the ſeat
from which he was never to riſe. Before his hands
and his feet were made faſt, he made a preſent to
the executioner, and twice embraced the man.

BOOK VI.
1618.

who was bathed in tears, as a token that he bore him not any ill will on account of the office he was about to perform. Then, making bare his neck, he yielded his limbs to be bound, with the utmost compofure. The inftant this operation was performed, he reclined himfelf backwards [11], and while he was in the act of recommending his foul to God, his head was in a moment fevered from his body. As the laft impreffions are commonly the ftrongeft [12], men forgave and forgot the imperioufnefs of his former conduct and behaviour, and thought and fpoke only of that mixture of humility and fortitude, that patience and piety, which he difplayed in the laft ftage of his life [13].

The counfels of Spain had, for many years, been diftinguifhed by a fingular union of a defire of power, with a love of peace: but it was found impoffible to gratify at once thofe oppofite paffions. The intrigues of ambition excited the violence of arms. The commotions of Italy were followed by thofe of Germany. A war was kindled, the moft fignal and deftructive in modern

---

[11] In Spain, traitors alone are beheaded with their faces downwards. The Spanifh word, is degollar, couper la gorge. The executioner performs his office face to face with the fufferer.

[12] Sed plerique Homines poftrema meminere. Julius Cæfar, Ap. Salluft. [13] Savedra, Devifas Politicas. Amelot de la Houffaie, Difc. Hift. Article Calderona. Hiftoria de Don Felippe IV. por Gon. de Cefpedes, lib. ii. cap. xxvii.

annals. Famine and pestilence succeeded to the destroying sword, and the direful power of hunger equally overcame the strongest antipathies, and violated the tenderest affections of nature: so bloody was that tragedy which concluded so happily for the liberties of Europe, in the famous peace of Westphalia!

The male line of Maximilian II. having terminated in Matthias, Maximilian, and Albert, who were now advanced in years, without progeny, the succession to the hereditary dominions of Austria in Germany, might have been claimed, on plausible grounds by the king of Spain [14]. But a natural love of tranquillity, the desire of preserving in his house the imperial crown, and the dread of that dignity devolving on the head of a heretic, determined Philip to comply with the request of the Austrian princes, and to yield up his pretensions in favor of those of Ferdinand of Gratz, great grandson of Ferdinand I. and distinguished by his zeal for the Catholic religion. He, accordingly, made a solemn cession of all his rights to the Austrian provinces, to Ferdinand and his brothers, and their issue male. But, if that should fail, it was stipulated, that the provinces should return to the house of Spain, of which the females were to be preferred before those born in Germany. On this occasion, Philip and Ferdinand entered into a family-compact, the object of which was not only to maintain the strength of

[14] The son of Anne, daughter of the emperor Maximilian II.

Margin: BOOK VI. 1618. Origin of the thirty years war in Germany, that terminated in the peace of Westphalia.

BOOK
VI.
1618.

their common stock, but to extend its branches over the neighbouring nations. They made a league, offensive and defensive. They engaged to support their respective rights and claims, by reciprocal succours; and to prefer the general interest of the Austrian race before any particular or transient advantage to any of its members. The date of these transactions was the year 1617. In the same year, on the seventh day of June, Ferdinand was raised to the crown of Bohemia, and in the year following to that of Hungary, with this reservation, that the regal power should remain with Matthias during his life.

The confederacy between the two branches of the house of Austria, and the steps that had been taken to continue in that family the imperial dignity, inflamed the jealousy that had long prevailed of Austrian ambition, and diffused among the protestants of Germany, a general alarm. Ferdinand had banished from his dominions all who persevered in the open profession of the reformed religion: a severity which prognosticated all the cruelty of religious zeal, wherever his power should be established. The apprehensions of men were increased, when they considered this strict alliance with the Catholic king, with whom he was connected by blood, by religion, and by interest. As he depended for support chiefly on the treasures and arms of Spain, so it was probable, he would be governed chiefly by Spanish counsels, whose constant aim was to wreath around the necks of mankind the yoke of religious and civil tyranny. As the power of the emperor would be strengthened by an alliance, or rather a species of union with the vaft monarchy of Spain, fo his claims, it was dreaded, would be increafed in proportion, and the enlarged prerogatives of the imperial crown, if the fucceffion to that dignity fhould not be interrupted on the death of Matthias, would defcend as an inheritance to the lateft pofterity of the family of Auftria.

'But the man on whofe mind thefe confiderations made the deepeft impreffion, was Frederic elector palatine, a prince young, high fpirited, and in power not inferior to any of the proteftants, the duke of Saxony perhaps excepted. He vifited all the members of the electoral college, to whom he reprefented, that as the prefent conjuncture demanded, fo it prefented a fit occafion of forming a barrier againft the progrefs of Auftrian ambition. He entreated them, by a timely interpofition, to check the growth of an authority which muft otherwife become irrefiftible; and by a fpirited and judicious exercife of their privileges, to perpetuate them in their families. The Catholic electors, as he had expected, he found attached to the houfe of Auftria: and thefe were four in number, while the proteftants were only three. But, in order to over-balance this inequality of numbers, Frederic with the confent and approbation of his proteftant brethren, made a tender of the imperial crown to the duke of Bavaria, not doubting but the archbifhop of Cologne, one of the Catholic electors, would intereft himfelf

BOOK VI.
1618.

BOOK VI.
1618.

in the fortunes of the duke, his brother, and be forward to promote his greatness. This plan in which there was not any thing subtle or profound, was the more solid and judicious, that it was obvious and natural. But it was disconcerted by a cause that was scarcely to be suspected. The duke of Bavaria rejected the proffered dignity of the imperial crown, and all that the policy and zeal of the palatine was able to effect, was a short delay in the election of a king of the Romans[15].

Description of Bohemia.

The sparks of discord which in other parts of the empire had produced only murmurs, jealousies, and intrigues, having fallen, in Bohemia, on more combustible matter, had, by this time, blazed into the flames of war. As that kingdom is the highest ground, the most mountainous, and by nature, the strongest in Germany, so its inhabitants had at all times been distinguished by the loftiness of their spirit, and the vigor and success of their struggles for civil liberty and religious toleration. It is bounded on the east, by Moravia and Silesia, the countries of the ancient Quadi and Marcomanni; on the west by Bavaria, part of the ancient Noricum: on the south by the ancient Pannonia, now Hungary, with other provinces of Austria; and on the north by Saxony. It is almost surrounded by the mountains of the famous Hyrcanian forest, whose sides broken into many sloping ridges, intersect this lofty and spacious amphitheatre, and form a landscape, bold,

[15] Batt. Nan. Hist. della Repub. Venet. lib. iv.

various, and of great beauty. This country is remarkably fertile, and before the spirit of the inhabitants was broken, and their industry checked by despotic government, so populous, that it was computed to have contained above three millions of souls.

The Bohemians of those times are represented by cotemporary historians, as a people of a ruddy complexion, and of enormous stature and force of body, and in their dispositions intrepid, fierce, proud, quick in resenting injuries, of a haughty mien, lovers of a rude magnificence and pomp, and addicted to revels and intemperance. The native language of Bohemia is the Sclavonic, which appears to have been the mother-tongue of the Tartars and their offspring the Turks; and of all the nations inhabiting those regions which extend from the northern parts of Russia to Turkey in Europe [16]. The metropolis is Prague, a city of large extent, stretching along the banks, and on either side of the river Mulda, adorned with many sumptuous edifices, and particularly two strong castles, one of which was the residence of the ancient Bohemian kings. The rich provinces of Silesia, Moravia, and Lusatia, were dependent on Bohemia, and formed a great addition to its power and importance in the scale of nations.

The authority of the church of Rome was never so great and universal as wholly to banish from

[16] Russia, Poland with Lithuania, Hungary, Transylvania, Sclavonia, Croatia, Istria, Wallachia &c. &c.

Origin and progress of the reformation.

BOOK VI.
1618.

the Christian world a spirit of inquiry and a love of knowledge. During the thickest darkness of the middle ages, a star appeared here and there in the firmament which reflected the light of ancient times, and formed a presage, that although the sun of science was set, it would return to enlighten bewildered nations. So early as the eighth century, Claud, bishop of Turin, sowed the seeds of reformation in the vallies of Piedmont, whence they were gradually transplanted into other countries. In the thirteenth century, the Waldenses, or Vallenses, or Albigenses, for by these and other names, the disciples of Claud were distinguished, had spread so far, and become so numerous, that the pope thought it necessary to exert his utmost efforts to suppress them. For this purpose, the first crusade was proclaimed of Christians against Christians, and the office of inquisitor was established. Such a war as had been waged with the infidels, was now carried on against these unfortunate heretics. In France alone, if we credit the authority of Mede[17], ten hundred thousand perished by the sword. According to an author less liable to the suspicion of aggravating the horrors of the inquisition, the Valdenses in that kingdom were either cut off by fire and sword, or dispersed into remote regions, or driven to the fastnesses of neighbouring woods and mountains. Some sought an asylum in the Alps adjoining to Provence, part withdrew into Calabria, part obtained refuge in Britain, and others turning

[17] Vide Mede in Apocalypsin. p. 503.

to the east, took up their abode among the Bohemians, and in Livonia and Poland[18]. In Germany they grew and multiplied so fast, that in the beginning of the fourteenth century, it is computed there were eighty thousand of them in Bohemia, Austria, and the neighbouring provinces. And so greatly had their number increased in the space of the next hundred years, that they avowed and maintained their religious tenets, in spite of the tyranny of the pope, supported by the power of the emperor. In 1410, Robert I. the count palatine being emperor of Germany, and Winceslaus, who had been deposed from that dignity, on account of his egregious misconduct, king of Bohemia[19]. The doctrines

[18] Thuani præfatio ad Henricum IV. p. 7.
[19] Winceslaus was continually immerged in debauchery, and in his fits of intoxication, frequently exercised the most enormous cruelties on people of all ranks. From a strange mixture of cruelty, whim, and indecency, he contracted an intimacy with the public executioner, whom he honored with the appellation of "gossip." His cook having offended him, he gave orders that he should be roasted alive. On account of these irregularities, and his selling the rights of the empire, both in Italy and Germany, he was deposed by the unanimous voice of the electors from the imperial throne. Winceslaus was so little mortified at the news of his deposition, that he said with the most perfect acquiescence. " We are overjoyed to be delivered from the burden of the empire." He sent a message to the imperial cities, requesting them to send him, as the last token of their loyalty, some butts of their best wine. He afterwards shut himself up in the castle of Visigrade in Prague, abandoning himself to the gratification of his appetites. Such a character was not likely to intermeddle in religious disputes.

BOOK VI.
1618.

of the Albigenses were maintained by the learning, eloquence, and irreproachable lives of John Hufs and Jerome of Prague. These reformers were condemned to the flames by the council of Conftance, and fuffered with the ufual fortitude of martyrs. A civil war was kindled from their afhes. The Bohemians revolted againft the emperor Sigifmond, who with many refpectable qualities was a zealous bigot to the catholic religion, and under the conduct of Zifca, defended their opinions not only with arguments, but arms. The emperor was defeated in feveral battles, by this bold leader, who gave law to the kingdom of Bohemia till his death, which happened in 1424. He gave orders that a drum fhould be made of his fkin, and what is equally extraordinary, his orders were faithfully carried into execution. Zifca's fkin, after undergoing the neceffary preparations, was formed into a drum, which was long the fymbol of victory. Procopius, a Catholic prieft, converted by the writings of one of the difciples of John Hufs, revived the fpirits of the Bohemian brethren, many of whom, after the death of Zifca, had retreated to caves and mountains. This champion, who, uniting the military with the facerdotal character, fupported the caufe of his party with great courage and bravery, fell in a battle with the Catholics. Yet, fo terrible had the name of the Huffites become to Sigifmond, that he allowed them the cup in the facrament of the eucharift (the deprivation of which had been the

main

main fource of their complaints) together with a general amnefty, and a confirmation of their privileges. But verbal and even written promifes are eafily retracted, where there exifts not any power of enforcing their accomplifhment: and a right avails nothing without a remedy. The difperfed brethren ceafed to be formidable. Sigifmond renewed his tyranny. His immediate fucceffors on the imperial throne were, like him, zealous Catholics. And the reformed in Germany were languifhing under the preffure of an arbitrary government, when Martin Luther raifed up nations to their aid, revived their drooping fpirits, increafed their numbers, and exalted their power.

Had the whole Chriftian world at the time when Luther began to preach againft indulgences been devoted to the Romifh faith, however abfurd the doctrines of the clergy, and however profligate their lives, it is impoffible that he could have met with any confiderable fuccefs: fo great is the power of eftablifhed authority, and univerfally received opinion! But the never-ceafing contefts between the popes on the one part, and the emperors with other fovereign princes on the other, diminifhed of themfelves the reverence for the papal jurifdiction; and alfo tended wholly to fubvert it, by roufing an inquiry into the grounds on which it was eftablifhed. This inquiry was facilitated by the revival of literature, which, fatally to the reigning church, explored the foundations both of its power and doctrines. The

BOOK VI.
1618.

discoveries of grave theologians and antiquarians were followed by the ridicule of wit and humor. And the learned and pious labors of Savonarola, Berengarius, and Wickliff, were aided by the raillery of Dante, Petrarca, and Erasmus. In the beginning of the 16th century, the primitive doctrines of Christianity had taken root in most countries in Europe. The materials for reformation were collected, and the foundations laid deep, before Luther and Calvin raised and completed the superstructure. The minds of men being thus prepared, the doctrines of these reformers spread far and near. In Bohemia with its dependent provinces, where similar tenets had been already adopted, and where ideas of opposition to the emperor, and contradiction to the pope, were so familiar and common, their progress was unusually rapid. And the number of Hussites and Evangelists, (appellations which cotemporary writers seem to consider as synonymous) soon equalled that of the Catholics, and was daily increasing. From their numbers they derived power, and from power a spirit of persecution. In Prague they committed many outrages on the property and persons of the clergy. The archbishop was driven from the city. And it was evident from the whole tenor of their conduct, that they aimed at nothing less than the whole power of government, both civil and ecclesiastic. Their encroachments received a check from the first Ferdinand, who, uniting vigor of conduct with lenity and moderation, asserted the rights of the established church, at the same time that he used not any other means for reclaiming the Protestants than the influence of authority, and the power of persuasion. He entreated them to submit to the decisions of the Christian fathers now assembled in council at Trent. And on the other hand, that the authority of the fathers might have greater weight, he took the liberty of exhorting that venerable order to take measures for reforming the lives of the clergy. He re-established in Prague, the exiled metropolitan, with other Catholic priests; and sent to their aid a strong reinforcement of Jesuits. The labors of these preachers, fostered and encouraged by the countenance of the emperor, sustained a while the declining interests of the Romish faith. The memory of Maximilian and Rhodolphus, the immediate successors of Ferdinand on the imperial throne, is stigmatized by Catholic writers with a coldness and indifference in matters of religion, which was extremely favorable to the growth of heresy. This charge, as far as it concerns Rhodolphus, appears not to have been wholly groundless. For while the protestant party on the one hand required an extension of their privileges, and the catholic on the other, begged that the heretics might be laid under closer restrictions, the emperor declined at first to gratify the desire of either. But a fortunate conjuncture gave weight to the applications of the protestants, and crowned them with success. Matthias, who had already usurped the government of Mor-

BOOK VI.
1618.

via Auftria, and Hungary, afpired now to the crown of Bohemia; and in order to pay his court to the proteftants, profeffed the principles of toleration, and affected a zealous concern for all their rights and privileges. By thefe arts he effectually attached to his intereft the leaders of that party, fo formidable for its numbers, boldnefs and difpofition to action. His indulgence to the reformed religion covered the violence of his ufurpations with a fpecious veil: and his proteftant partifans were not afhamed to fupport his unjuft pretenfions. Emboldened by the favor of Matthias and the juftice of their caufe, they took up arms, and in that hoftile attitude, prefented anew their petition to the emperor, for a confirmation of fundry privileges. Rhodolphus had hitherto exercifed over Bohemia the power of a fovereign; and though he had neither inclination nor ability to prolong that power by force of arms, he was not fo wholly indifferent to the attractions of a crown, as to refign it, if it could be retained by a few conceffions refpecting modes and doctrines of religion. The proteftants accordingly obtained a royal edict, authorizing a free exercife of their religion in Bohemia and the adjacent provinces; a confiftory or council for ecclefiaftic affairs, with other inftitutions relating both to the government and defence of the churches of the reformation, and alfo to the eftablifhment of fchools, colleges, and places of worfhip. It is reafonable to fuppofe, that the utmoft extent of this laft conceffion, was a permiffion to the proteſtants to build churches on their own lands. But they, interpreting it in the moſt comprehenſive ſenſe, began to build religious edifices even on the eſtates of the eccleſiaſtics: a freedom which appeared to the whole Catholic party an exceſſive outrage. Complaints of theſe encroachments having been carried to Matthias, who by this time had ſucceeded to his brother Rhodolphus, both on the Bohemian and imperial throne, a letter of royal authority was inſtantly iſſued, prohibiting the erection of all proteſtant fabrics on lands belonging to the church. In conſequence of this proclamation, one or two meeting houſes were demoliſhed. And the proteſtants were thrown into the utmoſt ferment, their reſentment againſt the emperor being exaſperated by the recollection of thoſe deceitful promiſes with which he had beguiled them when a candidate for the kingdom.

The Bohemian proteſtants by means of their Defenders, whoſe buſineſs it was to watch over the intereſts of the church, to ſpread an alarm in times of danger, and to concert meaſures for common defence [20], were enabled to combine in any effort that might be deemed neceſſary for the preſervation of the true religion. Henry, count Thorn, perceiving the force of this great machine, and alſo how eaſy it would be, in the

---

[20] The Defenders appear to have been the principal men of their communion, either in their ſeveral congregations, or in the different diſtricts of the country.

BOOK VI.
1618.

present juncture, to set it in movement, conceived the bold design of turning it against the house of Austria. This nobleman was indeed of an enterprising and turbulent disposition: but in the part he acted on this occasion, he was actuated not so much by any inquietude of temper, as by the passions of resentment, fear, and religious zeal. Deprived of his paternal inheritance by the tyranny of the archduke of Gratz, on account of his stedfast adherence to the doctrines of the reformation, and driven from his native country, he found refuge among the protestants of Bohemia. His zeal and his sufferings in the cause of the protestant faith, gained him the favor and confidence of this people, and the superiority of his genius their esteem. At the time when Matthias deemed it good policy to court the protestants, he affected a desire to establish the fortune of the count: and accordingly, when he seized the crown of Bohemia, he invested him with the command of Carlstein, a fortress in which were deposited the regalia of the kingdom. But when the power of Matthias was firmly established by the death of Rhodolphus, he threw off the mask of good-will towards the protestants, and openly patronized the faith in which he had been educated, and which was most favorable to regal power. The independent principles of count Thorn the emperor regarded with jealousy and distrust: for having determined to repress the pretensions of the heretics, he foresaw a conjuncture in which it would be dangerous to intrust places of strength in any other hands than those of catholics. That nobleman was therefore deprived of the government of Carlestein, which was bestowed on count Martinitz, a devoted instrument of both ecclesiastic and regal authority. The succession of Ferdinand to Matthias, afforded not to the exiled count any hope of preferment from royal favor: on the contrary, the bigotry of that severe prince threatened him with still further oppression. In these circumstances, he saw no resource but in civil commotion and revolution. These were justified to the count by the enthusiasm of religion, and the same passion, as has been already observed, conspired with others in rousing him to attempt them [21]. He flew to different quarters of the kingdom, and hastening from place to place, labored both in public assemblies and private societies, to rouse a sense of danger, and a spirit of freedom. The boldness of his genius, and the fervor of his zeal, inspired a like boldness and fervor in all with whom he conversed. The flame spread from breast to breast, formed a concert of wills, and united all ranks of men in a resolution to defend

---

[21] The principal authorities for this account of the origin of the troubles of Bohemia are these, Annales de L'Empire tom. ii. Heiss, Hist. de l'Empire. Batt. Nan. Hist. Lib. iv. ann. 1618. & passim. Gon. de Cesp. lib. prim. cap. v. et passim. Veritable Recit de ce qui s'est passé à Prague le 21 May 1618. Everhardi Waffemburgii Embricensis Comment. de Bello inter Imperatores Ferdinandos et coram Hostes, &c. Wilson's History of King James.

BOOK VI.
1618.

their religious rights with their lives and fortunes. And at his inftigation, the defenders, or chiefs of the proteftants, called a general aſſembly of the ſtates of the kingdom, for the expreſs purpoſe of concerting meaſures for the redreſs of grievances.

The emperor, confidering this fpirit of aſſociation as the forerunner of rebellion, iſſued a proclamation, debarring all aſſemblies of the ſtates, until he himſelf ſhould come among them in perſon, or ſhould give further orders to his miniſters. Notwithſtanding this prohibition, the Defenders, with numbers of other powerful barons, accompanied with armed ſervants and retainers, and a multitude of the inhabitants of Prague, convened at that city on the 20th day of May, and having heard a ſermon, and joined together in prayer, mutually pledged themſelves to defend their religion and their churches, not only in Prague, but in every part of Bohemia. It was alſo reſolved to publiſh to all the world an account of their preſent conduct and future views.

Manifeſto of the Bohemians.

A manifeſto was drawn up for this purpoſe. The exordium contained the ſtrongeſt expreſſions of loyalty to the emperor, as king of Bohemia. The general eſtates lamented the dangers which obliged them to take meaſures that appeared to ſuperſede an authority they wiſhed to preſerve inviolate. Their only deſign was to fruſtrate the pernicious projects of certain ſeditious and turbulent ſpirits, who had ſworn the ruin of their liberties, and of the fundamental laws of the kingdom; who had so far abused the confidence of the emperor and of Ferdinand, as to perfuade thefe princes to march againft Bohemian fubjects at the head of hoftile armies; in order to feize Prague; to kill or imprifon the greater number of the nobles, and deputies of ftates; to rafe their churches; and to abolifh the free exercife of their religion [12]. This manifefto being read aloud, was approved by the ftates, and a general murmur of applaufe was heard among the people.

In the midft of thefe tranfactions, an order arrived from the imperial miniftry, commanding the proteftant leaders to difperfe, and to retire to their refpective habitations. Upon this, count Thorn, attended by a number of other barons on horfeback and in armour, rode up to the caftle, and having fecured its gates, proceeded immediately to the hall, in which the minifters of Matthias were affembled in council on the prefent important emergence. Invective and altercation was foon followed by blows: and the count Martinitz, Slavata, and Fabritius, who held the principal offices of government, were thrown headlong out at the windows. Though they fell from a height of fixty feet, and that feveral fhots of mufquetry were fired at them as they fell, they efcaped, not only with their lives, but free from any material harm. The Catholics confidered this

---

[12] Everhardi Waffemburg'i Embricenfis Comment. de Bello inter Imperatores Ferdinandos II. et III. & eorum Hoftes.

BOOK VI.
1618.

remarkable prefervation of thefe three men as a miracle wrought by heaven in fupport of the Romifh faith. Minute defcriptions are accordingly given, in the writings of thofe times, of the wall of the caftle of Vifigrade, and of the tremendous precipice which intervenes between the bottom of the wall and the ditch. But proteftant writers difprove the alledged miracle, by obferving that the fpot on which the Catholics fell was covered deep with dung, and mud, and leaves of trees.

Revolt of Bohemia.

The Bohemians, now involved in the guilt of rebellion, determined to perfevere, and to feek from their own valor and good fortune for that indemnity which they had both little reafon to look for at the hands of Matthias, and ftill lefs from thofe of his fucceffor. Their minds opened to greater views than thofe they had entertained on the firft alarm of danger; and they now refolved to vindicate by the fword, not only their religious, but their civil privileges. In this refolution they were encouraged, whether they furveyed the internal fituation of their own kingdom, or caft their eyes abroad upon foreign ftates. There was nothing in Bohemia to refift their united force. Matthias, declining in health as in years, was not able, and perhaps would not be very willing to maintain, in oppofition to the juft pretenfions of a generous people, an arbitrary jurifdiction that muft foon devolve to an ambitious rival and hated fucceffor. The country was naturally ftrong and fertile, the people high fpirited nd warlike, and ready to encounter danger and death in defence of their religion. If paffing from their own, they contemplated the ftate of other kingdoms; circumftances not lefs animating prefented themfelves to their view, and fanned that generous fire which glowed in their breafts. The contagion of example, which more than reafon governs the world, difplayed its full force on this important occafion. The Venetian republic, and the duke of Savoy, had of late maintained their independence in oppofition to the pretenfions and power of that civil and religious tyranny, with which the Bohemians were now called to ftruggle. The proteftants of France formed of themfelves, as it were, a feparate ftate in the midft of a mighty kingdom. And the united provinces of the Netherlands, in fpite of the veteran armies of Spain, and the gold of the weftern world, had rifen from the loweft and moft diftreffing circumftances that could be imagined, to the greateft height of liberty and power. Thefe circumftances were ever prefent to the minds of the Bohemian leaders, and formed the chief topics in their public harangues, as well as in their writings, which were circulated all over the kingdom by means of the prefs, and which were full of eloquence and vigor. And as divers ftates animated the Bohemians by their example, fo all proteftant powers, it was probable, would fupport them with fubftantial affiftance. The fympathy of religion would render theirs the intereft of nations: and their companions at the altar would be their fellow soldiers in the field of battle [21].

The Bohemians having determined to infift on the reftoration of their ancient laws and conftitution, expelled the old garrifon out of the caftle (which was the royal palace) and replaced it by another in which they could confide. They appointed thirty perfons to govern Bohemia, with the title of Directors. Thefe magiftrates having, in the firft place, taken an oath of fidelity and allegiance, from the inhabitants of Prague, proceeded to the adminiftration of government. The firft act of their power was to banifh the Jefuits, and to confifcate their effects. They raifed an army of two thoufand horfe, and twelve regiments of foot, and gave the fupreme command to count Thorn. They addreffed a manifefto to the emperor; to the ftates of Silefia, Moravia, Lufatia; to the whole provinces and ftates of the empire; and to all the world; containing an account of their conduct, and invoking the aid of all the friends of religious toleration, and civil liberty.

Erneft, count of Mansfeldt, was the firft who efpoufed the Bohemian caufe, and the laft of its adherents who abandoned it. He was a natural fon of that count Mansfeldt, whom Philip II. appointed governor of the Netherlands. In his early years, he attached himfelf, like his father,

---

[21] Hiftoria de Don Felippe, &c. por Gon. de Cefpedes, lib. i. cap. vi. Batt. Nani, lib. iv. 1618.

to the houſe of Auſtria. The court of Vienna was filled with a juſt admiration of his talents and virtues; and, in a tranſient fit of favor, promiſed to inveſt him with the rights of legitimate birth, and to put him in poſſeſſion of the eſtates of his family. But a regard to intereſt violated a promiſe that had been made merely from generoſity: and as the moſt violent reſentments are thoſe which ariſe from diſappointed confidence, count Mansfeldt's hatred of Matthias was implacable. His averſion to the houſe of Auſtria he extended even to their religion. He renounced the Catholic faith, and openly profeſſed the doctrines of Luther. He abandoned the ſervice of the emperor, and entered into that of Charles Emanuel, the moſt active and enterpriſing of all the enemies of Auſtria. But the preſent ſituation of affairs in Germany, opened ſo full a career to the genius, the ambition, and the vengeance of Mansfeldt, that he could not forbear expreſſing to the generous prince whom he now ſerved, an eager deſire of offering his ſword to the revolted ſtates of Bohemia. The duke of Savoy, who conſidered the diſturbances in Germany as the ſureſt pledge of his own ſecurity, not only applauded the views of the count, but permitted him to levy two thouſand men, and alſo engaged to keep them in pay for him, for ſeveral months [24]. At the head of this ſmall force Mansfeldt marched into Bohemia, where he was received with the utmoſt joy, and inſtantly honored with the

[24] Batt. Nani, lib. iv. 1618.

charge of general of the ordnance. Thus the forces of Bohemia were intrusted to commanders who were both of them foreigners, both men of desperate fortunes, both breathing vengeance against the house of Austria, and both of them possessed in an eminent degree of military capacity and political discernment. Yet between the characters of these men there was a remarkable difference. Count Thorn, who had the talent of rousing, uniting, and wielding the minds of men, was the best fitted to govern a nation: Mansfeldt, so brave, enterprising, inventive, and refined, the best qualified to conduct an army. The military talents of this extraordinary person shone forth, indeed, beyond those of all his cotemporaries. Nor did ever any hero, in any age, exhibit greater boldness in encountering, or greater dexterity in escaping from danger. These fierce commanders took the field at the head of separate armies. The flag of rebellion was displayed throughout all Bohemia, and by a powerful contagion, incited a general insurrection in Silesia, Moravia, Lusatia, Hungary, and the Upper Austria [11].

The news of this revolution, distracted the emperor with opposite passions. The idea, which so naturally presents itself to monarchs in similar circumstances, occurred first to Matthias. But coercive measures might be as fatal to his own power, as to the liberty of Bohemia. He was not able to take the field in person: the command of an army would, of course, be claimed by

[11] Rushworth's Coll. vol. i. p. 7, 8.

Ferdinand: and so powerful an engine would place in the hands of that prince the whole authority of government. Moved by this confideration, he wrote, in the ftyle of the Catholics of thofe times, a paternal letter, requiring the evangelical ftates of Bohemia to lay down their arms, and diſband their troops, promiſing them, in cafe of obedience, indemnity and protection. This offer the revolted provinces regarded not as a mark of lenity, but as a proof of weaknefs ". They defpifed it fo much, that they difdained to anfwer it. Matthias then forbad all levies of troops in the empire, without the imperial permiſſion, and publiſhed to the world an elaborate account of the Bohemian revolt. A paper-war enfued between that prince and his revolted fubjects; and it was evident that the quarrel muſt be decided, as ufual in fuch cafes, not by the pen, but by the fword. Accordingly, with the aid of the princes, friends, and allies of his houfe, he raifed in Germany an army of ten thoufand men. The king elect of Bohemia, as had been forefeen, demanded the command of this force, and obtained it; but with fuch reftrictions, as betrayed the jealoufy of the old emperor, and left little more to the nominal chief than the fhadow of power. Ferdinand declined the exercife of fo limited an authority, and this the rather, that it would tend to heighten the difguft of the emperor, and might even induce him to take meafures

BOOK
VI.
1618.

... ria de Don Felippe III. por Gon. de Cefp. lib. i. c.:

BOOK VI.
1618.
Count Bucquoy appointed to the command of the imperial army.

for difappointing his expectations of the imperial crown. The command of the army was, therefore, with the confent of Ferdinand, intrufted in the hands of the famous count Bucquoy. This general took the field without delay, and, having reduced the town of Teutlbrod, fixed his head-quarters in Budovits, the only place of ftrength that now remained to the emperor in all Bohemia. Count Thorn advanced againft Bucquoy, reduced Krumlaw, with the fuburbs of Budovits, and held that city in clofe blockade. Various fkirmifhes happened of courfe between the oppofite armies; and fortune inclined fometimes to the one fide, fometimes to the other.

Various skirmishes between the Imperialifts and the Bohemians.

Whilft count Thorn was thus employed, in watching the motions of the imperial general, Mansfeldt carried on with fuccefs the fiege of Pilfen. This city was important for its fituation, as it commanded an extenfive and fertile tract of country along the courfe of a branch of the Mulda; and also contained great ftores and treafures. For this being the only place in that quarter of the kingdom, where the power of the Catholic predominated over that of the Proteftant inhabitants, thither the Jefuits and priefts, and many of the richeft citizens of the Bohemian capital had retired, with their moft valuable effects. The conditions on which the inhabitants of Pilfen furrendered, after an obftinate refiftance, were, that they fhould maintain two companies of evangelical foldiers; redeem the city from plunder by fixty thoufand florins; and take an oath of fidelity
and

and allegiance to the Proteſtant ſtates of Bohemia. Several Catholic ſoldiers as well as citizens, preferred exile with the loſs of all their goods, to this laſt condition. Mansfeldt having thrown into the city a ſtrong garriſon of both horſe and foot, continued his route in Bohemia, and took ſeveral places almoſt without reſiſtance.

During theſe tranſactions, continual overtures were made on the part of the emperor for peace. Matthias appeared in the ſingular character of a ſuppliant for power. He condeſcended to addreſs many promiſes and flattering expreſſions of regard to individuals [17]. The evangelical ſtates had at firſt, as had been already obſerved, treated the emperor's advances towards a reconciliation with a contemptuous ſilence; but after he had drawn his ſword, he became a more reſpectable correſpondent, and they deigned to honor him with a letter. This letter contained very ſingular matter. The whole was a bitter complaint of the ravages committed by the imperial troops in the kingdom of Bohemia. Matthias anſwered, that he was ſorry for what had happened, but that he would be under the neceſſity of ſending more troops among them, if they ſhould refuſe to lay down their arms. The Bohemians at this time endeavoured to incline the emperor to peace, by the mediation of the archdukes his brothers; and it is probable, that could they have obtained the reſtoration of their ancient

---

[17] Hiſt. du Regne de Louis XIII. Roy de France, et des princiaux evenemens arrivés pendant ce Regne dans tous les ſ.. du monde.

constitution, and the establishment of the protestant religion, they would have been willing to leave to Matthias, or to Ferdinand, all the power of a feudal king. But neither was the emperor inclined to rest contented with so confined an authority; nor, perhaps, could the difference have been composed if he had. All confidence between the contending parties was lost: and the matter now in dispute, was, which should retain the power of the sword? an arduous question, and which an appeal to the sword itself could alone determine.

Death of Matthias, and succession of Ferdinand.

Matthias had labored long under bodily infirmities and anxious cares, when the stroke of death laid him at rest, on the 20th day of March, 1619. Ferdinand, his successor, doubtful of his ability to reduce his subjects to obedience by force of arms, attempted to gain their confidence and voluntary submission, by argument and persuasion, and acts expressive of a tender regard for their happiness. He commanded Bucquoy to cease from all hostilities, and gave orders for a general suspension of arms throughout all his dominions. To all his revolted subjects he offered pardon and oblivion, a full confirmation of their privileges, and a full toleration in matters of religion. He added many expressions of good-will, and earnestly exhorted them to tread in the paths of peace. The exhortations of Ferdinand, were not more successful than those of his predecessor. Count Thorn having taken Iglaw, a frontier-town of Moravia, with several other places, and being reinforced by troops, not only from the provinces dependent on Bohemia, but also from Hungary, at the solicitation of several Austrian barons drew near to the Danube. Having been furnished with boats by those who favored his cause, he crossed that river with all his forces, and carried terror into the city of Vienna, as well as all the adjacent country. The whole garrison of Vienna amounted only to fifteen hundred foot and two hundred horse. This small force was under the necessity, not only of guarding the city from external attacks, but also from internal sedition: for count Thorn had a numerous party within the walls of Vienna, who had engaged to facilitate its reduction by securing one of the principal gates. Had that commander advanced on the present occasion with his usual celerity, the possession of the Austrian capital would, in all probability, have fixed the independency of the Bohemian states, and drawn after it other important revolutions. But trusting to the terror of his arms, and the influence of his partisans, he hoped to reduce Vienna, even without a struggle. He summoned that city to surrender. But while he lay two days at Fischen expecting an answer, the university armed five hundred students, and a reinforcement of several companies of cuirassiers having passed under false colors through the midst of the Bohemian squadrons, arrived from the grand duke of Tuscany. At this instant some zealots were in the act of shaking Ferdinand by the doublet, and demanding, with many imprecations, liberty of confcience. The trampling of horfes and the glittering of fwords and fpears relieved the king from the importunities of thofe rude petitioners, and filled them in their turn with confternation and terror [18]. Count Thorn now drew near the city, with a defign to befiege it; but, by this time, his prefence was thought neceffary in another quarter.

Count Dampierre of Lorrain had raifed four thoufand men in Hungary, with which he intended to join the army under the command of Bucquoy. Mansfeldt, having learned his defign, immediately refolved to attack him, before a junction of the Hungarians with the main Imperial army fhould render their united force irrefiftible. He was on his march for this purpofe, when count Bucquoy fell upon him from an ambufcade, and defeated him with great flaughter. Mansfeldt himfelf was among the wounded, and a great number were taken prifoners. The Bohemian army retreated to Breslaw, the capital of Silefia; and on occafion of this difafter it was deemed expedient to recal count Thorn, to oppofe the progrefs of the victorious enemy. Bucquoy, having reduced feveral places, retired to Budovits, where he waited for fome troops he expected from Flanders [19]. Count Thorn, having in vain endeavoured to bring the

---

[18] Gio. Batt. Nani, Hiftoria della Repub. Veneta dall' an. 1613. Sin'all' an. 1671, lib. iv. 1619.
[19] Conç. de Cefpedes, Hift. &c. lib. i. cap. 6. Hift. de Louis XIII.

Imperialists to an action, but having recovered some fortresses they had taken, set out for Prague, where the reformed of Bohemia, Moravia, Silesia, and Lusatia were assembled.

In this situation of affairs the archbishop of Mentz, as chancellor of the empire, proclaimed a diet at Frankfort for the election of a king of the Romans. The electors attended either in person or by their proxies, and, on the twenty-eighth day of August, Ferdinand was adorned with the imperial purple.

The Bohemian states had now been assembled for two months, and in the course of this period they formed a league offensive and defensive with the annexed provinces, and another of the same kind with Bethlehem Gabor, who, from the rank of a private gentleman, had been exalted, by the favor of the Porte, to the sovereignty of Transylvania. This prince the Bohemians engaged to support in an effort to mount the throne of Hungary; as he, on his part, promised to maintain their right to elect a king of Bohemia. For they had solemnly resolved never to recognise Ferdinand as their king; but to chuse a Protestant for their sovereign, and to shake off for ever the yoke of all the princes of the house of Austria. They justified their renunciation of Ferdinand by several arguments. "By preserving the forms of free government, they said, the monarchs of Europe had been enabled to conceal their progressions towards absolute power, and insensibly to impose

The Bohemian states fortify themselves by new alliances, and resolve to chuse a new king.

the yoke of slavery on their unguarded subjects. The election of Ferdinand, however formal it might appear, was certainly no other than an act of authority. Matthias, in the fulness of his power, had nominated his successor on the throne, and no individual had dared to oppose his will. Thus it was that the house of Austria trampled on the liberties of a free people, and abused the power which was intrusted in their hands for the public good, for the purpose of perpetuating it in their own family. But waving the question concerning the validity of his election, they maintained that Ferdinand had forfeited all title to the crown by violating the privileges of the states, particularly by endeavouring to fortify himself on the throne, by means of foreign aid; to control Germans by the arms of Spaniards." These were grave and solid reasons, but they added yet another, which appears very extraordinary, and even somewhat ludicrous; they said they had a right to chuse a new king, because Ferdinand had smoothed his way to the crown of Bohemia by means of Spanish gold; insinuating, that if they had sworn allegiance to that prince, they had been bribed to do so[*].

Such were the reasons of the Bohemians for deposing their king. Their motives for electing another were equally cogent. As they had not yet experienced the inconveniencies of an aristocracy, the election of a king did not seem necessary

[*] Harte's History of Gustavus Adolphus.

for the purpose of internal government, nor were they so much attached to regal dignity, as to chuse a king merely for the pomp and parade of a court. But the vigor of the prince who claimed the throne made it necessary for them to form by all means powerful alliances and connexions. They made a tender of their crown first to the duke of Savoy. That prince had already given them proofs of his good-will; and his superior genius seemed necessary to defend them against the threatened danger. But the duke declined to accept the crown, though he applauded the generous spirit of the Bohemians, and exhorted them to persevere in the noble course on which they had entered. They next cast their eyes on the elector of Saxony; but the hope of succession to the dutchy of Cleves restrained that prince from opposing the house of Austria. They now made an offer of the Bohemian throne to the elector Palatine. The spirit and zeal of this prince seemed not unworthy of a crown; and by his own force, and his connexion with prince Maurice [11], and the king of England, they imagined he would be enabled to preserve it. Frederic, after some little hesitation, which was easily overcome by his natural ambition, and the incitements of the princess his wife, who had great influence over him, accepted the offer, and, having levied an army of ten thousand foot and two thousand horse, marched into Bohemia in support of his new subjects.

[11] His uncle.

The elector Palatine accepts the crown of Bohemia.

BOOK VI.
1 9.
The nations alarmed at the appearance of a comet.

While the commotions in Germany drew attention from every quarter, and from interest, from affection, or from religion, interested all nations, a comet appearing towards the North in the heavens, aggravated the general gloom; and the minds of men were agitated at once by the alarms of war, and a superstitious terror. A belief in astrology was at this period universal in Europe as well as Asia. Pamphlets were daily published, containing interpretations of the comet. While the vulgar considered it as ominous of domestic and particular events, men of genius and learning, deriding such absurd comments, supposed that a general sympathy pervaded the universe; that nature at certain periods was in a kind of commotion; and that, in such a crisis, the minds of men were naturally moved also [12]. And, if the languor of inoccupation be the great curse of human life [13], it may be affirmed that at no time was there ever a greater portion of felicity diffused throughout the world.

The contest between the emperor and the prince Palatine seemed at first altogether unequal. A spirit of disaffection and resistance had gone forth throughout the whole of Ferdinand's dominions. His crowns tottered on his head, and that of Bohemia seemed already fallen. The small

---
[12] Bart. Nan. Hist. lib. iv. Wilson's History of King James, ann. 1619. Hume's Hist. vol. viii. p. 109.
[13] See L'Abbe du Bois, and Ferguson's Essay on Civil Society.

army under the command of Bucquoy was all that he had to oppofe to the different forces of the Palatine, of count Thorn, and of Mansfeldt. A new and more terrible enemy advanced upon him from the Eaſt. The prince of Tranſylvania, under the auſpices, and with the promiſe of powerful aid from the Ottoman Porte, marched rapidly into Hungary; reduced the capital; aſſumed the crown, with the title of king; made himſelf maſter of all that was important in the kingdom except Javarrin and Comorrha; formed a junction with count Thorn; and threw a bridge over the Danube, with a reſolution to carry the war into the heart of Auſtria.

In this extremity the native courage of Ferdinand was ſupported by the treaſures, the arms, and the authority of Spain. In a cauſe which involved at once the greatneſs of his family, and the ſupport of the Catholic religion, the Spaniſh monarch advanced large ſums of money, and levied a powerful military force. A body of eight thouſand men marched from the Low Countries to reinforce the Imperial army under count Bucquoy. And Spinola, with an army of thirty thouſand, compoſed of Italians, Spaniards, Walloons, and Iriſh, prepared to invade the Palatinate[14]. The powerful aid of Spain encouraged the electors of Saxony and Bavaria to appear on that ſide which ſeemed now to be ſtrongeſt, and by adhering to which they might look

BOOK VI.
1620.

The cauſe of Ferdinand ſupported by Spain.

[14] Batt. Nani, lib. iv. 1619. Hiſtoria de Don Felippe, &c. por Gon. de Ceſpedes, lib. i. cap. 9. 11.

for the higheſt advantages. The views of Saxony have already been mentioned ". And as to the duke of Bavaria, he was invited by a promiſe of receiving the eſtates as well as the dignity of his kinſman the elector Palatine. The example and influence of the Bavarian, the authority of the whole houſe of Auſtria, and the common intereſts of the Romiſh faith, united all the princes of the Catholic league in a reſolution to ſupport Ferdinand with their lives and fortunes. The pope, beſides his ſpiritual benedictions, contributed a pecuniary ſupply; and ſeveral eccleſiaſtics as well as princes of Italy followed his example.

" A writer of great reputation ſuppoſes that the duke of Saxony may have been actuated by a jealouſy of Frederic, who of an equal was to become his ſuperior; or, that he may have been afraid leſt the princes of the houſe of Weymar, who were the warmeſt partiſans of Frederic, ſhould, by the aſſiſtance of that prince, if victorious, regain the poſſeſſion of Saxony, the ancient inheritance of their family. [Pauli Piaſecii Chronica Geſtorum in Europa ſingularium: apud Amelot de la Houſſaie Diſc. Hiſtor.] It is of no importance to inquire whether theſe conjectures be well founded or no. It is often a difficult matter, it muſt be owned, to aſſign the real motives of the actions of princes, their conduct being often determined by ſecret, and ſometimes trivial cauſes. As to the matter in queſtion, I ſhall only obſerve, that I do not find any hiſtorian who is inclined to give credit to what Saxony himſelf affirmed: which was, that he would ſupport the juſt claim of Ferdinand, in oppoſition to the pretenſions of Frederic; becauſe a contrary conduct would bring a ſtain on the Proteſtant religion. Batt. Nan. lib. iv. 1619.

An army was quickly raised for the defence of the ancient religion. The command was given to the duke of Bavaria. The protection afforded by the Ottoman empire to Gabor, interested the king of Poland also in the prosperity of Ferdinand; and in an instant ten thousand Cossacs, fierce and savage auxiliaries, over-ran Moravia, and joined the Imperial army under Bucquoi [16].

The eyes of all Europe were now turned to the kings of England and France: the first interested in the fortune of Frederic from the connexion of blood as well as sympathy of religion; the second bound by the strongest ties of policy and ambition to oppose the progress of a proud and hated rival. But the indolent disposition of James, his reverence for the rights of kings, an eager desire to effectuate a marriage between the second infanta and the prince of Wales, and a conceit withal that the whole world entertained a profound respect for his love of justice and great learning; these circumstances inclined him, as usual, to embrace pacific measures; and he sought to promote the greatness of the Palatine, not by the sword, but by embassies and negociations [17]. Lewis was neither ignorant of the interest of France, nor did he want that spirit which was necessary for pursuing it with vigor. But that prince, who was one of those modest characters that are apt to pay a deference to capacities inferior

[16] Batt. Nan. lib. iv. 1619.
[17] See Hume's History of Great Britain, anno 1619.

BOOK VI.
1620.

to their own, was at this time under the government of the duke of Luines. That favorite was induced, by the artifices of the Spanish ambassador, to sacrifice at once the interests of the Palatine and of France to private ambition. The rich heirefs of Pequigny and Chaunes was educated at the court of Bruffels. It became the policy of Luines, by the favor of the archdukes, to pave the way for a marriage between that lady and his brother Honorius. He entered into a confidential correfpondence with thefe princes, and eafily acquired their good graces by engaging to favor, in the prefent critical juncture, the views of the houfe of Auftria. The veil under which he covered his fecret defigns from the eyes of his prince, was, that if the elector Palatine fhould eftablifh himfelf on the throne of Bohemia, he would undoubtedly protect the Hugonots, with whom he maintained a correfpondence

June,
through his uncle, the duke of Bouillon. An ambaffador was difpatched from France to the city of Ulm, where there was held a diet of the empire. In this affembly the Catholic and Proteftant parties were prefent, and alfo deputies from correfponding ftates and princes. The ambaffador declared the refolution of Lewis "to obferve an exact neutrality in the prefent difpute, and expatiated on the mifery and folly of war and bloodfhed, between parties who were not impelled to hoftilities by any caufe of mutual animofity or contention. The only quarrel, he faid,

was between the emperor and the elector of the Palatinate. Let thefe princes, therefore, fight out their own battles. But if the minds of princes be too ftrongly agitated by the prefent conjuncture to embrace fuch moderate and pacific councils, at leaft let not the ravages and defolation of war be fpread over all Germany. On the contrary, let them be confined within the narroweft poffible bounds: and, as the kingdom of Bohemia is the only fubject of contention between the parties principally concerned, fo let it be the only fcene of all military operations that may be undertaken in fupport of their refpective claims by their friends and allies." A treaty was accordingly framed in which it was fettled that neither the Evangelical Union, nor the Catholic League fhould directly or indirectly invade or attack any electorate, principality, province, or city of the empire, Bohemia alone excepted.

Treaty of Ulm.

The emperor was now in a fituation in which he could act with the utmoft vigor. The mere good offices of England were a general fubject of derifion [11]. He was fecure from the attacks of France. The Proteftant princes and ftates of Germany were animated indeed with a hearty averfion to Ferdinand; but their affembly at Nuremberg had already proved how much they were divided by political jealoufies [12] and religious

---

[11] Hume's Hiftory of Great Britain, Reign of James I, an. 1619, 1620, 1621, 1622.
[12] Hift. della Rep. Ven. Batt. Nan. lib. iv. 1619.

disputations [20], and how little reason there was to imagine they would ever unite in any effectual measures for the support of Frederic. The treaty of Ulm offorded the emperor a farther pledge of security from their attacks, and set him at liberty to pour an irresistible force into the kingdom and dependent provinces of Bohemia. Emboldened by these circumstances, he thundered forth against his rival the ban of the empire, and committed the execution of that decree to the archduke Albert, and to the dukes of Bavaria and Saxony.

The marquis of Spinola invades the Palatinate. August. Don Lewis de Velasco being left with fifteen thousand men for the defence of the Austrian frontier towards the United Provinces, the marquis of Spinola, with a Spanish army, as has already been observed, of thirty thousand men, but these under the colors of Albert, marched directly into the Palatinate, and halted at Coblentz, at the confluence of the Rhine and the Moselle. As this invasion of Spinola was a manifest infraction of the treaty of Ulm, the princes of the Evangelical Union reproached the Catholic party with their perfidy. The elector of Mentz, adding mockery to breach of faith, said, that the house of Austria was not bound by that treaty, as it was not comprehended in the Catholic League [21]. The princes of the Union, alarmed at the proceedings of the Austrians, and provoked at their

[20] Hist. de Don Felippe, &c. por Gonc. de Cespedes, lib. i. cap. 9.
[21] Amelot de la Houssaie, Disc. Hist.

insolence, opposed to the marquis of Spinola an
army of twenty-four thousand foot, under the
command of the marquis of Anspach ⁴². This
force was joined near Worms, on the first day of
October, by two thousand horse, and four hundred musketeers, under the command of prince
Henry of Nassau, and by an English regiment of
infantry, conducted by Sir Horatio Vere, consisting of two thousand four hundred veterans ⁴³.
This single regiment, with some scanty supplies
of money, was all that the king of England contributed to the support of his son-in-law. Nor is
it probable that he would have adventured to
send out even this small force against the Austrians, if he had not, from the timidity, or the
facility of his nature, deemed it expedient to make
a show of corresponding to the zealous attachment
of his people to both the person ⁴⁴ and the cause
of Frederic. The Spanish ambassador at the court
of London managed so dexterously the hopes and
fears of James, that for the small assistance he afforded to the Palatine he made ample compensation. At the very time the armies of Spain were
battering the English, and the other friends and
allies of his son-in-law, in Germany, Sir Robert
Mansell, vice-admiral of England, was carrying
ordnance and naval stores to the Spanish arsenals,

⁴² Hist. de Don Felippe III. por Gonç. de Cesp. lib. 1.
c⁻⁻. ' ı
⁴³ The History of King James, by Arthur Wilson, Esq.
⁴⁴ Hume's History of Great Britain, anno 1619.

and protection to the Spanish trade and coasts from the rapine of the Turks [45].

When the marquis of Spinola arrived at Coblentz, he learnt that Anspach was encamped at Oppenheim [46], a post, one of the most important that could have been chosen either for the defence or the command of the Palatinate. In order to draw the enemy from this advantageous station, and to pave the way for taking possession of it himself, the Spanish general made such movements and such dispositions as seemed at first to indicate an intention of making an attack upon Frankfort on the Main, and afterwards, to make it dubious whether his design was against that city, or against Worms. In the course of these operations he reduced the towns of Creutzenach and Altzeim. The stratagem of Spinola had the intended effect. At the earnest request of the inhabitants of Worms, Anspach hastened to their relief with his main army, leaving Oppenheim under the protection of a moderate garrison. Upon this Spinola, who had set his face against Worms, wheeled suddenly about, and with an amazing rapidity advanced to Oppenheim, which he took by assault, together with great quantities of military stores and provisions. In this important place he formed his magazines; and, having strengthened it by a numerous garrison and new fortifications, threw a bridge over

---

[45] History of King James, by Arthur Wilson, Esq.
[46] Bat. Nan. Hist. &c. lib. iv. 1620.

the Rhine, and paffed over into the Lower Palatinate. In this principality he reduced upwards of thirty towns and caftles in the courfe of fix months ".

When we confider that this commander not only reduced, but kept firm poffeffion of the greateft part of the Palatinate, in fo fhort a time, and in the face of an army equal in numbers to his own, and, perhaps, not inferior in bravery; we cannot but conclude, either that his capacity muft have been far above, or that of his adverfary far below the common ftandard of human nature. All hiftorians agree, that the conduct of Spinola in this, as in his other campaigns, difcovered the moft confummate military fkill; yet their accounts of his conduct are, in feveral inftances, materially different, and, perhaps, all of them, in many refpects, wide of the truth. The evolutions of armies, their marches and countermarches, and all the various operations of war, are not to be defcribed with fufficient accuracy, either from the hafty and partial compilations of the day, or from a comparifon of works better entitled to the name of hiftories. The general himfelf, or his confidential friends, can alone give an account of his views and defigns; and, as to the viciffitudes of an engagement, they are not always known, even to the experienced officer prefent in the field of action. The utmoft therefore that any other perfon can afpire to is, to

" Gon. de Cefp. lib.vi. cap. 12, 13. Batt. Nan. lib. iv. cap. 16. 20. Hift. du Regne de Louis XIII.

BOOK VI.
1620.

illustrate the advantages of vigilance and foresight; to display the power of discipline, of habit, and of opinion, and, perhaps, to point out a few of those causes which surprise the hearts of men, and fill them with the passions of courage or of fear.

But, if it is impossible, by tracing the designs, to do justice to the genius of Spinola, it is an easy matter to discover that he had not a formidable rival in the marquis of Anspach. As an example has been given of the capacity of the one general, so an example shall in like manner be given of the incapacity of the other. On the third day after the arrival of the Dutch and English troops, the marquis of Anspach marched, with an intention of surprising Altzeim, at the head of four thousand horse and six thousand foot, with a suitable train of artillery. The marquis of Spinola, unwilling that his reputation should be tarnished by suffering any of the places he had taken to fall again into the hands of the enemy [47], hastened to its relief. Anspach, informed of the march of Spinola, suddenly turned about to give him battle; but Spinola had by this time learned that the army he had designed to attack was greatly superior to his own in numbers; he therefore drew his cannon up to the summit of a neighbouring hill, from whence it played on the enemy's cavalry, that had begun to press him, with such success as forced them to retreat. Upon this the princes of the Union also drew

Incapacity of Anspach, general of the forces raised by the princes of the Union.

---

[47] Gon. de Cesp. lib. i. cap. 13.

their artillery up another hill, on the right hand
of Spinola. There was a wide valley between
the armies, and in the midst of that valley a
third hill, covered with cottages and vineyards.
By this hill the hostile armies were mutually concealed, and it was only from the summit of this,
that the one general could review the situation
and movements of the other. As soon as the
princes of the Union perceived that the Spaniards were glad to fortify themselves in a strong
position, they rightly concluded that the enemy
were inferior to themselves in numbers and
strength; and therefore resolved to attack them.
It was agreed on, that the English should begin
the charge. Horatio Vere had for this purpose
selected eighty musketeers out of every division of
the regiment. The whole army, full of ardor,
stood impatient for an engagement: but the evening approached, and the men still lay on their
arms. The English general, wearied with this
delay, rode up the hill of vineyards, accompanied
with the earls of Oxford and Essex, to survey the
posture of the enemy. They were retreating in
good order, and in deep silence. The foot marched first, the waggons with the baggage proceeded next, in two ranks, as a species of fortification to the infantry, and the horse brought
up the rear. In this order they marched with all
possible speed to Oppenheim Anspach was posted
nearer to that city than Spinola and it was
in his power either to reduce that important
place, or to force the Spaniards, under a mighty

disadvantage, to come to an engagement. The earl of Essex flew to the marquis of Anspach, and entreated him with much emotion and importunity to improve the important and favorable conjuncture. But the marquis replied hastily, and in an angry tone, "There is a fort between us and Oppenheim, and we cannot pass to that place without being at the mercy of the enemy's cannon." Sir Horatio Vere exclaimed, "And when shall we fight, if we shun the cannon "?" The season of winter had now arrived. It was uncommonly rigorous. The frost was so intense, that the English officers burnt a great many of their waggons: and as to the common soldiers, they lay in heaps on the ground, close together, like sheep covered with a fleece of snow. One would naturally imagine that the rigor of the season must have been severely felt by the Italians and Spaniards. If we may give credit, however, to the authority of a celebrated Spanish author, those inhabitants of the southern climates bore all the severities of the campaign better than the Germans and the English ".

Progress of the war in Bohemia.

While the affairs of the emperor prospered in this manner in the Palatinate, they were still more fortunate in Bohemia. That vigilant prince had learnt that Osman, who now filled the Ottoman throne, had promised to occasion a diversion of the Austrian forces, in favor of the Palatine and Gabor, in the next spring, by invading

" This account of the inglorious conduct of Anspach is chiefly taken from the History of king James, by Mr. Wilson, who was an eye-witness of what he reports.
" Hist. de Don Fellipe III. &c. por Gon. de Cesp. lib. i. cap. 12. 14.

Poland; he, therefore, urged the dukes of Bavaria and Saxony to collect their forces, to advance upon the strength of the enemy, and, by operations equally rapid and decisive, to determine the issue of the war, before time and accidents should turn the tide of fortune, and strengthen the hands of Frederic. Saxony instantly took the field with twenty-four thousand men, poured into Lusatia, laid Budissen, the capital, in ashes, and quickly reduced the whole province under the authority of the emperor. Having accomplished this object, he dispatched fourteen thousand troops into Silesia. This force reduced Glosgaw, a city on the Oder, which, by opening a communication with the Baltic, secured a firm footing in a fertile and extensive country.

In the mean time, the duke of Bavaria, at the head of twenty thousand foot and four thousand horse, marched into the Austrias. The Lower Austria immediately returned to its allegiance, and was received into the protection of the emperor. The Higher, at first, disdained to follow this example of submission. A garrison of two thousand soldiers, thrown into Lintz, the capital, by count Mansfeldt, had inspired the states with a degree of confidence and resolution, which was not to be overcome by an apprehension of danger, while it was yet distant. But the near approach of Bavaria struck them so forcibly, that, although their own force was not diminished, nor that of the duke greater than they had all along suspected, they sent a message desiring conditions of peace. Bavaria, contemning their late applications, took Lintz by assault on the 4th of August, punished the chief authors of the rebellion with death, imposed on those he spared, the burden of a strong garrison, and chastised the whole country with the ravages of war. As there was not in the whole province any castle or fortress that was able to withstand the conqueror of the capital, all the chief men either submitted to the emperor or fled into Bohemia. Having thus re-established peace, together with obedience, in Austria, Bavaria passed on, in order to join count Bucquoy, who opposed, with various fortune, the Bohemian army, whose head-quarters at this time was Egleburgh [50]. The count, according to orders from his prince, marched from Langlovits to Budovits. Here he was joined by the duke of Bavaria: and the two generals having had a short conference, the different armies continued their march, by different routes, towards Prague. On the 10th day of October, they both of them, whether by concert, or by accident, drew near to Pilsen. Hitherto their divided forces had reduced every place that was situated in the tracts through which they bent their courses: and the footsteps of the Cossacs were every where marked with blood.

[50] Gon. de Cesp. lib. i. cap. x. Batt. Nan. lib. x. 620.

But Pilsen resisted their united power, being defended by the subtilty and refinement of Mansfeldt. The count being summoned to surrender to the combined armies of his imperial majesty and the duke of Bavaria, demanded a cessation of arms, and proposed a treaty of accommodation. He insinuated, in a letter which he wrote to the duke and Bucquoy, some general complaints of the injustice of fortune, and of his own hard fate, which had doomed him to struggle with difficulties, and to be rewarded with ingratitude and disappointment. The commanders to whom these hints were addressed, considered them as an advance on the part of Mansfeldt, to surrender the town and garrison of Pilsen, upon those conditions which politicians sometimes take the liberty of holding out to soldiers of fortune. A circumstance had taken place, which shall by and by be mentioned, that enabled them to comprehend, as they imagined, the count's meaning, and which inclined them at the same time to give easy credit to his sincerity. They did not hesitate, therefore, a moment, to transmit to Mansfeldt a very friendly letter, in which they endeavoured to restore him to the interests of the house of Austria by the most liberal promises of preferment and fortune. But Ferdinand had not treasures sufficient to bend the inflexible spirit of that gallant hero; nor was it in his power to have set before his eyes so glorious an object at once of ambition and revenge, as that which he now pursued. Mansfeldt, however, counterfeited a satis-

BOOK VI.

1620.

Count Mansfeldt amuses the imperial generals.

faction in the assurances that had been given him: but he declined to surrender the place, and the troops he commanded, without saving his honor, by making a show of resistance. The imperial generals perceived at last that they had been the dupes of artifice [11]. There was no reason to despair of being able to reduce Pilsen by force of arms: but the obstinate valor of Mansfeldt, it was probable would render the siege tedious, and, in the present crisis, every moment was precious. After being amused for thirteen days, they pushed on towards Prague, and, at Raconits, encountered with the Bohemian army, which was now conducted by the marquis of Anhalt and count Hollach, his lieutenant general. These men were but little acquainted with military affairs; but they possessed the ear of the Palatine, who, passing by the distinguished merit of the counts Thorn and Mansfeldt, bestowed his confidence where he had placed his favor. This was the circumstance which gave credit to the pretences of Mansfeldt, and enabled him to impose on his adversaries at Pilsen.

Adjoining to Raconits, on the west, stood a hill, covered from the bottom upwards, to the middle, with a thick and intricate forest of pine and fir trees, whose close and feathered branches intwined with one another, and reaching to the very ground, formed a shade impervious to the rays of the sun, and a retreat to wild beasts. In this natural fortress, Anhalt resolved to make a

---

[11] Batt. Nan. lib. iv. 1620.

stand, and to wait the approach of the enemy. He formed a camp for the infantry on the upper part of the hill, and defended the approaches to the whole, by the cavalry, and five hundred mufketeers. As it would have been dangerous to have advanced to Prague, leaving fo great a force behind them, the imperialifts refolved to affault the hill on all hands, and, to provoke the enemy, if poffible, to an engagement. But, if, in this attempt, they fhould be unfuccefsful, they hoped af leaft to derive fome advantage from that fpirit which is infufed by an attack, and from that depreffion of courage, and lofs of reputation which the Bohemians would fuffer by declining an action. The moft defperate efforts were accordingly made to diflodge the Palatine, by fetting fire to the vegetable rampart that protected him, and opening avenues for the afcent of the imperial troops, by the hatchet. In this attempt, many officers as well as private men fell, and Bucquoy himfelf was grievoufly wounded. On the 5th of November, Anhalt perceived the imperial army in motion. Upon this, he difpatched count Thorn with a confiderable force to Prague, to ftrengthen the city, and to fortify the wavering minds of the inhabitants. He himfelf, followed foon after with the main army. He left his baggage behind, and, by forced marches, through unfrequented paths, accrofs the mountains, arrived before the imperialifts, at the Bohemian capital. The vaft extent of that city, which was open in many places to

BOOK VI.
1620.
Battle of Prague.

hoftile invafion, determined Anhalt to poft his army on the Wifemberg ⁵¹.

The Wifemberg, or White Hill, is of no great height or circumference, but, being cut and broken by crags and deep ravines, it is of difficult accefs, except on that fide which looks towards Prague, where an inclined plain, of equal fertility and beauty, extends from its fummit to the walls of the city. The lower part of this declining fpace was covered with a range of houfes, or rather a ftraggling village, which formed part of the fuburbs of Prague; the middlemoft was an extenfive park, adorned with a wood, and a royal palace, called the Star; the higher overlooked, and in many places commanded the capital In this ftrong pofition, the Bohemian general drew up his forces, and here he determined to abide the affault of the enemy. The various projections and incurvations of the hill, improved by art, feemed to defy the boldeft affailants. And that the men might not be tempted to abandon fo advantageous a ftation, Anhalt ordered the gates of the city to be fhut, and fignified what he had done, to every divifion of the army. Having taken this precaution, he ranged his troops in order of battle, and waited the approach of the enemy ⁵².

⁵¹ Gon. de Cefp. lib. i. cap. 14. Batt. Nan. lib. iv. 1620.

⁵² Hift. de Don Fellipe III. per Gon. de Cef. lib. i. cap. 14.

The imperialists, who had by this time advanced within half a league of Prague, were struck with the advantageous situation of the Bohemians, and deliberated, whether or no they should give them battle. But the advanced season would not permit them much longer to keep the field; and in the spring, thirty thousand Turks [14] would be added to the number of their enemies. All the friends of Ferdinand had already taken an active part in his cause, and his whole force was now in exertion. The powers, on the other hand, that formed the natural allies of Frederic, from causes that could not be permanent, stood many of them aloof, as if indifferent to his fortune, but would assuredly join in support of his cause, if the sovereign authority should be confirmed in the hands of that prince by length of time, as well as by actual possession. In many cases it was more prudent to guard against disaster than to run any great risque for the sake of victory. But in cases of rebellion there was not room for delay, for the loss of time was equal to misfortune in the field of battle [15]. The enemy was, indeed, strongly posted: but the fate of battles depended on accidents, not to be foreseen by human prudence; and the steady valor of

[14] Hist. du Regne de Louis XIII. Roy de France, et des principaux evenemens arrivés pendant ce Regne dans tous les Païs du Monde.

[15] In di cordiis civilibus nihil festinatione tutius, ubi facto magis quam consulto opus est. Nec cunctatione opus, ubi perniciosior sit quies, quam temeritas. Tacitus.

the Imperialists, was more likely to bear up under any unforeseen and adverse circumstance, than the tumultuous courage of the undisciplined Bohemians. There was yet another consideration, which, of all others, had the greatest weight in the present question. The sermons of father Dominico, a bare-footed Carmelite, who assured the army that the Lord of Hosts would go forth with their standard in his own cause, had infused into the soldiers an impatient ardor to charge the heretics: so important, in those days, was the office of a military chaplain "! On the whole, it was resolved to storm the hill: the troops were formed in order of battle; the Imperialists on the right hand, and the Bavarians on the left. They advanced upon the enemy by the way of Stratzis, the only way that was practicable. Pursuing this course, they were obliged to march in a file over a bridge, and then, before they should arrive at the bottom of the Wisemberg, a miry valley. The younger Anhalt, son of the general, perceived the advantage to be derived from this embarrassing situation, and was all on fire to improve it. He proposed, after allowing such numbers of the Imperialists to pass the bridge as should greatly weaken the main body of the army on the other side, to attack them before they should be formed, and while struggling with the difficulties of marshy ground. This plan of young Anhalt, which was not less prudent than

---

" Batt. Nan. iv. 1620. Gon. de Cesp. lib. i. cap. 14.

courageous, appeared to Hollach, the lieutenant-general, the effect of youthful impetuofity. The Imperialifts were allowed to extricate themfelves from their embarraffment, without any other inconvenience than what they fuffered from the Bohemian artillery. In order to avoid this, they haftened their march, until the prominencies of the hill afforded them protection. Then, having put themfelves in the beft order that the time and the nature of the ground would admit, they preffed up the Wifemberg with deliberate valor, and made a furious attack upon the enemy. The fhouting of the foldiers, the noife of trumpets and drums, and the roaring of artillery, reverberated from the inflections and cavities of the hill, announced the commencement of the important onfet, and fhook the country for many leagues around with terror. Prague, as being nearer to the dreadful fcene, was more fenfibly ftruck with its horrors, and trembled in awful expectation of the eventful iffue. Frederic, on whofe account the contending armies profufely fhed their blood, beheld from the battlements of his palace [17], on the one hand the fpacious capital of Bohemia, and on the other the fierce engagement that was to difpofe of the Bohemian crown [18]. At the beginning of the conflict, fortune feemed to fmile on the Bohemians; for young Anhalt, fupported by count Slich, repulfed

[17] In the Star Park already defcribed.
[18] Batt. Nan. lib. iv. 1620. Gon. de Cefp. lib. i. cap. 14.

BOOK VI.
1620.

with great slaughter the first assault. This assault was made by count Tilly, lieutenant-general to the duke of Bavaria. But the veteran troops, which formed the strength of the Imperial army, sustained this disaster with that firmness which results from discipline, and a glorious reputation. On this occasion the wounded Bucquoi signalized his own spirit, and re-animated the hearts of the fearful. He had been carried in a litter to his tent in the camp, there to wait the event of the action. But he no sooner saw the Imperialists hardly pressed by the Bohemians, than he jumped out of his carriage, and feverish as he was, mounted the first horse he found, put himself at the head of his troops, and attacked the Hungarians with such fury, that he left near two thousand, as was computed, dead on the spot [59]. The Walloons, commanded by William Verdugo, next to Bucquoi, had the honor of restoring the battle. They took young Anhalt and count Slich prisoners, and having made themselves masters of a redoubt, with three pieces of cannon, turned the artillery with prodigious effect against the thick squadrons of the enemy. The panic that was struck among undisciplined troops, by this sudden reverse of fortune; the fright and confusion that had taken place among the Hungarian cavalry, from the yelling of the Cossacs; together with a steady and unremitted fire both of cannon and musquetry, in spite of the

---

[59] Hist. du regne de Louis XIII. et des évenemens, etc.

exhortations, the threats, and the example of the generals and other officers, threw the whole Bohemian army into irrecoverable diforder and terror. A general rout enfued. All was loft, but the honor of having made a brave refiftance. Anhalt, having firft difpatched a meffage to the Palatine, provided for his own fafety. The regiment of count Thorn was the laft that quitted the field. The Wifemberg was covered with the arms of the fugitives, and the bodies of the flain. Multitudes feeking to efcape from the edge of the fword, perifhed in the Mulda. Five thoufand Bohemians, that had been pofted in the Star Park, threw down their arms, aad caft themfelves upon the clemency of the victors. The generals were willing to give them quarter; but the Coffacs remaining equally deaf to the orders of the commander, and to the cries of the flying victims, fheathed the fword only when the arm was weary with fhedding blood [60].

This important victory reftored to Ferdinand the crown of Bohemia, and rendered the authority of Auftria over that kingdom more abfolute than ever. Whatever privileges and immunities the Bohemian ftates had formerly enjoyed, whether as their ancient rights, or the conceffions of their kings, were, by a royal edict, abolifhed or revoked. The electoral dignity, and afterwards the eftates of Frederic were, by the mere authority of the emperor, transferred to the duke of Bavaria. His principal adherents were profcribed;

[60] Batt. Nan. lib. iv. 16.0.

BOOK
VI.
1620.

and all thofe rigors and feverities exercifed againft the profeffors of the reformed religion, which were to be expected from a vigorous, unrelenting, and bigoted conqueror. The misfortunes that awaited the elector Palatine were fingularly affecting; nor, has ever the tragic mufe invented fcenes more fitted to purge the minds of men with fympathetic forrow. In the filence of the night that followed the fatal 9th of November, he fled with his wife and little children into Silefia, where he met with the common reception of unfortunate princes. His abode among a people, determined to make their peace with his mortal enemy, was as fhort as it was comfortlefs. He wandered with his family from place to place, ftill fondly hoping to retrieve his fortune by arms, or by negociation. In the midft of his peregrinations, two domeftic events of contrary natures equally diffolved his foul into the tendereft anguifh. At Brandenburgh, whither he had retired from Silefia, he was reminded how much his family had fuffered from his imprudent ambition, by the birth of a fon[a]. The fame reflection occurred, in all its bitternefs, fome years after, on a journey to Amfterdam. As he was paffing over the Harlem-mer, in a dark and tempeftuous night, the light veffel in which he failed foundered on another, againft which it was driven by the fury of the wind and waves. Before the fhip funk, the Palatine, with fome other

[a] Hift. du regne de Louis XIII. et des évenemens principaux, &c.

paffengers,

passengers, made their escape to that other vessel; but the prince, his son, was unfortunately left in the foundered vessel, which they durst not approach, though they heard the cries of the boy, calling for the help of his father. The next day, when the tempest abated, they found him frozen to the mast, which he had embraced as his last refuge[11]. While the unfortunate Frederic was thus wrestling with adversity, his friends and allies left him, one after another, and sought to reconcile themselves to the emperor. Even the brave and active prince of Transylvania, who, after the battle of Prague, had the courage to march his troops to the frontiers of the Lower Austria, maintaining his army by the plunder of the Catholic subjects of his enemy, even he would have abandoned the common cause, and given up the interests of his ally, if he could have exchanged the crown for the viceroyalty of Hungary[12]. Count Mansfeldt alone, with a small army, which he subsisted chiefly by pillage and free quarters, still maintained the cause of Frederic; and his successful boldness encouraged duke Christian of Brunswic, and the marquis of Baden Dourlach, to appear at the head of armies on the same side. These princes were defeated by the Imperialists under count Tilly. But Mansfeldt, though much inferior in force to his enemies, still maintained the war, and discovered,

BOOK VI.
1620.

Courage and constancy of count Mansfeldt.

[11] History of King James, by Arthur Wilson, Esq.
[12] Bat. Nan. lib. iv. 1620. Gon. de Cesp. lib. i. cap. 15.

at once, the moſt wonderful caution in ſecuring his own troops, and the greateſt valor in annoying thoſe of the enemy. For the ſpace of two years, he defied, with a ſmall flying army, the whole houſe of Auſtria when in the zenith of its power, and would probably have prolonged the conteſt to a more diſtant period, if the Palatine, at the inſtigation of the king of England, had not, under color of ſubmiſſion to the emperor, diſmiſſed him from his ſervice. The count withdrew his army into the Low Countries, and there entered in the ſervice of the United Provinces ".

At the ſame time that the treaſures and arms of Spain were employed, with ſo much ſucceſs, in ſupporting and extending the authority of Ferdinand in Germany, the duke of Feria, by the ſubjection of the Valteline, conſolidated the territories of both branches of the Auſtrian race into one extenſive and mighty empire.

Revolt of the Valteline.

The Valteline extends from the lake of Como, in Milan, winding in an eaſterly direction between two ridges of lofty mountains, to the county of Tyrol, and of the vallies of Sol and Munſter; from which regions it is ſeparated by the hills of Braulio, which may be croſſed in the ſpace of ſix or eight hours. On the north, it is bounded by the Alps, and, on the ſouth, by the territories of the Venetian republic. Its length is ſeventy miles; its breadth, if we reckon from the

" Hume's Hiſtory of Great Britain. Reign of James I. anno 1622.

summits of the enclosing mountains, forty; but, if from their roots, on a medium, not above six. It is watered by the river Adda, and being exceedingly fertile in cattle, corn, and wine, it abounded in towns and villages full of people. The inhabitants of this valley are said to have been of a mild and difpaſſionate temper; their manners to have been uncultivated and ſimple; their language and cuſtoms Italian. The Valteline was in former times a part of the principality of Milan; though by this time it had fallen, through various revolutions, under the dominion of the Grifons: thoſe republicans governed this dependent province with a rod of iron, the antipathy that naturally takes place between a conquering and conquered people, being exaſperated by that of religion. They interdicted their religious rites and uſages, baniſhed the Jefuits, annihilated the juriſdiction of the ſecular clergy, and converted their churches into places of worſhip for the Proteſtants. Colleges were founded, and profeſſors of divinity were brought from Geneva, at the expenſe of the king of England. And, as the Grifons tyranniſed over the minds of this unfortunate people, ſo they in reality enſlaved their bodies. They deprived them on various pretences of the fruits of their induſtry, and even of the patrimony left them by their anceſtors. All thoſe who were in the ſervice of the leagues [11], might commit the greateſt enormities

[11] The civil conſtitution of the Grifons is a democracy. A certain number of towns and villages compoſed a community

212 HISTORY OF THE REIGN OF

BOOK VI.
1620.

July.

on the Catholics with impunity. The government of the Valteline resembled that of Turkey, by Pashas and Janissaries; or the dominion which is now exercised by European merchants over the princes of Asia ".

Animated at once by the resolution of despair, a zeal for religion, and private assurances for the most effectual support from the governor of Milan, the Catholics of the Valteline, in one day flew to arms, and surprised and massacred the unwary Protestants. The magistrates, and men of distinction and property were, as usual in all similar commotions, the chief object of their rage. Upwards of three hundred fathers of prosperous families were put to the sword; and their goods, houses, cattle, and estates, seized by the insurgents. Immediately the Catholics chose new magistrates, and, with the aid of money from Spain, erected several forts, which were also garrisoned by Spanish troops. The Grisons, assisted by the wealth of Venice, which enabled them to hire some companies of Swiss, made an effort to regain the Valteline; but were repulsed

---

or corporation; several communities, a league; and three leagues, assembled by their deputies in a general diet, possessed the supreme power of the republic. The Grisons are represented by writers of those times, but Catholics, as a fierce and intractable people, venal, inconstant, and delighting in blood; and in all respects as the reverse of the simple natives of the Valteline.

" Batt. Nani, lib. iv. 1620. Gon. de Cesp. lib. i. cap. 16.

by the Catholics, supported by near five thousand Spanish foot and horse, with a train of artillery. Thus the conquest of the Palatinate by Spinola, having opened a passage for the Spaniards through Flanders into the heart of Germany; the Spanish territories in Italy being linked to those of Ferdinand by the reduction of the Valteline; and a communication having been already established between the Milanese and Spain, through the ports of Monaco and Final, on the Mediterranean; a chain seemed to be formed for holding the fairest portion of Europe in subjection to the house of Austria.

Among the fortunate events of this year, may be ranked the preservation of Naples from the attempts of the duke of Ossuna. How soon that singular man conceived the bold design of converting his delegated into sovereign power, is uncertain. His resolution was fixed the moment he learnt that the court of Madrid intended to deprive him of his government; but it is probable that fluctuating and transient ideas of independency on that court had occupied his mind at an earlier period; for when matters were brought to a crisis, it was only by pursuing his usual tenor of conduct with unusual alacrity, that he endeavoured to accomplish the object of his lofty ambition. It appears that he entertained a hearty contempt for the feeble capacity and temper of his sovereign[17]. He characterized this prince by an

[17] Batt. Nan. lib. III. anno 1617.

image very natural in the mouth of a military man. Talking of Philip, he was wont to call him, "The great drum of the monarchy" as if he had been merely an inftrument for communicating the orders of the duke of Lerma ". This contempt of the king, and the diftance of Naples from Spain, were perhaps the circumftances which firft fuggefted to Offuna ideas of raifing himfelf to independent power. Thefe ideas appear to have been uppermoft in his mind, when he fcornfully declined to folemnize the double marriages, and courted popularity, by diftributing the money that had been collected for that purpofe among a number of poor virgins.

The means by which this duke, who paffed with many for no other than an ingenious madman, endeavoured to bring about his ends were fo refined and artful, that a brief account of them will not appear unentertaining to the reader.

The order of nobility, accuftomed to look back, and to reverence antiquity, he reafoned, would be averfe to innovation, and difpofed to fupport the crown, which they confidered as the fource of their own eminence in fociety. He therefore endeavoured by all means to humble the nobles, and by ftudied infults to diminifh that refpect which was paid to their rank by the people. He excluded them from all places of power and truft, and even plundered them occafionally of their property. His chief friends

" Anecdotes du miniftere du comte duc d'Olivarez.

and confidents were ſtrangers. Wherever he found a man of courage and genius, whom want or crimes had made deſperate, he received him into his boſom, and loaded him with ſuch favors as infallibly attached him to his perſon. On pretence of quelling commotions, which he himſelf had induſtriouſly excited, he introduced a military force compoſed of foreigners, who were entirely devoted to his will, and who acknowledged no other maſter. He had alſo ſhips of war under his command, which roved the ſeas, not under the flag of Spain, but that of the family of Oſſuna. In this manner he propoſed to train up a naval force, that from habit ſhould look up to him as the only power entitled to direct their motions.

The prizes made by his fleet, and the plunder he raviſhed from the nobility, he employed in bribing the council of Spain to connive at his enormities, and in increaſing his popularity, both in the army and among the great body of the people. Throughout the whole kingdom of Naples he had agents who fomented the natural malignity of the people towards their ſuperiors, and aſſured them that the duke of Oſſuna was the only perſon to whom they could look up for protection againſt the tyranny of the court, and the inſolence of the nobles. He it was who would relieve them from oppreſſive taxes, and eaſe them of all their burdens. One day as he paſſed by a place where the officers of the revenues, in order to adjuſt the tax, were weighing certain articles of provision, he drew his sword with great appearance of indignation, and cut through the ropes of the scales, signifying by that expressive action, that the fruits of the earth ought to be as free as those celestial influences from whence they spring. At the same time that he was assiduous to gain the favor of the Neapolitan people, he also labored to conciliate the friendship and to secure the support of foreign nations This purpose he hoped to effect by doing them all the mischief in his power. For this end he left nothing unattempted that might tend to embroil the Spaniards with all their neighbours, and to render their very name hateful to the world. He endeavoured, as has already been observed, to bring the Infidels into Italy, harrassed the fleets and coasts of Venice, and committed piracies on the ships of almost all nations without distinction. In the mean time he entered into a secret correspondence with the Venetian senate, and the duke of Savoy, and assured them that all the hostilities he had committed were the effects of the most positive orders from the court of Madrid. He invited them to join with him in a design he had formed of restoring the liberty of Italy, by driving the Spaniards beyond the mountains. The republic, averse to such hazardous exploits, would not so much as hear the duke's proposal. But Charles Emanuel thought it worthy of consideration, and instantly communicated it to the court of France. In consequence of this, a person was sent by the marechal Lesdiguieres to learn the real situation of affairs at Naples ".

The designs of Ossuna did not escape the court of Madrid. The council was unanimous that he ought immediately to be recalled: but whether he would submit to their orders they very much doubted. It was therefore resolved to attempt his removal by stratagem. Orders were instantly dispatched to the cardinal Don Gaspar de Borgia, to hasten from Rome to Naples, to take upon him the government in the room of Ossuna. The cardinal, agreeably to instructions from Madrid, having previously secured the countenance of the governor of Castel Nuovo, introduced himself into that fortress in the silence of the night; and the thunder of the cannon which welcomed the arrival of Borgia, next morning announced the disgrace of Ossuna.

But the duke, even while he stood on this precipice, did not resign his power without a struggle to maintain it. He attempted, by means of his emissaries, to rouse an insurrection both of the populace and soldiers. But the possession of the castle, the constant roaring of artillery, expressive of the will and authority of Spain, the acquiescence of the nobility, and those in the civil departments of state; these circumstances operated with irresistible force both on the soldiery and the people, and prevailing over their attachment to Ossuna, maintained their reverence for

" Greg. Let. Hist. Osson. Butt. Nan. lib. iv. 1619. Anecdotes du ministere du Comte Duc d'Olivarez.

BOOK VI.
1620.

Defeated.

BOOK
VI.
1620.

that power which they had been accuftomed to obey. The degraded viceroy returned by flow journies into Spain. When he went to court, Philip withdrew his eyes from him, and turned his back. The high-fpirited Offuna, furveying the monarch with contempt, muttered to thofe who ftood neareft him, "The king treats me not as a man but as a child." This difcountenance was all the punifhment that was inflicted by the meek and gentle king, on a man who had attempted to deprive him of a kingdom. But, in the firft year of the fucceeding reign, he was thrown into prifon, where he died of a dropfy[70].

The brilliant fuccefles of this year, which diffufed through the Spanifh nation a general joy, made but a faint impreffion, where it might naturally be imagined it would have made the greateft. So deep a melancholy had overcaft the mind of the king that it would not be brightened up by the greateft national profperity. In order to revive his fpirits by a change of air and of objects,

April 22.

by the advice of his new minifters he fet out on a journey into Portugal, accompanied with the prince and princefs of Spain, the infanta Maria, feveral of the nobility, the gentlemen of his bedchamber, and his confeffor. The towns through which he paffed teftified their joy at his prefence by acclamations and triumphal arches. On the feaft of St. Peter he made his public entry into

---

[70] Hift. de Don Fellippe IV. por Don Gon. de Cefpedes, lib. fegundo, capitulo fegundo.

Lisbon. The river was covered with all kinds of vessels, which were gaudily decorated, and exhibited the greatest profusion of riches. Thirty-two triumphal arches, adorned with gold and precious stones, displayed in a manner still more pompous the wealth of the capital of Portugal. Philip, struck with so magnificent a spectacle, said, " He never knew before that he was so great a king. " Having assembled the cortes, or estates of the kingdom, he received the crown, with the homage of his subjects. The king in return, agreeably to ancient custom, swore that he would preserve inviolate the rights and privileges of his people. The cortes also swore fealty to the prince, as the heir apparent. This they did in conformity to the wishes of the king. For that good prince, convinced that his end was approaching, was anxious to establish his family in peace and comfort. He remained at Lisbon for some months; but, through the infirm state of his health, did not appear much in public. On his return to Madrid he was detained for some time by a severe fit of his distemper at Casa Rubios. Having somewhat recovered he pursued his journey, and employed the short remainder of his life in the settlement of his family. The infant Don Ferdinand, his third son, at the age of ten years received a cardinal's hat, and with the approbation of the pope, was raised by proxy to the see of Toledo, the primacy of Spain, and the richest benefice in Europe.

On the twenty-fifth day of November the marriage was confummated between the prince and princefs of Spain. And on the fourth of December the prince was introduced to the councils of ftate, in order to learn the importance, and how to difcharge the duties of the crown. This meafure the king adopted in imitation of his father's conduct with regard to himfelf In imitation of the fame example he left, for the ufe of his fon, fome inftructions in writing [71].

{Feb. 23. 1721. Illnefs of Philip.} In the month of February the king's illnefs returned in all its malignity. Soon after his return from the chapel he was taken with a fever, which continued with various intermiffions about the fpace of a month. During all this time his fpirits were depreffed with the deepeft melancholy, and he perfevered, notwithftanding fome encouragement from the phyficians, in expreffing his full affurance that he fhould die. He defired that the image of the Holy Virgin of Antiochia fhould be carried about, which was performed on Sunday the twenty-eighth, in a folemn proceffion, at which the counfellors of Spain and many of the other nobles affifted. In the evening of that day commandment was given to all the churches of Madrid to place the bleffed facrament upon the altars. On Monday, about four o'clock in the evening, the king grew worfe than ever. He had before been feized at different times with a violent

March.

29th.

---

[71] Hift. de Don Fellippe, &c. por Gon. de Cefpedes, lib. i. cap. 7. 16. 18. Anecdotes du miniftere du Comte Duc d'Olivarez. Amelot de la Houffaie.

vomiting and a diarrhœa. Blisters now appeared on his limbs and other parts of his body; and the physicians feeling his pulse, said unanimously, "That they undoubtedly assented to the king in the opinion he entertained of his infirmity." He then, in the presence of his confessor, with other divines, the grandees of Spain, the presidents of the different councils, and the first lord of his bed-chamber, authorized the president of Castile to affix in his name, for his hand shook greatly, the royal signature to a codicil he dictated in addition to his testament, which he had already made at Caso Rubios. This being done, he gave orders that other presents, besides those he had already appointed, should be given to his confessor, and to his servants. After this, his physicians persuaded him to take some food; they also advised him to compose himself for sleep; but he answered, "On so long a journey, and in so short a time for performing it, I must not rest." He now desired as the last action of his life, to see, to address, and to bless his children. He told the prince that he had sent for him that he might behold the vanity of crowns and tiaras, and learn to prepare for eternity. To the child Don Carlos he spoke long and in a low tone of voice. He then said aloud to the prince, "I recommend the child to your protection. It grieves me that I should leave him unprovided; but I hope that I leave him in the hands of a good and affectionate brother." Then appeared the infanta Maria, and the infant cardinal.

At the approach of the infanta he burst into tears, and said, "Maria, I am full sorry that I must die before I have married thee;" but this thy brother will take care of: and turning about he said, "Prince, do not forsake her till you have made her an empress." He then spoke to the cardinal infant, whom he had appointed, when he should be of a fit age, to be archbishop of Toledo. He should be much grieved, he said, if he thought that he would not undertake, and faithfully discharge the duties of that sacred office. He also sent for the princess of Spain; but she fainted away as soon as she entered the king's bed-chamber, and was conducted back to her own apartment. It was not thought proper that she should make a second effort to see the dying king, as she was now in the fourth month of her pregnancy. When what had happened to the princess was reported to the king, he was melted into compassion, and greatly affected at so striking an instance of sensibility and filial love. He professed a firm belief that the princess loved him as well as any of his own children. She would lose a good father, he added, and that he had always loved her tenderly. Afterwards, giving them all his blessing, he dismissed them with many prayers for their happiness, both here and hereafter. The blessed sacrament was administered to him about midnight. He received the extreme unction at two o'clock in the morning. During the whole time of his illness he made a constant confession of his sins, and implored divine mercy. He confessed to all around him that he had often been guilty of dissimulation in matters of government; he regretted his supine indolence, and blamed himself greatly for having devolved the cares of the state on his ministers; and when he reflected that he had not in all things made the will of God the rule of his government, he trembled, crying out at different times, "Oh! if it should please heaven to prolong my life, how different should my future be from my past conduct!" But in the midst of his troubled thoughts he found consolation in the mercies of God; and embracing a crucifix, he expressed his hope, that the Redeemer of the world would not leave his soul in hell, but that, after many ages of painful purification, he would receive him at last into the mansions of the blessed. At devotion so affecting the spectators burst into tears; and at that instant father Jerome of Florence came up to the bed on which the king lay. The father, unwilling to bruise a broken reed, held up to the view of the pious monarch the consolations of religion, and expatiated on the exemplary purity of his life, and that zeal which had appeared throughout the whole of his reign for the Roman catholic religion. The alternate tumults of hope and fear that had so long agitated the mind of the king, at last subsided into a gentle calm, and he died in all the tranquillity of faith, on the last day of March, in the forty-third

His death

BOOK VI.
1621.
And character.

year of his life, and the twenty-third of his reign [72].

The pliant, mild, and religious difpofition of this prince would have well entitled him to the praife of *pious and good* [73], if the natural benevolence of his temper had not been controlled, in many important inftances, by the bigotry, and his piety deeply tinctured with the follies of fuperftition. His amiable and inoffenfive manners would have adorned a private ftation; but he was adverfe to the trouble, and deftitute of the talents for governing a great kingdom.

Review of his reign.

The difpofition of the minifter, upon whom, on his acceffion to the throne, he devolved the honors and the cares of government, was, like his own, gentle and pacific; and pacific meafures were neceffary in the exhaufted ftate of the empire. But a fpirit of domination had taken root in the councils of Spain; the confidents and veteran commanders of Philip II. ftill breathed war; war was the general voice of the nation; and, though peace was the intereft of the monarchy, its predominant paffion was the love of glory. The nobles had recovered in the prefent, a confiderable fhare of that importance which they had loft during the two preceding reigns.

[72] A letter from Spain touching the manner of the death of king Philip III. directed to Gondomar, the Spanifh ambaffador here in England, A. D. 1621, found among Dr. Birch's Collection of Manufcripts in the Britifh Mufeum, Nº 4108. Gon. de Cefpedes, lib. i. cap. 18.
[73] FELLIPPE PIO Y BUENO.

And

And if the king was governed by the dukes of Lerma and Uzeda, thefe minifters were themfelves obliged, in all momentous affairs, to comply with the general bent of the kingdom. The ambitious maxims which had been impreffed on the ductile mind of Philip, from his earlieft infancy, the bigotry of a falfe religion, and the warlike temper of the nation, prevailed for many years over that love of tranquillity which diftinguifhed both the king and his minifter, and alfo over the interefts of the nation. The war was profecuted, but not with fuccefs. The military difcipline, valor, and fkill of the Spaniards were yet undiminifhed; but vigor and prudence were wanting in their counfels. No attention was paid to the trade and manufactures of the Netherlands, Portugal, or Spain. The chief object with adminiftration, was to bring home in fafety the treafures of America; remittances, which diftance and the naval power of the enemy rendered infinitely flow and precarious, and which paffed with rapidity, through a thoufand channels, into the hands of their induftrious enemies. The refources of war were dried up; the public finances were deficient; yet, even in this fituation of affairs, plans were formed for exciting a rebellion in France; and an armament was equipped for the conqueft of Ireland. The attention of the Spaniards was thus diftracted by different views, and diverted from that which, while they chofe to purfue it, ought to have been its only object.

BOOK VI.
1621.

The attachment to liberty, the enthufiafm of religion, laborious induftry, with public and private economy prevailed, but not till after a ftruggle of near half a century, over the wealth, the reputation, and difciplined valor of the numerous armies of Spain; and this haughty nation was obliged at laft to hearken to terms of accommodation. It was indeed in a great meafure owing to mifconduct and want of vigor on the part of the Spanifh minifters, that the war had not been attended with greater fuccefs; but they had judged wifely in refolving to bring it to a conclufion. Nor was there any reafon to doubt that the truce would prove as advantageous to the Spaniards as to the Dutch, if thofe who held the reins of the Spanifh government fhould afterwards conduct themfelves with that prudence, moderation, and wife economy, which they might have been taught by paft experience.

But the world was yet ignorant that domeftic induftry is preferable to extended dominion. This doctrine, which was but juft beginning to influence the cabinets of princes, in the period under review, was fcarcely thought of; nor has it yet had any vifible influence in the counfels of Spain, after its truth has been proved by the experience of near three centuries. That the ftrength of any country chiefly confifts in the induftry and number of its inhabitants, is indeed a truth deducible not only from experience, but from reafon. A kingdom, compact and populous, has a mighty advantage over one thinly inhabited and of great extent. The former refembles a garrifon within the narrow limits of a well conftructed fortrefs, which is able to refift the affaults of fuperior numbers without, and often to make fuccefsful fallies: the latter, a fortification on too large a fcale, whofe extenfive works cannot be defended with effect, againft all the attacks of a vigilant and active enemy. This important truth is illuftrated in a very ftriking manner, by the circumftances of the Spanifh monarchy during the reign of Ferdinand of Arragon, contrafted with its fituation in that of Philip III. In the firft of thefe periods the dominion of Spain extended over the kingdom of Naples, and all the iflands of the Mediterranean, from the Straits of Gibraltar to the fouthern extremity of Italy, befides Tripoli, Bugia, Oran, Mazalquivir, and other towns on the coaft of Africa. The fmall kingdom of Portugal, though governed hitherto by its native princes, it was eafy to forefee, would fooner or later be reduced by policy or by arms, under the power fo that greatly preponderated in that peninfula, of which it formed a part. The viciffitudes of fortune had never confpired more harmonioufly with the operations of nature to form a mighty and durable empire. The branches were not fo ponderous, or ftretched out to fo great a length, as to fall off and to lacerate the parent ftock; but, on the contrary, they were fuch as returned the nourifhment they drew, with increafe. The populoufnefs, the induftry, the martial fpirit of Spain, rendered it at that period the moft powerful monarchy in

BOOK VI.
1621.

Europe, and formidable to all its neighbours. But in the reign of Philip III. the imperial power of Spain, which extended over a greater part of the globe than that of Rome in the zenith of her power, was foiled in a contest with a small territory, peopled with manufacturers and merchants.

The Spanish nation, after this mortifying defeat, sought to conceal its want of power by an increase of pomp and splendor [74]; and to recover, and even extend its authority by intrigue and negociation. The first of these arts, in the present times, appears somewhat frivolous. It ought, however, to be considered, that in those days the ancient hospitality and magnificence still remained, and were considered as very important circumstances in government [75]. As to the second, never certainly were intrigues and negociations conducted with more address, or crowned with greater success. The Spanish ambassadors generally governed the courts at which they resided: and it was in the reign of the feeble Philip III. that those chains were forged, which for so many years alarmed the nations, and which if they had not been burst asunder by the vigorous arm of Gustavus Adolphus,

---

[74] See Appendix, C.

[75] Chamberlayne mentions, as a proof of the moderation and economy of the elector Palatine, that when he came to England to pay his court to the princess Elizabeth, he had a small train of sober well-fashioned gentlemen, servants and all not exceeding one hundred and seventy. Birch's Collection of Manuscripts in the British Museum.

and the generals trained up to war under his standard, would have extended the authority of Austria over Europe.

While few nations from the Euxine and the Baltic to the Pyrenean mountains, escaped the calamities of war, Spain enjoyed the supreme blessing of profound peace. The success of her arms in Germany retrieved that loss of reputation which she had suffered in the Netherlands. And as it is the prerogative of military renown to dictate many circumstances of custom and fashion, the dress and manners of Spain were very generally imitated by other nations [x]. The magnificence of the court was supported at an incredible expense; and the Spaniards were still esteemed the first nation in the world. This splendid face of things had an imposing air abroad; but the nation at home, oppressed with taxes, suffered for all its acquisitions and triumphs.

[x] As it is common to say of a man of fashion, on his return from the continent, that he is very much Frenchified, so in these times travellers generally became very much Spanishified. "Mr. Ruffingham, says Mr. Chamberlayne, is come home so Spanishified that I hardly knew him when he saluted me." Birch's Collection of Manuscripts in the British Museum.

APPENDIX.

(Vol. I. Page 136.)

A journal of the Conference betwixt his Majesty's Commissioners, and the Commissioners of the King of Spain, and Arch-Dukes of Austria, Dukes of Burgundy, &c. at the treating and concluding of a Peace with the aforesaid Princes at Somerset-House in London, Anno 1604.

May 1604.

SUNDAY the 2d of this instant the earl of Dorset, lord high treasurer, the earl of Nottingham, lord high admiral, the earls of Devonshire and Northampton, and the lord Cecil, principal secretary, being appointed commissioners by his majesty to treat with Don Juan de Taxis Conde de Villa Medina the Spanish ambassador, and signor Alexander de Rouida a senator of Milan, commissioners, authorized on the behalf of the king of Spain and the count of Aremberg, the president Richardot, and the audiencer Verniken authorized in the like manner on the behalf of the archdukes of Austria, Burgundy, &c. to treat about the making and concluding of a firm peace and amity betwixt his majesty's kingdom and subjects and the aforesaid princes' subjects and dominions, their lordships repaired to Somerset-house, the lodging of the said Spanish ambassador, and there, with the rest of the other commissioners, entered into a common conference concerning the said business.

APPENDIX.

A fair great chamber, heretofore used for the council-chamber in the said house, was expressly prepared by his majesty for the said meeting, and it was thought fit to give the said commissioners the place of the right hand at the table, in respect of the great honor done to his majesty in sending of the said commissioners to treat here within this realm.

The said commissioners being placed together on the right hand of the table, and their lordships on the left hand in the same manner, the earl of Northampton in a speech in the Latin language, fraught according to the manner of the times, with many quotations and allusions to the sacred scriptures, and the Grecian and Roman literature, among other things, congratulated his audience on the prospect of peace; set forth the pacific dispositions as well as prosperous fortune of his Britannic majesty; expatiated on the duty of sacrificing all passions, whether of individuals, or of the times, to the general good of mankind; mentioned several circumstances which ought naturally to conciliate peace and good will between the king of Spain, and the princes of the house of Burgundy on the one part, and the king of Great Britain and Ireland on the other; and expressed, in conclusion, his ardent wishes and hopes that not only would a good correspondence be re-established between those princes, of which he did not entertain any doubts, but that all grounds of animosity, jealousies, and contention would be removed from the breasts of their respective subjects.

APPENDIX.

After the earl of Northampton had ended his speech, the senator of Milan made also a speech in Latin at greater length, and more religious, learned, and elaborate than that of Northampton. In this speech, among other particulars, he reminds the commissioners of the marked proofs of sincere congratulation which his master the king of Spain, had given to his Britannic majesty, on his accession to the crowns of Scotland, England, and Ireland, and of the professions of friendship and amity, which on that occasion his most serene highness the king of Great Britain had made to his most Catholic majesty. The mutual professions of good will which then took place between those princes seemed to the senator of Milan to resemble that " rushing of a mighty wind" which preceded the descent of the Holy Spirit on the Apostles, and therefore he exhorts them to banish from their councils all passions and prejudices of every kind, animadverts severely and fully on certain denominations, and classes or kinds of men ¹, who would endeavour all that was in their power to obstruct the present negociation for peace; calls to mind the ancient habits and bands of friendship which had subsisted between the kings of Great Britain and the princes of the house of Austria; bestows the highest praises on king James on account of his pacific disposition; expresses the utmost satisfaction and joy at the general appearance of a pacific disposition throughout Europe; exhorts all the European princes to peace among themselves, and animates

¹ Hominum Genera.

APPENDIX. 233

them to a common refiftance of the Turks, the common enemy of Chriftendom. He prays for a return of peace and commerce with all their bleffings; he promifes his utmoft endeavours for effectuating fo defirable an object, and appeals to God for the fincerity of his declarations.

The prefident Richardot made a fhort declaration in French, to the like effect, of the affectionate defire of his princes to continue and maintain the good amity which had been ever between his majefty and them; and that to that end, and not to fail in the performance of any kind and loving office towards his majefty, the faid princes his mafters fent to congratulate his majefty's coming to the crown. So becaufe it hath heretofore fallen out, either in refpect of the unhappinefs of the former times, or by God's juft judgment for our fins, or by other occafion, that there have reigned great diffenfions between the kings of England and the princes of the Low Countries, now poffeffed by the faid princes, which heretofore could not be determined, their defire was both for the affurance of the public quiet of Chriftendom, which hath received no fmall interruption by thofe differences, and to renew the ancient amity and friendfhip which hath been ever carefully cherifhed between this ftate and the faid provinces, to conclude fuch a firm peace and folid amity between his majefty and the faid princes as might be for the common utility of both their ftates, which they hoped would accordingly fucceed to the effect defired by them, out of the trial which they have always made of his majefty's princely and Chriftian inclination to so good a work; and out of the same assurance for the like respects of interest, they had solicited the king of Spain to join in common treaty with them, which he prayed God to bless with a happy and fruitful success.

The several speeches being made and ended, it was signified by the lord Cecil that their next proceeding ought to be, according to their use and order, to exhibit their several commissions to each other's considerations. Whereupon the same was accordingly done of all parties, and the Spanish ambassador did first read the immediate commission which was granted by the king of Spain to the constable of Castile, whereby not only absolute power was given to himself to treat and conclude a peace, but also a farther authority (as they did enforce) by the words, *tratar y hazer tratar*, to constitute and sub-delegate other commissioners according to the power whereof they declared that the said constable had sub-delegated, by another special commission from himself which was also showed and read. The said Spanish ambassador, and signor Alexander Rouida to be in his absence commissioners for the king of Spain, to proceed in the said treaty; and furthermore, the said ambassador produced a letter written from the king of Spain unto himself whereby he did nominate and appoint him to be a commissioner in the said treaty; that being done the lord treasurer proceeded in the reading of his majesty's commission; and afterwards the count Arembergh did in the like manner read the commission of the archduke and the Infanta and copies were delivered interchangeably to each other, of all their commiffions.

Their lordfhips, conceiving to have caufe to note fome defects in the Spanifh commiffions, as well in that it appeared by the fame, that they were to treat with fub delegates, whofe authority was derived from the power of the conftable's commiffion, as alfo for that it feemed to them that the words *tratar y hazer tratar* were fomething weak to authorize the faid conftable to fub-delegate other commiffioners under him, their lordfhips did therefore think fit to withdraw themfelves to the lower end of the chamber, to advife of the objections that were neceffary to be made to the faid commiffioners, and after fome fmall time of conference among themfelves thereupon, they returned to their former feats, and it was fignified to them by the lord Cecil, that although their lordfhips could not deny that they had caufe to receive great contentment in the honorable and forward difpofition which both the king of Spain and archdukes had fhowed to effect the conclufion of a firm peace and amity between his majefty and them, wherein his majefty was willing to anfwer them with the like correfpondence of his part, yet notwithftanding that they hoped that it would not be difpleafing unto the faid commiffioners that their lordfhips, in careful difcharge of their duty towards his majefty and the truft repofed in them, in a matter of fo great weight and importance, did acquaint them with thofe things wherein their lordfhips in their judgment held themfelves bound to be better fatisfied, as being, firft, derogatory to the king's honor, that themfelves reprefenting the quality which they did of principal counfellors to the king's majefty, fhould be referred to treat only with commiflioners fub-delegated by derived power of the conftable of Caftile, who although he were to be acknowledged a perfon of good blood, and chief quality, yet that he was not to be confidered for other than a fubject of Spain.

And fecondly, for that their lordfhips were doubtful whether the words of *hazer tratar*, were to receive the conftruction of giving power fufficient thereby to the conftable to fub-delegate other commiffioners; and that, though it were true, that the commiffioners of France treated at Vervins with others authorized by the archduke; being a prince, made a difference therein: and moreover that there was no other meaning at the firft meeting of the faid commiffioners at Vervins, fave only for the prefent to handle matters by way of conference and propofition, fo as it was not taken fo behoveful to infift upon the due formalities of an exact commiffion; and therefore, his lordfhip prayed the commiffioners to give their lordfhips anfwer to the aforefaid objections, where their lordfhips conceived it to be very material and fit to be fatisfied.

Hereupon the Spanifh and archdukes' commiffioners withdrew themfelves to the lower end of the chamber, and after fome conference among themfelves, they returned to their former feats, and the fenator of Milan, in the name of them

APPENDIX.

all, delivered this anſwer, that it was far from the meaning of the king of Spain, by any proceedings of his in this matter, to caſt any diſhonor upon the king's majeſty, but rather, that his intent appeared to be the contrary, by the choice which he had made of the perſon of the conſtable to be employed in this buſineſs, which he would accordingly have performed by his own preſence, if he had not been prevented by his indiſpoſition of body, the which neceſſity was cauſe that he had made the ſaid ſub-delegation, being unwilling that a buſineſs of ſo great importance ſhould receive any delay; and that as the ſaid conſtable intended to aſſiſt at the concluſion of the treaty, it would in part anſwer the other objection touching the inſufficiency of the words *hazer tratar*, which in the Spaniſh tongue they held neverthelefs to be ſtrong enough to give authority to depute and ſub-delegate others, and that it was to be remembered, that, the like exceptions being taken to the ſame words by the Engliſh commiſſioners at Boulogne, they were afterwards allowed for good and valid; that in the commiſſion given to the archduke for the treaty of Vervins thoſe words were clean omitted, and yet, notwithſtanding, no exception taken, but the honor of the prince therein contracting truſted; but that any ſuch doubts were chiefly ſatisfied, in that the treaties which were made were afterwards to receive their ſtrength and virtue by the confirmation of the princes.

Their lordſhips ſaid they would acquaint the king with the objections made by them, and the answers made to the same, and therein receive his majesty's resolution, without the which they durst not further to proceed for the present in a matter of so great weight, and so took leave of them for that time.

On Tuesday the 22d of this instant, their lordships repaired again to the said commissioners at the place of their former meeting, and it was then declared unto them by the lord Cecil that their lordships had acquainted the king's majesty with the doubt moved by them upon the view and consideration of the Spanish commission, and with the answers made to the objections, and that thereupon it had pleased his majesty to give them directions to signify unto them, that though his majesty was resolved to be ever truely sensible of any thing that might concern him in honor, yet that out of the reality of his mind he chose to prefer substance before circumstances, and therefore was not willing to insist upon other formalities with them, than only to note unto them, that the manner of their commission did give cause to those which desired not the perfecting and countenance of this amity to disgrace the proceeding therein, for that it was requisite, that, according to the ordinary use, more persons than one should have been joined in the original commission to supply the absence of any one in case of sickness or otherwise, and especially that the omitting to join the Spanish ambassador in the said commission, showed that the order for the foresaid sub-delegation was rather out of purpose disesteeming than by accident;

and although it was sought to be colored with the authority of a special letter written by the king of Spain to him, by the which he was appointed to be a commissioner in the said business, yet that the same doth far differ from the necessary form of a due and powerful commission so as his majesty might be justly moved to appoint commissioners to treat by a like answerable power of sub-delegation: nevertheless because his majesty found that there was no want of authority to treat in the original commission, or reason to doubt of the constable's speedy coming to supply the defect of the said sub-delegation, the Spanish commissioners, after having had some conference among themselves, made answer by the mouth of the senator of Milan.

That they were glad to find, by this real proceeding of the king with them, a confirmation of that noble disposition in confidence whereof their princes had been induced and encouraged to enter into this treaty with him, for the which they did acknowledge both in their masters and in their own name all thankfulness unto his majesty, and particularly also unto their lordships for being a means to reconcile the difference in question, protesting that there was no meaning to proceed otherwise than with like sincerity and integrity also of their part, as they hoped to receive the like measures from their lordships.

Hereupon it was agreed to proceed to the handling and debating of the point of the treaty, and it was moved by the earl of Northampton that they would begin to make the firſt propoſitions of their part, whereunto they aſſented; and it was ſignified by the ſenator of Milan, that the king of Spain did, at the coming of the king's majeſty to this crown, lay open the affection of his heart unto him by ſending to congratulate with him and to deſire the eſtabliſhing of a ſincere and intrinſical friendſhip with him.

And becauſe of the chance of times between his ſtate and the kingdoms of England and Scotland, the ſaid king deſired for his part that the friendſhip of the ſaid kingdoms might be now ſo ſtraitly conjoined, as that there might be made a league offenſive and defenſive between the ſaid princes, to be friend to each other's friends and enemy to their enemy.

The lord Cecil yielded them thanks for the great good will and affection which by their offer they expreſſed unto his majeſty; but gave them to underſtand that it could no ways agree with the preſent ſtate of his majeſty's affairs to make ſuch league with them at this time as was propoſed by them, as well in reſpect that his majeſty ſhould thereby declare and engage himſelf againſt thoſe of his own profeſſion of religion, as alſo for that he ſhould therein violate his amity with France which already did ſtand between them upon condition of a league offenſive and defenſive: therefore, that the ſaid propoſition would be more proper for ſome other time hereafter, and for the preſent that it would be beſt to adviſe to eſtabliſh a firm amity for the aſſuring of the liberty of trade and free intercourſe between the kingdoms and ſtates. It

APPENDIX.

It was hereupon anfwered by the fenator of Milan, that the king of Spain was moved to tender the aforefaid offer unto the king, out of the affection which had been before declared, and to witnefs unto him that he would prefer his amity before all others, but if it fhould be thought inconvenient, for any difficulty, to proceed in thofe terms of condition, that they would forbear further, to urge the fame in that manner: but becaufe they would be glad to make a peace that fhould extend further than to the effect of an intercourfe, they defired their lordfhips to open themfelves what kind of peace the king would make to the princes their mafters. The prefident Richardot ufed a fpeech to the like effect on the behalf of the archduke.

The lord Cecil made anfwer, that they did all agree in the acknowledgment of the mutual and real affection of their mafters, for the which he did the more hope that God would blefs their work; that their lordfhips did conceive that it did ftand with good order firft to conclude and eftablifh a general amity between kingdoms and ftates whereof the effects are afterwards to enfue, and that in the perufing and digefting of the fmall points of the treaty, the matters of privileges and cuftoms and other neceffary provifions which might be thought fit to be fpoken of as they fhould fall out, would be beft handled in their order and courfe.

The fenator of Milan anfwered, that it was far from their meaning to except againft any thing which had been formerly spoken of, and that it was not otherwise meant to press the order for making of a league offensive and defensive, than as should stand with the king's own good liking, and not to be prejudicial to other princes and states; but he prayed their lordships again to explain themselves what kind of peace the king should make with their princes, their several natures being reduced under those three divisions, either to make a general league offensive and defensive, or else a particular league defensive *sine offensione*, which should bind to assist each other in case of being invaded by a third person, or lastly to make a peace of firm amity and friendship with condition not to attempt any thing to the other's prejudice and wrong.

The lord Cecil answered again, that their progressions had been hitherto to good purpose in that they had declared themselves thus freely to each other, and cleared the doubt of their commission, and that their lordships would be as willing also to give them resolution in this matter of their propositions; because they desired, for the avoiding of misunderstanding, to be clearly instructed of the king's purpose therein, when it was fit, his majesty being so near at hand, to acquaint with a matter of so great importance and weight, their lordships prayed them to give them time to receive his majesty's resolutions upon that point; and that their lordships would return to them again to proceed in the business as soon as the affairs of the parliament, which they were also

neceffarily to attend, would give them leave: with
the which anfwer they refted fatisfied, and fo they
took leave of each other for that time.

Friday the 25th their lordships repaired again to
the faid commiffioners in the afternoon, and the
lord Cecil then firft declared unto them that their
lordfhips had acquainted his majefty with the point,
whereupon they paufed at their laft meeting, and
whereupon they thought fit to receive refolution
from his majefty's own judgment, and that now
they were come to make known his majefty's
pleafure therein fignified to them; wherein firft
their lordfhips held themfelves bound to declare
truely that which they found of his majefty's gracious and willing inclination to entertain good
amity and fincere friendfhip with the king of Spain
and the archduke; and touching the point of
making a league offenfive and defenfive, that his
majefty having underftood from them the arguments which were made by their lordfhips, not
only againft the fame, but alfo againft the fecond
propofition for a definitive league, his anfwer to
both the faid points fhortly was, that there ought
not to be ufed much argument to debate thofe
things which were directly to be refufed, for not
being of condition which might receive fatisfaction; that ftrict forms were neceffary where doubt
ought to be made of the parties difpofition to
obferve the conventions; but as his majefty did
not refufe the former propofed leagues for want
of good affection, fo the faid former commiffioners were to confider the integrity of his majefty's

disposition, that was not willing to enter into a thing that could not yet be accomplished, as his majesty desired, in respect of being otherwise engaged of honor; and therefore, considering the present state of things, that it was fit to resort to the third point for making of a firm peace and amity; but because it would be a fruitless name if the particular conditions were not agreed upon, that it would be necessary first to enter into the consideration of the conveniency of the conditions to be resolved on, and afterwards to frame the form thereof according to the use in cases of marriage, wherein first the articles of covenant are handled between the parents, by way of admission, upon presumption of a future liking to follow between parties whom it is sought to join in marriage. This he declared to be the effect of his majesty's answer to their propositions, with assurance of all kind and loving affection unto the princes their masters.

After the said commissioners had conferred sometime among themselves, the senator of Milan made answer in the name of them all, that the princes their masters did hold themselves confident in the assurance of his Majesty's good will and love towards them, out of the proof which they had formerly made of the same, and being therefore desirous for the better confirming and strengthening of that amity, that the unkindness and difference which had formerly reigned between this state of England and the said princes might be now abolished; the said princes were moved to make the aforesaid proposition, either by the making of a league offensive and defensive, or only defensive; the first whereof was propounded of good will, and the second to show that there could hardly be entire friendship between any but that they ought to be sensible of each others harm and wrong: but seeing neither of the said propositions could now be accepted, for the reasons which had been before alledged, they desired to reserve them to other times, and better occasion, and in the mean time to proceed to the making of a firm peace and amity in the third, whereof it had been before spoken; and because of the mention made of former treaties to be an impediment of the leagues before recited, he desired their lordships to declare themselves better, whether there were any incompatibility touching the peace to be made with the princes their masters, and any other treaties already made with the king, and to show what those treaties were, and what peace the king would require; for that they knew not that the princes their masters were in difference with *any* other prince or state of Christendom, but only sought the confirming of their own, without any other ambitious desiring. To the said propositions touching matters of treaties, the lord Cecil made answer, that though the king himself might, before the entrance into this kingdom that had in former times difference with others, and treaties thereupon made, he could not now conveniently do any thing that might be in prejudice thereof, whereby they might judge to what interest we stood still engaged of the time past.

The senator of Milan desired their lordships to satisfy them more certainly, what kind of friendship the king would make with their princes for not offending each other, and not ministering help to their enemies, to the end there might be no scruple to hinder the peace, because *in generalibus non est scientia*.

The lord Cecil made answer, that as he did well perceive the force of this argument, so he was willing to give him satisfaction in things which should be reasonably urged; as namely, that there ought to be observances of kind friendship between the said princes, and not to be offensive to each other; but for the expressing of further obligations, and courtesies, in case of the falling out of any differences between either of them and a third prince, that it was not to be looked, that princes would otherwise intermeddle themselves in any such sort than as they should be moved upon occasion of very good desert, but rather that they would be careful for the good of the state still to maintain their necessary interest of intercourse with any such other prince.

The president Richardot said, that it was necessary that they should open themselves more clearly to each other, in order to come to an end of the business: that the example of other princes which had been before mentioned was nothing pertinent to their case, because the princes their masters had amity with all the world, but only the rebellious subjects of Holland, whose protection it was desired that his majesty would quit, and the same was the

APPENDIX.

point whereupon their princes defired to contract a peace with his majefty: That the archduke did only feek juftly to reduce their lawful fubjects to their due obedience, and howfoever thofe of Holland had hitherto forgotten themfelves in their duty, that the archduke would be content to receive them upon any reafonable conditions, to the end to avoid the further profecution of an unhappy war; and the faid archduke would be very glad, that it would pleafe his Majefty to be judge and arbitrator in the caufe between them; or in cafe thofe of Holland fhould refufe to fubmit themfelves to any conditions of reafon, that he hoped his majefty would not think them worthy to be fupported by this ftate; and he defired that it might be remembered, that the performance thereof was agreeable to the proteftation made by the late queen to the world, not to undertake the protection of them longer than they might obtain conditions of reafon.

The fenator of Milan made a fpeech to the like effect, of the difference that was to be made of the cafe of another lawful prince in war, and the condition of rebels, who ought rather to be by all means disfavored, than that an intercourfe of trade fhould be entertained with them.

The lord Cecil made them anfwer, that he was drawn by their laft fpeech to fpeak of the Hollanders wherein they plainly difcovered their object and intent. That it was true, were it not for the diftraction growing by their late occafion, there was no color for any difference to be between the king and the princes their masters: he desired that he might not be pressed to dispute whether they were rebels or not; but that he would boldly affirm, that the contracts which were made by the deceased virtuous and pious princess, whose memory he was bound to honor, with them which called themselves by the name of the United Provinces, were done upon very just and good cause. He desired that they would proceed to agree to the peace that was to be made, and if they thought it not fit to take any other conclusions until they were first satisfied whether they would continue to trade with Holland or not; his lordship prayed to understand from the said commissioners, whether they held that point to be so essential as that the peace could not be proceeded on without receiving, first, a resolution therein, or otherwise to be accidental, that necessarily required to have a proposition made for it.

The senator of Milan answered, that he must still insist upon the difference that was to be made of rebels, in regard of whom the said trade might be considered to be essential or accidental, according to the greatness or smallness thereof.

The lord Cecil answered that during the time the king's majesty was only king of Scotland, he being in firm league and amity with the princes their masters, did nevertheless, use a continual course of trade with those of Holland, as in the like manner France and Denmark and all other states had ever used, and that there was no reason he should do himself the wrong to undergo now a worfe condition therein, than heretofore he had done and others now did.

The fenator of Milan now anfwered that we were to live by laws, and not by examples.

That it was true they were in peace with Scotland, when neverthelefs Scotland ufed to trade with the Hollanders, and though they had reafon to except againſt the fame, yet becaufe they held not the fame trade to be great, they thought not fit to break their peace thereupon, which would have been of great inconvenience to them, that now it was not only a far greater trade by the union of the kingdoms of England and Scotland, but alfo the making of a new peace, wherein it was requifite to provide a remedy againſt inconveniences of the times paſt.

The earl of Northampton anfwered to the feveral parts of the fenator's fpeech; that though we were to be governed by laws and not by examples, yet that examples were the means of interpreting the laws; that the king of Scotland did bring with his own perfon the privileges which he formerly enjoyed, and that good or evil was not to be meafured by proportions, but to be efteemed by the juſtice or injuſtice thereof.

The fenator of Milan alledged that it could not be denied but that trade was an affiſtance, and thereby repugnant to the treaties of amity, and in that refpect the ufe thereof unlawful.

The earl of Northampton anfwered him, that if it were not heretofore unjuſt for the king to ufe that liberty being king of Scotland, then that there was no reason to except more against it now, that the king's majesty takes no other course therein than was used by the king of Spain himself, who was content to admit and entertain a trade with those which he called his rebellious subjects, which, as it might be alledged to be done chiefly for his own utility, and not for any respect done to them, so his majesty did profess only to regard therein only his own necessary interest.

The lord Cecil added further that it was good to let them plainly know that the trade with those provinces was of so great importance to us, that we could by no means spare the same; and moreover, that the king was no less tied by the weight of other considerations, not to renounce, the holding of further correspondence with them, in due care not to lose the great debt which they owed him, and the possession of the towns which he held among them, and therewith also not to make themselves desperate, to betake themselves unto other protection, which might be more dangerous both for Spain and England, and therefore, he told the said commissioners, that they were not to expect to receive satisfaction upon that point.

The said commissioners answered, that they had respective meaning not to seek to restrain our trade to our prejudice; but only to bar their rebels from partaking also by our means, of the fruit of our trade with their princes, for the prevention whereof that it was fit to advise how to limit our trade in due sort, and they prayed their lordships to propound some reasonable means for the same.

APPENDIX.

The lord Cecil defired the faid commiffioners, that they would rather explain unto their lordfhips their defire therein; but becaufe the time grew late, it was agreed to refpite the further handling of that point unto their next meeting, and fo they took leave of each other for that time.

Thurfday the 31ft, their lordfhips repaired again unto the faid commiffioners, and firft excufed unto them their long abfence, by the occafion of other important bufinefs, and then defired to proceed in the determining of the bufinefs laft in communication between them, and to receive the faid commiffioners anfwers therein.

The fenator of Milan anfwered, that the laft fpeech was concerning matter of trade, wherein they were willing to conferve our former liberties unto us, fo as their rebels might not be benefited by the ufe thereof, and therefore they defired their lordfhips to propofe the means of a middle remedy unto them.

The lord Cecil faid, that their lordfhips being perfons of honor did not defire to *merchand* the point with them; but thought fit to let them know that there was no poffibility of yielding to reftrain the trade of his majefty's fubjects into Holland, and likewife of the Hollanders trade unto his majefty's dominions, which he did not entertain for their fakes, but only for our own good; and, confidering that all other princes take their liberty, that there was no reafon to reftrain the fubject of his majefty; who, for the confiderations which had been before expreffed, was much more interefted to maintain the fame: and therefore he wished that there might be no further argument upon that article, but to pass over upon some other.

The president Richardot alledged, that their last treaty made with France, was strong in general terms, to restrain the French from ministering such help and assistance to their rebels as the use of trade did import, and like assurance had been since given for the revoking of their ambassador out of those ports; but howsoever that the same had not been observed, it ought to justify the wrong that they had received therein.

That their intent was to be careful of our lawful interest, and they desired us to have the like consideration of theirs, and therefore prayed that their lordships would propose some reasonable way of remedy therein.

The lord Cecil answered him, that it was yet unknown unto us, what benefit we should receive by the trade of Spain, but that we were assured that the trade of the Low Countries, was of greatest importance unto us; notwithstanding, to show that their lordships were most willing to accommodate themselves to reason, that their lordships would assent to prohibit the carriage of all materials of war to those of the United Provinces, upon pain of confiscation of the same commodities.

The senator of Milan desired their lordships to explain themselves, whether their lordships understood thereby, that it should be also lawful for the subjects of England to carry the commodities of Spain into the Low Countries, and so likewise of the Low Countries into Spain, because their meaning was not to allow that favor unto the Hollanders, howfoever they might otherwife agree to approve our trade with them; neither alfo that it fhould be lawful for us to trade in their fhips, and in any fort to color the faid Hollanders goods.

The lord Cecil faid, that he found their reafons to be very allowable, in that they fought to impeach their enemy's good, and he hoped likewife, that they would acknowledge it to be as reafonable that we ought to feek to receive benefit by the peace, or otherwife, that it would be better for us to remain ftill in war, in refpect of the fortunate purchafes which we had made at the fea. But becaufe it was fit that their lordfhips fhould receive informations from the merchants concerning this point, before they did further determine thereof, he defired that they would proceed to fome other matter and leave that queftion to fome other time, which was affented unto; the point of intercourfe with Holland and Zealand being admitted in general, and the queftion referred to further confiderations whether we ought to be reftrained to vent the commodities of Holland and Zealand into Spain, and fo likewife of Spain into the faid Provinces: and it was defired by the faid commiffioners, becaufe they had already made two propofitions of their part, that their lordfhips would now exprefs themfelves concerning their demands.

The lord Cecil faid, that their lordfhips would be willing to give them fatisfaction therein; and therefore, firft, that he would begin with the complaint of the great wrong and grievous vexations, which were committed upon our merchants trading into Spain by the authority of the inquisition there, whereof he defired that they might from henceforth be difcharged and cleared, and a free liberty of trade to be granted to his majefty's fubjects in all the dominions of the king of Spain and the archduke.

The fenator of Milan anfwered, that they were to yield to any thing which was in the power of their commiffion in the favor of the trade of his majefty's fubjects, but under that generality, that they could not promife other matters for the which they had no authority, namely, that they would promife and undertake for a liberty of trade to be granted in the king of Spain's dominions of Spain, Portugal, and Italy, and fo likewife in the territories of the archduke; and concerning the inquifition, he alledged that it was to be held for a general ground, that the inquifition took no notice of any fault, but where there was a public fcandal given, the which order the king would be careful to recommend to have duly obferved according to that rule, and if they might receive informations from our merchants of the particulars of the grievances whereof they complained, that they would endeavour to procure them redrefs thereof.

The lord Cecil made anfwer, that their lordfhips would be glad to receive better fatisfaction from them to the two points propofed by their lordfhips, becaufe their lordfhips did conceive that there fhould have been a general admittance and permiffion of trade into all the dominions of the

APPENDIX. 255

king of Spain; by nominating of some countries and omitting of others, it seemed that there was a meaning to use a restriction therein, which did not answer to the condition of a general and reciprocal free trade, which ought to be granted between the princes: for the other point concerning the inquisition, that his majesty was not willing to exempt his subjects from punishment for any offences which they should commit by public scandal given by them, but there was no reason that they should be otherwise subject to the passionate censure of the inquisition, to be so strongly dealt with by them as ordinarily they had been, where the like severity was not practised in any part of Italy, nor in the proper dominions there of the king of Spain, where it was conceived that he had as great a power to exercise the authority of the inquisition; and therefore, if order were not taken therein, that his majesty should be forced to make the subjects of the king of Spain to undergo the like severity here.

The senator of Milan answered, that for the matter of trade, they did not design for the better demonstration of the freedom of the intercourse in the king and archduke's dominions; but that now he would more particularly explain himself, that our subjects should have trade in any place of the king's dominions where he admitted any other prince to have intercourse with him; and for the matter of the inquisition, that the king of Spain had as great authority to exercise the form of that law in his dominions in Italy, as in Spain, but that it could not be dropped; that some judges might want discretion in their proceedings, for that princes might make judges, but could not give them discretion.

The lord Cecil said, that concerning the answer made for the granting of such a liberty of trade unto his majesty's subjects as was allowed unto other princes, they were not acquainted with the interest of other princes, of whom some had more private considerations than others; but for us, which were of another constitution, that it was no way fit for us to be restrained in our trade, and that we expected liberty granted us, to trade to the Indies, and desired to know whether any just reason could be alledged for excluding us from them.

The senator of Milan confessed, that their meaning was to restrain us from the trade of the Indies, which could not be imputed to be a wrong unto us, because it was never before granted us in any former treaties, never hitherto permitted by the king of Spain to any of his own subjects, or nearest kindred, or so much as to any of his children, therefore he prayed to be excused, for that it was not in their power to give their lordships satisfaction in that matter.

The lord Cecil answered, that the king was resolved to maintain all things which were necessarily belonging to a lawful trade, and he hoped they would not urge unreasonable restrictions upon him which had no example; that he desired trade with all the world, but so, as it might be also accompanied with liberty to distribute the said
merchandize

merchandize afterwards into any ports to the beſt behoof of the merchants; that they were content that any goods which ſhould be taken belonging to the Hollanders, ſhould be ſubject to confiſcation, whereof it ſhould not appear by good proof, that they properly had been before changed, and the right of the ſame to be ſince in any of his majeſty's ſubjects to tranſport goods in any of the Hollanders veſſels upon the ſame penalties, but that other harder reſtrictions ought not to be impoſed upon them. The earl of Northampton told the ſaid commiſſioners further, that he did conceive them to be ſo reaſonable, as they would not impoſe other laws upon us than themſelves would willingly admit in a caſe of their own like intereſt, there being no reaſon to hinder to vend that to his beſt commodity in any other place, which he had adventured to fetch home to his great hazard; beſides, that his majeſty ſhould receive a notable prejudice therein in the ſtate of his cuſtoms, for that there ariſes a far greater benefit to him by the tranſportation of commodities out of the realm.

The ſenator anſwered, that they did not ſeek to impoſe laws upon us, but only to provide for their own ſecurity; that by our means the Hollanders might not enjoy thoſe things which they did reſtrain from them; and conſidering that there might be found vent for the ſaid commodities in other parts, as Poland, Denmark, Dantzick, &c. that ought not to be held unreaſonable to be yielded unto.

The earl of Northampton anſwered, firſt, that the generality of the words expreſſed not in this treaty only, but in thofe of former times, gave a more free fcope and freedom of accefs to the ports and dominions of the kings of England and Spain, than a conftruction againft the plaineft purpofe and fenfe of their words themfelves ought to qualify, for it was true that *omnia intelliguntur permiſſa quæ non funt expreſſe prohibita, &c.* (every thing is underftood to be permitted, that is not exprefsly mentioned in the lift of exceptions and prohibitions, &c.) That the treaties between Lewis the VII. and Maximilian, and between Henry the VIII. and the emperor Charles, at Cambray, Bruxelles, &c. did afford freedom of trade to Englifhmen, with thefe words, *ficut proprii fubditi, ficut in fua patria,* (as his own fubjects, and as if in their own country &c.), And fecondly, that though the king of Spain might moderate the defires of his own fubjects, or of thofe princes in whom he had a greater intereft for many fpecial refpects, yet might the king of Britain ftand upon the fame terms that the queen of England did with Don Aires the Portugal ambaſſador, prefling earneftly a prohibition of Englifh merchants upon the fame grounds and motives that their lordfhips do now, which were that in this cafe fhe could not condefcend with honor, to the king of Portugal's requeft, left his fcope of trading univerfally in her dominions fhould be more abfolute than her's in the dominions of Portugal thus limited; that if ports, which by the law of nations ought to be free to all men in refpect of trade and ufe, though not of jurifdiction and property, might be fhut up to any, it was to be either for hoftility as the Civilians demonſtrate, or in refpect of infidelity; but that in the firſt degree, the king of Britain's fubjects could not be ranked in refpect of league; nor in the fecond, becaufe the differences there are in religion between the princes reached not fo far; but by the judgment of Hoſtienſis, a learned canoniſt, it was required that there fhould be either *falforum & plurium deorum, aut utriufque teſtamenti rejectio;* (a belie for worfhip of falfe, or a plurality of gods; or an abjuration of both Old and New Teſtament); therefore, againſt us the Spaniards ought neither to fhut up their ports nor their harbours; that the laſt will of a Chriſtian made in the *ports* of a Pagan prince was fufficient in law; becaufe thefe were holden *juris publici & jure gentium ad ufum communem tenere*, (to belong to the great republic of the world, and by the law of nations to be fubfervient to the common good of all.) Whereas, all teſtaments that are made within the *dominions* of a Pagan prince were by law reverfible: that therefore, it was holden by the Civilians, that in cafe a man would lay the charge out of his own purfe of making or unbarring a haven, which is the greateſt merit that induſtry can perform, *etiamfi ædificia funt ædificantium tamen ipfe portus debet effe communis*, (although all ſtructures are the property of thofe who raife them, ports themfelves ought to be common.) And that fo far were the Civilians from barring princes out of ports, as that they feem rather to be *portuum vindices*, (the affertors of the freedom of ports), in purging the seas from piracy, and that their ports were a protection in *omnibus maribus*, (in all seas); besides, that if any body may bar us from trading into those parts, the right of that exclusion belonged properly to those Indian princes themselves, to whom the seas did belong, as the Civilians averred, in property and jurisdiction, that confine upon their state, and which did possess those places wherewith he desired to trade, for that the Portuguese did not possess the 20th part of that which is open; 1000 leagues, lying sometimes between one part possessed by them and another, and they paying to those Indians pier-custom and tribute for their freight, &c. That those princes were so far from barring and excluding, as they did rather allow all the world to trade, and if they did not, that the worst part must be ours in adventuring so far without sound warranty; and these arguments were further added by him; first, that in universal societies there ought to be an equality, and therefore a reciprocal, free intercourse was to be admitted by the law of society.

Secondly, that a contract, to be gainful to the one part without commodity to the other, was *leonina societas*, (a society of lions). Thirdly, that our kingdom consisted more of navigation than others did, and therefore, that their answer for having denied it to other countries was nothing pertinent to us.

Fourthly that our people was a warlike nation, and having been accustomed to make purchases on the seas, could not better be reduced than allowing them a free liberty of trade.

The which he enlarged with this further amplification, that the other princes forbearing this trade was no lawful bar to the king of Britain; because it was rather for want of means than liberty in them; but the providence of God having fitted this state more for trade than any other, in the making of ships, the situation of the monarchy, the capacity of ports, the disposition of men, the strength of their constitution, and the convenience of all ordinary means, would tax us in a manner both with sloth and idleness, in case we should forbear to make our advantage by that means which nature offered; wherefore since we could not, without error and absurdity suffer those wooden walls, as Apollo gracefully termed them, which are the ramparts of Brittany to rot for want of use, there was great reason that the king of Spain drawing them from employments of hostility, should leave them to the general and ordinary course of trade, whereby they might be maintained, the subjects enriched, and the state fortified.

The senator of Milan answered, that though ordinary societies by leave should be equal, yet that they might be limited by conversions, and that the same ought not to be found strange in this case, because the said Indies were a new world; and touching argument of inequality of condition, that it could not be so reputed, because the subjects of England should have the liberty of commerce of thirteen kingdoms belonging to him, for the three kingdoms of England, Scotland, and Ireland; and therefore, that it could not be said to be *Leonina focietas;* that the king of Spain had ever denied the liberty of that trade to all his own fubjects of what country foever, though depending as much upon navigation as we did: laftly, whereas it was argued that the liberty of the faid trade would contain our people in better terms, that there was no reafon that our men which had before benefited themfelves by the fpoils unjuftly, fhould now have for recompence a trade which had been denied to all others, even to the king of Spain's own kindred and brethren.

The lord Cecil faid, that he found, by the former fpeech of the faid commiffioners, that they were not authorized to give any further fatisfaction touching this point, and therefore, that he thought it fit to refer the refolution thereof to the coming of the Conftable of Caftile, to whom he hoped it would appear that he had not fo much reafon to deny the liberty of that trade as his majefty had to infift upon it.

The commiffioners anfwered, that the conftable was no more authorized to give fatisfaction therein than they were, being a matter which they did not expect would ever have come in queftion, and fo their lordfhips conference ended with them at that time.

Friday the 1ft of June, their lordfhips repaired again to the faid commiffioners, and the lord Cecil declared unto them, that their lordfhips held it to be the beft courfe to the end, to bring the treaty to a more speedy and orderly conclusion, to take the view and form of other precedent treaties, and to select out of the same such rules as were necessary for the present time; that it was agreed of the form of the amity, and that the princes should not minister occasion of offence to each other, and that since there had been question of moderating our trade, which they termed to be an assistance to those of Holland, that their lordships since last being with them, had due consideration of the matter, and did protest not to be willing to insist upon any liberty to pleasure the Hollanders for the bettering of their condition, but because if they should admit the restrictions which had been proposed by the said commissioners or merchants, they should be bound to undergo infinite inconveniences and vexations by the perils which the same would draw upon them, for that it was impossible so clearly to distinguish of the sort of merchandise according to the several places of their making, but that it would breed a confusion of questions, and difference and endless troubles and molestation to the merchants; and therefore, that there was no reason to make any goods of Holland subject to confiscation, after such time as the property of them should be changed.

The president Richardot answered, that it was not so hard a matter as it was conceived, to discern and distinguish of the places where any commodities were made, as well by the fashion itself of making, as also by the applying of some seal and mark, the which considered, that there was no reason but that they should confiscate the merchandise of Holland from what place soever the same should be brought.

The lord Cecil told him, that contrariwise, it would be infupportable to our merchants, which would grow thereby, and we were moreover to have respect to the prejudice which we should otherwise receive by that means in our trade with France, who finding that we had covenanted not to vent the commodities which they might tender unto us, though being of foreign growth, would also hereupon interdict the receiving of our commodities into that country; therefore he wished it might be forborn to dispute further of that matter for the present, and to pursue his first motion to make a selection of articles out of former treaties.

The senator of Milan answered, that they had some other special demands first to make, whereunto they desired to receive answer, namely, that they desired to be restored to the towns which were held belonging to them in the Low Countries.

The lord Cecil told them, that the king's majesty did not pretend any interest of right to the said towns, and wished it were lawful for him to restore them to the true proprietary, but that he held them as pawns for good sums of money owing to this crown, and that there were no reason he should dispossess himself of them till he were satisfied of the said debt.

The senator of Milan answered, that we received the said towns from those that had no right to pledge them.

The lord Cecil said, that the king should be much wronged to deliver them to others than from whom he received them; and if they would confider it well, that it would be safer for them that the said towns should be continued in his majefty's hands, than be reftored to the ftates.

The senator of Milan propofed it as a doubt how, if he would not reftore the said towns presently, it might ftand with the continuance of the peace? For their defiring to reduce the iflands to their obedience, might lead them firft, for their better entrance, to begin with the towns.

The earl of Northampton told him, that the deceafed queen poffeffed herfelf of the said towns by the like juftice as the king of Spain took towns in France, and did ally herfelf with Holland and Zealand by the fame right, as he did with the houfe of Guife, fo as it ought no more to be difputed with us than it was in their cafe, whether they took the towns and poffeffed them from *vero domino* (the right owner), or not, whereof mention had been made by them.

But their lordfhips obferved, that the great difference was to be made between the right of reftoring of towns conquered, and fuch as were delivered for the fatisfying of conditions of pledge and affurance.

The lord treafurer added further, that great difference was to be made between the bounds and contracts of private men, and thofe of princes; that in the one the ftrict rules of private law, as was expreffed, might have place; but in the second there was not only respect to be had of the laws, but also of public utility and princely honor, and of the equity that ought to be between great states: wherefore, in as much as the deceased queen of England did, as a public princess, enter into contract for the said towns, that the king's majesty was now still to hold them, and might not in honor deliver them; besides, that it was for the good of the archduke that they should rather fall into our hands than into worse.

The senator answered, that the ignorance of the law to whom the said towns belonged, ought not to be available to him that should have informed himself by better knowledge, as well concerning the right of private interests as of public; but if it should be admitted to yield profit to him for the time, it ought to be only for the benefit of the mere fruits, and not for the detaining of the thing itself; and whereas it was alledged, that it was happy for the archduke that the said towns fell into so good hands, that it would now appear by the restoring of the said towns; or otherwise, that we only respected our own interest, and nothing the good of the archdukes.

The president Richardot answered, and pursued the same argument; only adding, that the king's right for his money might be sufficiently preserved against the parties that engaged the towns, and that they would assist us therein: that it would be dishonorable for their princes to make a peace, and to leave the said towns in our hands, and that they desired to know whether, if they should

APPENDIX.

attempt the recovery of thofe towns, it fhould be taken as a breach of the peace.

The lord Cecil told them, they had reafon' to feek to fortify their demands, but that their lordfhips had more reafon to maintain their denial if their lordfhips fhould be forced to profecute the further reafons which had been delivered unto them of ftate and honor, and plainly they were to underftand, that it was a thing that the king would not do; that they ought to content themfelves with the making of a firm peace with us, without cafting us thereby into greater inconveniences than we were before fubject unto by the war with them, that if they had purpofe to attempt any thing againft thofe iflands, they fhould not be therein impeached by us, but only we would look to the guard of our towns.

The earl of Northampton purfued a fpeech to the fame effect.

The fenator of Milan anfwered, that they know no difference between the right of a private man and of a prince, but that a prince could not be compelled to make reftitution; and whereas it was faid that thefe things could not be determined by the ftreams of law, that they required the faid towns by the law of nations, which did yield to every man his right: but becaufe it was alledged that the king fhould violate his oath and honor, in cafe he fhould affent to the prefent reftoring of thofe towns, they confeffed it was *regiæ poteftatis*, (a matter of fovereign power,) and therefore, that they would not further infift upon that demand:

but they defired to be anfwered to their former propofition, whether in cafe they fhould be forced to the reduction of the towns, it would be held a breach of the peace, which they defired to have continue inviolable, and defired fome provifion to be made for it.

The lord Cecil faid, that their lordfhips were willing to concur with them to affent to any thing that might be reafonable for the reconciling of this difficulty, but that it was fit to proceed in the matter with great moderation, left it might otherwife give interruption to the peace, and if they already advifed of any unreafonable propofition to be made of their lordfhips, they would be glad to underftand the fame, or otherwife, that it might be confidered of againft the time of their next meeting, which was approved by the faid commiffioners.

The earl of Northampton told them, that he would briefly remember unto them before their departure two confiderable things: firft, that their lordfhips had yielded unto them in all confiderable matters, and given them no interruption; and fecondly, how unwilling their lordfhips were, by way of argument, to receive the remembrance of the old differences, whereby they could fufficiently anfwer the point of the prefent propofitions.

Tuefday the 5th of June, their lordfhips repaired again to the commiffioners, and the lord Cecil declared unto them, that their important bufinefs which hindered them from coming fooner to them, forced them ftill to begin with excufes for their long abfence; that they had acquainted his majefty with the point that remained laft in difference between them; and that they were commanded by his majefty to make them that anfwer to the fame, whereof he defired they would make good interpretation; that he was wi'ling to give their princes all good affurance and fatisfaction of his defign to entertain firm amity with them, but that he had reafon chiefly to look to proceed in the making of the peace with the fafe-guard of his honor, which he held in no lefs recommendation than his life, namely, concerning the cautionary towns, which he was refolved not to deliver over unto them for the reafons which had been before declared unto them, and that his majefty did find exceeding ftrange, that they fhould feek to exact more of him in that behalf, than they had done of their bafe and barbarous mutinied foldiers, with whom they had lately compounded, and had been contented that they fhould deliver back unto the State's hands the town of Grave, which they had received from them; but if they thought that there could be no peace made with his majefty, if he continued to hold the faid towns, he would be willing, fo as they would find the means, how he might be reimburfed his money, to deliver them back into the States hands according as by contract he was bound; that thereupon their princes might afterwards take fuch courfe as they fhould think fit for the recovery of them.

The fenator of Milan anfwered, that the propofitions made for not reftoring the towns were the reasons of honor and utility: honor, for being otherwise engaged by contract to them from whom we received them; and of utility, in respect of your debt; that they did not desire to wrong the king in his honor, but because the holding of the said towns by the king, would be an impediment to the observing of the peace; therefore, that they would be glad that some reasonable means might be proposed how the one might be preserved with the other, which they thought might well be by suffering the king to keep the said towns in his hands some three or four years: in the which time it were to be hoped that the Hollanders might be reduced to obedience either by his majesty's mediation, whereof they had good hope, or otherwise, by the good work of God; and if they were so, all difficulties would be removed, and order might be taken for satisfying of the king's debt; but if they should still remain in disobedience, then there would be no cause why the king should longer respect his promise to the Hollanders, finding them to continue so obstinate, and he was desirous that by this contract now to be made, the king would promise them to restore the said towns unto their princes.

 The lord Cecil said, that knowing the king's heart to be so full of integrity as they did, their lordships should much fail of their duty, if they should not return an answer worthy of their proposition; if there was not a third person interested in this case, the difficulty for the restitution of the towns might much more easily be cleared; but it

APPENDIX.

was apparent to every man's reafon, that a thing depofited could not be delivered over in the prejudice of a third perfon, and a thing fimply depofited could not afterwards be reftored upon conditions; that the covenant now to reftore the towns at a limited time hereafter, imported as much as the prefent reftoring of them; that it were better therefore to advife of fome other means; and that the king's majefty, to witnefs that he would be willing to give the faid princes all the fatisfaction that he might, would ufe all good endeavours to draw the Hollanders to a peace; and becaufe, as their neceffity fhould increafe after having loft the favor of his majefty's protection, they would be then the moft conformable to reimburfe the king's debt: that whenfoever they might be drawn to fubmit themfelves, the king would make it appear that he likewife for his part would not ftand, upon any reafonable matter of money, for the reftoring alfo of the faid towns, to bring the war to an end.

The prefident Richardot afked, whether it was not intended to yield to any limitation of time for the reftoring of the faid towns, but to refer it to the uncertain reducing of the States, and fo to continue to a time infinite.

The lord Cecil anfwered him, that there was no reafon to expofe the king's majefty to the difcredit of a difhonorable treaty for yielding to a limited time, feeing they were affured to reduce the faid Hollanders within a fhort time after they fhould want the benefit of his Majefty's affiftance. The earl of Northampton added further, that if the like reason of equity, after five years, should remain as now, for the not delivery of the said towns, why should they more urge the delivery to be then made than now? that it could not be denied that the Hollanders should be less able to withstand and to resist the archduke, being separated from us, than now; and therefore it was to be judged they would be reduced: but if contrariwise, by despair, that people should be forced to seek other protection, it were to be considered whether it were not better for the princes, that the king's majesty should join with them for the defence of his pledges, than to leave them to desperate men without having his interest in them. Hereunto the senator of Milan replied, that though the said arguments had been in part before, and might be again sufficiently answered; yet that they would not insist upon further disputation, but rather desired to bring the point to a conclusion; and therefore, because it was alledged that it would touch the king no less in honor presently to covenant for the restoring of the towns at a certain time hereafter, than it would be to do it presently; and seeing on the other side, it would be dishonorable for their princes that there should a peace be made without providing for this point in some sort, they offered to their lordships consideration the framing of the said promise in this or like manner: that if within some certain time to be limited, those of Holland, &c. should not conform themselves at the king's solicitation, that then the king would

APPENDIX.

would be left to his liberty to difpofe of the towns, according as fhould be agreeable to juftice and good amity.

The lord Cecil told them, that it was fit their lordfhips fhould acquaint the king with the faid overture, before they gave them a conclufive anfwer thereunto, in refpect that the king had been fomething diftafted with the motion that was formerly made, and fo their conference ended for that time.

Thurfday the 7th of June, their lordfhips repaired again to the faid commiffioners; and the lord Cecil declared unto them, that their lordfhips had at large acquainted the king with the arguments which were particularly handled by them of both fides, touching the point of the rendering of the towns: and the king's majefty took in fo good part the moderation which they had ufed in being careful to temper the matter, that his honor might not be wronged, as he protefted to be in trouble between the care how to fhow himfelf thankful to their mafters for the due refpect therein had of him and of the other fide not to do a thing which might be difhonorable to him upon confideration of precedent contract made between the deceafed queen and the United Provinces, which he was bound to obferve: he did find that he ftood fo ftrictly engaged in honor towards the States, that he could not yet (as they do now ftand) enter into a covenant for the delivery of the faid towns to their mafters; but that he conceived the beft expedient would be, that he fhould enter into a new communication with the States, and to profess unto them, that if they should not either take order for the payment of their debt by a certain time, or else conform themselves to the obedience of their princes, that then the king's majesty would be at liberty to take such course with the said towns as should be agreeable with honor and justice; which assurance of the king's good inclination toward them in this course might well content them without urging the king to a more expressed promise.

The senator of Milan answered, that they never doubted of the king's affection for the good amity towards their princes; and therefore, that they held themselves bound to be the more careful to use their best endeavours for the tempering and accommodating of the point in question, so as the honor of both princes might be preserved; which they, by way of discourse, and not otherwise conceived, might be, by the assigning of a time convenient unto the Hollanders, wherein they should conform themselves, or else the towns to be restored to their princes; but that now it was added further, that if the States would pay the money in the mean season, that then they should receive the towns again, which could not be contracted by them, without prejudice to their princes honor; and therefore, he referred himself to the president Richardot, to declare the interest of the archdukes upon that point; who signified, that it could not stand with the honor of their master to make any such contract.

The lord Cecil told them, that all that hitherto had been spoken, was by way of discourse, to the end, to seek to reconcile this question, that as they were not to admit any mention to be made of restoring the towns to the States, because they conceived they should thereby approve either the States possessing of the said towns, or their fact to be lawful, so the king his master would be as loath to covenant any thing which might prejudice or discredit his own contracts with the States, in that he had accepted the said towns; therefore, as before had been declared, that the king did hold it to be the best course to summon the States to enter into a new conference and contract with him, whereby he might provide, that if they should not conform themselves within a convenient time, that he would be at liberty to take such course with the said towns as should be agreeable with honor and justice: and other promise than this, that he could not for the present make, till he had freed himself of the contracts with the States which did now stand in force.

The president Richardot desired, in the name of all the said commissioners, that they might have some time given them to consider of the said proposition; and withal that some form of an article might be conceived for that purpose, to be delivered unto them, which was allowed of, and agreed to pass over to clear the point of the trade, which had been formerly handled.

Concerning the said matter of trade, the lord Cecil told them, that their lordships having had conference with the merchants thereof, they did all protest, that the restriction that was sought to be imposed upon them for not transporting the commodities of Holland and Zealand into Spain, would be of so great vexation and trouble unto them in their trade, as would be to their ruin, if they should be forced to undergo the inconvenience thereof; and therefore his lordship desired the said commissioners not further to urge the said condition, and the rather, considering that the benefit thereof would nothing be so great unto them as the prejudice would be great unto us: that we were content to give them satisfaction to yield, that our men should not make use of the Hollanders ships or mariners, whereby they would be exceedingly distressed.

The president Richardot answered, that the trouble would not be so great as was pretended; and that our merchants might be furnished of the same commodities out of the archdukes provinces, which they fetched out of Holland and Zealand, which might well be distinguished by a seal from those of Holland.

The lord Cecil told them, that our trade could not be soon settled in their provinces; and that the States would moreover give impeachment to our trading with them, as they did to all other princes and states of the world, pretending that they could not admit of any trading with the archdukes without their manifest ruin; and that we did expect to receive their protestation upon that point.

It was said by the commissioners, that the States

would not dare to impeach our trade, if we would take the courses which we might do, to be sensible thereof; but it was told them, that it could not be done without plunging ourselves into a new war; and it was desired by their lordships to leave this question of trading with them, to be handled in its proper place and course, and to clear the other point first spoken, touching the transporting of Spanish wares of those princes into Spain, concerning the which the lord Cecil signified unto them that, if it would please them to be satisfied in the effect of that which they desired, he would propose an offer unto them how it might be done, and our merchants freed from molestation, which should be, that the king's majesty should prohibit the transporting of the commodities of Holland and Zealand into Spain; and so likewise of Spain into those provinces, by any of his majesty's subjects, upon pain of confiscation of the same commodities, and of incurring further, punishment; and, for the better observation thereof, that some seal should be appointed to design the commodities carried out of England. The said commissioners desired to take time to consider of the said proposition, and so brake off their conferrence for that time.

Friday the 8th of June, their lordships repaired again to the said commissioners; and it was moved by the lord Cecil, to know their resolution touching the point which had been last handled.

It was answered by the said commissioners, that they were content to agree to the passing of our commodities into Spain, upon ſtrait order and prohibition to be made by the king's majeſty, according as was offered, that none of the commodities of Holland and Zealand, ſhould likewiſe be under that color tranſported by his majeſty's ſubjects into Spain, upon confiſcation thereof; and for the better avoiding of fraud in that behalf, that the merchandizes of England which might be ſubject to queſtion, being of the ſame kind and making as thoſe of Holland, ſhould be diſtinguiſhed by the marks and ſeals of the towns where they were made, and having that teſtimony, that they ſhould not be ſubject to viſitation, for the merchandize which ſhould be marked, but there have their allowance.

It was then moved by the lord Cecil, to know what proviſion they would require for the merchandizes which ſhould be brought out of Spain, for not tranſporting the ſame into Holland and Zealand.

The ſenator of Milan ſaid, that we might be diſcharged of giving any caution in paying the impoſt of thirty upon the hundred; but it was anſwered by the lord Cecil, that we did not now only expect to have the impoſt aboliſhed againſt us, but alſo to be reſtored to our former privileges and liberty of trade with them.

The ſenator of Milan declared, that their care was to give their lordſhip ſatisfaction, by all means to make it appear what affection they did bear unto the peace: and therefore, although there were an order eſtabliſhed for payment of thirty upon the hundred, for all goods issuing out of Spain, unless the same should be carried unto the archdukes provinces, that the said imposts should be remitted for such merchandizes as should be brought into England only.

The lord Cecil answered, that though we must interpret every thing for a courtesy from them, wherein they would show to make a difference between us and others, yet that we found it would be a hard condition unto us, to be restrained not only from carrying the commodities of Spain into Holland, but also into France: which haply might be an occasion also to impeach the liberty of our trade with France in respect of our admitting a condition of such prejudice unto them. But notwithstanding that their lordships were contented not to dispute the reasons of their interest, and would admit the said condition, upon protestation that the restraint for the transporting of Spanish commodities into France should not stand longer than till the present differences which were between France and their princes for matter of trade might be compounded, wherein that the king's majesty would be glad to do some good office between them, to take away those interruptions which might grow thereby to the state of the common trade of their subjects, that it followed to be the next question, what caution should be given for the observance of the foresaid restraint for such commodities as should be brought out of Spain.

It was answered by the senator of Milan, that

they required the caution which was provided by their placard for the giving of affurance in Spain for the payment of the impoſt of thirty upon the hundred, if a certificate ſhould not be afterwards brought of the landing of the ſaid goods in England, and not for carrying the ſame to the prohibited places.

The lord Cecil told them, that there was no meaning to yield to give fuch affurance, in refpect of the inconveniences and vexations which the fame would draw upon our merchants; befides, that it was diſhonorable for the king to yield unto it, that he was content to make ſtrict prohibitions to the contrary upon pain of incurring fevere penalties, and if any further caution were to be given, that it were rather neceſſarily to be taken here in England; that in fuch cafes, where a proviſion could not be conveniently made without occaſion of greater inconveniences otherwife, there ought to be repofed a truſt in the honor and word of the prince, and upon complaint that ſhould be made by the ambaffador of Spain refiding here of any contrary actions in that point, that there ſhould be redrefs thereof.

It was earneſtly preffed by them to have fome better proviſion; but in the end, after much debating, it was agreed to put off this queſtion till fome other time without refolution of either part.

It was afterwards propounded by the fenator of Milan, to clear the point alfo touching the impoſts which our merchandize ſhould pay, which were to be carried out of England into Spain, becaufe the

APPENDIX.

impoſt of thirty upon the hundred did ſtand ſtill in force againſt us.

The lord Cecil told him, that we undertook to bring the trade to the ſame ſtate of payment of both ſides, as it was before the breaking out of the laſt troubles.

The commiſſioners anſwered, that their princes were content to remit unto us the impoſt of thirty upon the hundred, and that our merchants ſhould not be ſubject to pay any other dues than were eſtabliſhed by the time of the publiſhing of the laſt placard of thirty upon the hundred; and that they did not hold themſelves to be authorized to look further backward for the taking away of any impoſt, than till the ſaid time; ſo that there was no reaſon that we ſhould ſeek to exempt ourſelves from thoſe impoſitions which were before eſtabliſhed, and which are generally payed by the ſubjects of all other princes and other ſtates whatſoever, and even by their own ſubjects; but if there hath been any thing particularly impoſed more upon our nation than upon others, then, that we had to ſeek the aboliſhing thereof, and not otherwiſe.

It was anſwered by their lordſhips, that if the ſaid commiſſioners were not authorized, as was alledged by them, to yield to any moderation of the impoſts for longer time than till the ſetting out of the laſt placard, there was no reaſon for the preſent, to ſpeak further thereof; and touching the other point, that we ought in reaſon, to ſubmit ourſelves to the ſame general payments as all others did.

That the same was no good argument to be used to us, to whom there ought to be a more particular respect, in regard that we ever had in ancient times a more strict alliance and amity with them than other nations had, which was an occasion to move princes in favor of such an extraordinary friendship, to grant more special privileges and immunities to some nations than might be challenged by others, that could not pretend the like consideration, as it might be exemplified by the ancient convention made between France and Scotland, wherein the Scottish then had more beneficial privileges granted unto them than any other nation; that in our treaties with Burgundy, it had been provided to set down our particular privileges, and care had been taken to use us always with the same respect of favor in Spain, where our friendship had been the same; and therefore, that their lordships found it strange that they would not make the treaty to have reference to the former time of amity, rather than to the latter more confused and troubled time wherein the interruption grew.

The said commissioners protested, that they knew not, for their parts, what other impositions had been established since the time of the last troubles, besides the impost of thirty upon the hundred; and therefore, that it was to no purpose to argue longer upon an uncertainty, which could not be determined without better information of that point: whereupon it was thought fit to break off their conference for that time.

APPENDIX.

On Wednesday the 11th of June their lordships repaired again to the said commissioners, and it was signified unto them by the lord Cecil, that their lordships expected to hear from them what other propositions they would make, of their part, to proceed to the conclusion of the treaty.

Whereupon it was answered by the senator of Milan, that it was best, before they entered into any new matter, first, to recapitulate and clear the points which had been before discussed and agreed on for matters of trade, namely, touching the goods of Holland and Zealand into Spain, and so likewise of the merchandizes, &c. we should carry out of England, or the archdukes provinces into Spain, and so likewise out of Spain into England or the archdukes provinces only; that they should be exempted from payment of the impost of thirty upon the hundred, and the provision to be accepted which was offered; and the king's majesty should restrain the transportation of the commodities of Holland and Zealand into Spain, on pain of confiscation, and further in testimony that the said merchandize should be known to the English, that the same should be marked and distinguished by the seals of the places where they were made; but for such merchandize as should be transported out of Spain, he enforced it to be necessary that our merchants should enter in bond to the value of thirty in the hundred, not to carry the same to other places than only to England or the archdukes provinces, and upon any confiscations grown for any thing done contrary to the foresaid order, the king of Spain to be satisfied out of the same; the value of the said imposts of thirty in the hundred, and the rest due to be answered into his majesty's exchequer with the allowance of the half part thereof to the informer.

It was answered by their lordships, that in Spain there had been lately raised another impost of twelve in the hundred, upon wines and oils, which were shipped from thence, wherein his majesty's subjects did sustain the greatest grievance, for that they did most deal with the said commodities; and therefore, that his majesty's subjects should not receive any benefit by the trade of Spain, unless the said impost might also be taken away.

It was alledged by the commissioners, that the said impost of twelve in the hundred, did extend to all other nations, and even to their own subjects, and therefore, could not now be removed.

But it was answered by their lordships, that there was no reason to comprise us under that generality, to whom there belonged a more particular regard, for restoring us to the privileges and customs which had been anciently accorded between us and them.

The others insisted earnestly upon the maintaining the lawfulness of the said impost; so as for that time, nothing was concluded upon that point.

Afterwards there was speech of the caution which our merchants should give, which the said commissioners required, with sureties concerning the merchandize which they should bring out of Spain, for the not venting of the same contrary to the placard, but it was utterly refused by their lordships to subject our merchants to so troublesome a caution; and their lordships only assented to the giving of simple caution to the value of the said impost.

On Wednesday the 13th of June, their lordships repaired again to the commissioners, and it was moved unto them by the lord Cecil, that it might be granted, to the end our merchants might receive comfort in the trade; to take away also the impost of twelve in the hundred, whereof speech had been before, as well as of the other of thirty. But it was answered by the commissioners, that the present state of their masters affairs could not permit the same to be done.

It was then demanded by the lord Cecil, that if they would not yield to the release thereof, how they would otherwise recompense it in some other thing, seeing in justice we ought to be exempted from the payment thereof, though their necessity would not permit it.

They said, that they had already gratified by the remittal of thirty in the hundred, and that they would in like manner submit themselves to the ordinary impositions of the state, and so it was forborn further to prosecute that point at the time.

Afterwards the lord Cecil prayed the said commissioners, to resolve their lordships, for the better clearing of the point of trade, whether their meaning was, to limit us to carry the commodities of Spain only into England, and other the king's dominions, and the provinces under the obedience of the archdukes, and not to any other parts of Christendom, as France, Denmark, &c.

The said commissioners answered, that free liberty should be allowed unto us to bring any commodity of Spain, either for their own use, or to carry it into the archdukes provinces, without paying the imposition of thirty in the hundred, and to all other places, paying the said impost, &c.

Thereunto the lord Cecil answered him, that the king's majesty found, that if the placard should continue still in force, it would deprive his subjects of the benefit of a free trade, and generally interrupt the liberty of the commerce of all Christendom: therefore, that the king would be willing, to do a good office, to mediate an agreement between them and France, concerning the differences now depending between them for matter of trade, and the placards thereupon set forth, the one against the other, to the end there might be a convention of the said placards, whereof the trade might be restored to its former state.

The senator of Milan answered, that for the point of their placards which did directly concern his majesty's subjects, it was resolved to exempt them from the payment of the said impost; but for the other point which touched other princes, although it was a thing unexpected by them, that the interests of other princes should come in question, and be handled in this treaty, yet that they could not but thankfully accept the king's most gracious offer to be a means for the compounding of the differences between their masters and others, and removing of the impediments grown about the said placard, wherein as they know their princes would more repose themselves upon confidence of the king's majesty's kindness and sincerity, than of any other prince's, so they would be willing to grow to any resolution upon the point of the placards, when the king should with due regard of the honor of their princes, work the effecting of his intention for the compounding the said differences.

The lord Cecil told them, that they might assure themselves the king's majesty would not deceive the trust of their princes in that behalf, and would be careful so to handle the matter as to propose it to the French ambassador, without any prejudice to the honor of Spain, and as it had been casually moved unto them, so that the ambassador should be dealt with in the like sort, and moved to procure commission to treat thereof, as it was desired, that he would do the like from the constable of Castile, to the end the matter might be presently proceeded in; in the mean season, that it would be best also to suspend the motions which had been made upon the point between their lordships, and the said commissioners.

The senator of Milan desired, that the other intended course might be no impediment to the determining (for the mean time) of the present question between them; but their lordships refused to give them any further answer till they were better instructed of his majesty's pleasure therein.

It was then demanded of them by the lord Cecil, whether they had any other propofition to make?

Whereunto was anfwered by the prefident Richardot, that they had a particular motion to make, in the name of the archduke, for reftoring unto him of the ancient jewels of the dukes of Burgundy, which were engaged to the late queen by thofe which had no right to difpofe of them; and in refpect that the faid jewels had ever been preferved and left in fucceffion to the dukes of Burgundy, that they defired the recovery of them more in that refpect than the value of them.

It was anfwered them by the lord Cecil, that the faid jewels were engaged by moft of the principal provinces of the Low Countries for good fums of money; therefore, that the king's majefty could not deliver the faid jewels without their liking and agreement, and order to be taken for the reimburfement of his fum of money, for the which hereafter fome better expedient might be found than could be now; and the archdukes might affure themfelves, they fhould find the king's majefty very willing to ufe them with kindnefs therein, and his lordfhips fignified unto them, that their lordfhips were alfo to make demand in behalf of the king's majefty for the reimburfement of other monies, which were lent by the deceafed queen to thofe princes, for the appeafing of the troubles, at the time of the pacification of Ghent; which money the deceafed king of Spain promifed afterwards, by his letters, to pay intereft of, it being for the ufe and benefit of his fervice.

The

APPENDIX.

The commissioners alledged, that the satisfying of that debt did not properly belong unto their princes; and the rather, for that there followed no observation of the pacification made at Ghent, and so for that time their conference ended.

On Monday the 18th of June, their lordships repaired to the commissioners, and it was signified to them by the lord Cecil, that their lordships, out of their desire to bring the treaty to an end, thought it fit to conceive and frame certain articles agreeable to the points which had been hitherto treated on; and because there had been something insisted on which had reference only to some considerations of the present time, with the which matters it were not fit to clog the other general and perpetual conventions of the treaty; therefore, that their lordships thought it best to make some provision for those temporary restrictions, by private articles to be passed between the princes.

Hereunto it was agreed to read the articles which were conceived on both sides, which was pursued till it came to the article in the which they designed in what countries of the king of Spain's dominions intercourse and traffic should be permitted to the king's majesty's subjects, and for that the naming of some parts of the dominions of Spain and excluding others shewed that they had a meaning to exclude us from the trade of the Indies, it was desired by their lordships to agree that point concerning the Indies before they proceeded any further, and therewith it was declared unto them, that if they could show any ancient treaty wherein the like restrictions had been used, then that their lordships would yield to reason therein; otherwise, that there was no cause but that the trade ought to be accorded unto us in the article in the said general terms as had been unto all others in former time.

It was answered by the senator of Milan, that they conceived the said article to be made according to their former conference with their lordships, seeing no mention was therein made of the Indies one way or other; nevertheless, if their lordships did mislike any thing in the form of the words thereof, that they would be content the same should receive alteration, so as there might be a provision that the trade of the Indies might not thereby be permitted.

The lord Cecil said, that to speak clearly unto them, as their lordships did conceive they would be unwilling to grant us the freedom of that trade, so they prayed them to understand that their lordships were not less resolved not to assent to be more restrained now from the liberty of using that trade, than we had been by former treaties.

The senator of Milan answered, that howsoever ancient treaties had been penned by neglect, yet that observation showed that the use of that trade had never been granted to us, and seeing the taking of that liberty by color of those words, might breed occasion of war again, it was convenient so plainly to express them at this time, as that all peril might be avoided, and nothing left that might give interruption to the peace.

APPENDIX.

Their lordships answered, that it was not their meaning now to dispute the king of Spain's right to the Indies, or whether he might lawfully restrain our trade thither or not; but that the king's majesty would not so wrong his honor as to yield to be more restrained in that freedom than France and other provinces were by the conventions made with them.

The senator of Milan answered, that France never made that question for the liberty of the trade for the Indies as we had done; but seeing that the king's majesty would not admit a public article of restriction in such sort as they desired, because the same might be prejudicial to him in honor, that they would be content to pass the article in the same general terms with us as they did with France, so as the king would promise by some private article that he would not approve his subjects trading thither; but if any should offend in the contrary, that he would both punish them himself for the same, and allow the king of Spain to do the like.

It was told by their lordships, that the king would be satisfied with the general article which was passed with France, and that he could not otherwise assent to any private article whereby to yield to exclude himself from the said trade, only he would be content not to mislike that the adventurers into those parts should be left with the peril which they should incur thereby; or otherwise, that they would accord to forbid his subjects to trade unto any of the places which were now possessed by the king of Spain in the Indies, so as the said king would not give interruption to our trading to any other places which were not precisely under his obedience.

Then it was urged by them to declare by a private writing, that he would leave the adventurers to their own perils, in such sort as had been before spoken of; but it was refused to engage the king to make any such promise by writing.

Hereupon it was alledged by the said commissioners; that they having seriously advised how to reconcile the point of difference, they knew of no other means to do the same than to pass the article in general words, for the licensing our merchants to trade to all such places where formerly they had used to do.

Their lordships insisted still to have the article to pass in absolute general terms, without any manner of restrictions, and told them, that if they thought it fit, there might be protestations made thereupon of both sides: of their part, for not intending to allow us the trade of the Indies; and for our part, for our not assenting to be excluded from thence.

But the said commissioners refused to yield thereunto, alledging that they could not further enlarge themselves than as they had formerly declared, and protesting vehemently, that if the said matter should be stood upon, they should be forced, to their great grief, to break off the treaty, which they referred to the consideration of his majesty, whereupon their conference ended for that time.

APPENDIX.

Thursday the 21st of June, their lordships repaired to the said commissioners, and it was declared unto them by the lord Cecil, that their lordships did acknowledge, that the form of the proceeding of the said commissioners with them had been so good, and agreeable to honorable dealing, as their lordships wished that it were also in their power to make them some requital to their liking; therefore, that their lordships would not seek, according to the custom of ministers in like cases, to value themselves by many diligences of reservedness, but would plainly let them know that day, what they would grant them next; for the which cause, although there was a breaking off the last time upon the point then in question concerning the Indies, so as thereupon occasion of scruple might arise which partly should ruin the conference; yet that their lordships were not willing to stand thereupon: but to return to debate that argument with them to a further reconciliation, if it might be, for the concluding of the peace. And first, to make them answer by the king's commandment, to those things which had been the day before proposed to his majesty by the archduke's commissioners in their audience with his majesty, concerning the licensing of men to pass from hence to the service of the States, the which numbers he said had not been raised by any assistance of the king's authority, but only by the private gathering of a few voluntaries together; nevertheless, because the public passing of them at that time from the city gave scandal unto the said commissioners, that order was taken by the king to restrain the transportation of any further numbers, at that time, from this place: but that the king must plainly let them know, that he could not deny his subjects the liberty to employ themselves in service abroad, in all places which were in amity with his majesty, to the end to preserve the peace and quietness of his state, which abounding of people, he could not restrain them from seeking to make their fortune by service abroad, and that the king would therein show no partial affection to the States, but would give the like free liberty to the archdukes to draw any numbers from hence, which they should require for their service; and withal, it was remembered unto them, that there was no reason to limit in that point more his majesty's subjects, than those of France and other countries, which did ordinarily go to the service of the States.

The senator of Milan protested, how great satisfaction they received by their lordships honorable proceeding with them, and prayed their lordships to conceive that they had no other meaning but only to refer the matter which was in difference to his majesty's consideration, and to be reconciled by his majesty's better wisdom and judgment; and he reinforced to the president Richardot, to make answer to the other parts of lord Cecil's speech, because he had dealt in the said matters with the king.

The said president acknowledged, that they had received good satisfaction from his majesty, by

APPENDIX.

the anfwer which he had made them of not having been acquainted with their levies of men which had been complained of by them, and by the promife which it pleafed him to make, to take order therein; and touching the offer made to furnifh their princes in the like fort, in any number which they fhould require for their fervice, they gave their lordfhips thanks, faying, that they would advertife their princes thereof; but defired that under that color there might not be liberty given to their enemies to draw men from hence, which would be directly againft the peace; and for the proceedings of France, that we were not to take example by them, for that, howfoever they brake with them in that point, yet they being charged therewith, did not ftand to the juftification thereof, but alledged for their excufe, that they were but banifhed men that put themfelves into that fervice; and moreover, that at the making of the peace, the French king did publicly prohibit that any of his fubjects fhould afterwards ferve there.

The lord Cecil faid, that he found that the faid, anfwer which was made by them, confifted of two points; firft, of the inconvenience that might grow thereby to them, then of the anfwer made for France. For the firft, although it could not but be in fome fort inconvenient for them, that ourfelves fhould retain within the realm, a fuperfluous number of idle and loofe perfons, which by that means were routed abroad, we were rather to refpect the avoiding of a greater mifchief thereby unto ourfelves, than a lefs prejudice that might grow to others: and touching that which had been laid of France, that howsoever others would largely promise without respect of performance; yet, that the king's majesty had that just regard unto his honor and word, as he would promise nothing but that he would duly perform; and therefore, that he would freely profess beforehand what liberty was fit for him to take for the good of his state: besides, that there was great difference to be made between us and France, in respect of a nearer interest we had with the States for the towns which the king held in caution, and otherwise, which necessarily as yet required the holding on of a correspondence with them.

The earl of Northampton pursued a speech to the same effect, comparing the politic body of a commonwealth to the natural body of a man, wherein it was often necessary to purge superfluous and ill humors, which otherwise might endanger the health of the body; so also that if it were meant to spend abroad loose persons, as they grow to abound in a commonwealth, the retaining them could not be without danger of the safety of the same.

The commissioners answered, that there might be means for them to serve abroad in other places, though not in Holland and Zealand, to their prejudice, and that they had ever grounded themselves upon the king's promise, that there should be a restraint for going thither.

Whereunto their lordships shortly replied, that men were most willing to repair thither, where

APPENDIX. 297

there did occur most action and matter of employment, as at this time there was in the Low Countries; neither would they, as counsellors, advise his majesty otherwise to restrain his subjects; and so they brake off for that time, till his majesty's pleasure might be better known therein.

Wednesday the 27th their lordships repaired again to the commissioners, and the lord Cecil signified unto them, that their lordships had made the king acquainted with the matter which remained in difference between them, at the time of their last conference touching the restraining of voluntaries to repair to the service of the States, and how they urged a promise made in that behalf to some of them by the king; and also, for revocation of the number which were now there: whereunto the king's majesty did answer, that he was sorry to have been so misunderstood, but would be loath to enter into any question thereupon with an ambassador, for that he would not acknowledge that he had promised any such thing without doing himself great wrong; but if, out of the liberty of a free mind, and a good affection towards them, he had said in discourse, that if he should hereafter find the States to persist still in their obstinacy, that then he might be moved to press more straightly against them in such course as had been spoken of, there were no reason that any such discourse which was ever used by him with reference to the respective conditions of a peace, should be urged as a promise which would bind himself presently to satisfy.

The count of Aremberg defired that he might explain himfelf, that he did not charge the king to have made any fuch direct promife, but only to have ufed fpeech to him, whereby he thought to have reafon to conceive hope of fuch an affection in the king towards the archdukes. And the prefident Richardot, prayed their lordfhips to confider, that if that article were not accorded, it would be directly to crofs the purpofe of a peace, and contrary to all former treaties; and thereupon he produced precedents of former treaties which were all made with ftrict cautions refpecting that point.

The lord Cecil anfwered, that the king had not fo ill a purpofe to prejudice them by that liberty of that article as they feemed to conceive jealoufy, but only to avoid inconveniency to himfelf, and that there was not fo precious regard to be had to that which the formalities of the law did require, as what did more nearly concern the king in his private and particular interefts, the ufe being always to make the conditions of peace agreeable to the confiderations and refpects of the time prefent; and therefore, that the king's majefty prayed them to be fatisfied that the prefent ftate of his affairs would not permit him to allow of that article of reftriction.

The fenator of Milan anfwered, that they perceived that the king's majefty had an honorable meaning not to do any thing that might tend to a violation of the peace; but only to avoid being bound to reftrictions which might touch him in honor: therefore, he wished that the articles might be preserved which had been conceived, and that they might be so framed as that the honor of both parties might be preserved. Whereupon it was agreed to read the articles which had been offered by the said commissioners. And their lordships finding cause to except against his strictness of them in sundry points.

It was declared unto them by the lord Cecil, that the king's majesty was not of the disposition of other princes that seek to make evasions by the subtilty of words; but contrariwise, was sincerely minded, as he desired, that the treaty might be made in so clear words as might breed no ambiguity, or doubt of interpretation; and therefore, as the king would be willing to yield to reasonable things, so he desired that the treaty might not be compounded of unnecessary and superfluous articles, as their lordships conceived some of those to be, which were delivered by the said commissioners.

The said commissioners answered, that they would agree to any reasonable amendment, but first, they desired to be satisfied from their lordships, what order should be taken for the revoking of the regiments of his majesty's subjects, and commanders which were in the service of the States; for that it would not stand with the conditions of a peace, to suffer them to continue longer there: and therefore, desired, that it ought to be agreed to revoke the said troops by a public edict.

Their lordships prayed them seriously to consider,

whether it would not be much more inconvenient to the king to yield to their demands therein, than the forbearing thereof would be advantageous to them, both in respect of the greater pester and burden which he should draw upon the realm by the revoking of the said troops; and the rather, for that most of them had great sums of money owing to them by the States, for the discharge of their accounts and reckoning; and in as much, likewise, as by that means he should so much discontent the Hollanders, as might move them out of despair to practise to recover from his majesty the towns which he held there, whereby there would not remain unto them either credit or power, to mediate with them to reduce them to obedience; that the number of his majesty's subjects now serving there was not great, and of them, few which were persons of account. But, for their satisfaction, that the king's majesty would be content to disavow hereafter, the repairing of any persons of quality to the service of the States, and to endeavour to divert them from going thither.

The said commissioners answered, that to make it appear that they would not press the king in any thing to his prejudice, they would satisfy themselves with the forbearance of the said public revocation, so as the king would promise that there should be some private means used to persuade them to return, which was thought reasonable to be promised by their lordships to be done so far forth as the parties serving there could be induced thereunto; and thereupon the articles were so reformed as should neither import any such public revocation, nor to restrain the going of voluntaries thither; and upon that conclusion taken, their lordships ended their conference for that time.

Friday the 29th of June, their lordships repaired again to the said commissioners, and it was moved by the lord Cecil, that there might be a review of the articles which were formerly agreed on, to be thoroughly perfected, that afterwards they might proceed to the determining of the other points of the treaty, which was accordingly performed; and after some amendments of the articles given on either part, they resolved upon the draught of the general articles for peace, and in what form the commission for the cautionary towns should pass, and that the garrisons of those places should give no aid or assistance to the Hollanders.

This being finished, they proceeded next to speak of some provision to be agreed on between them, for security of our merchants against the dangers of the inquisition of Spain.

To the which it was answered by the commissioners, that it was out of the king of Spain's power to make any particular conventions against the inquisition; but that they would pass a general article, whereby his majesty's subjects should be provided for, not to be subject to danger for matters of religion, so as they gave no cause of public scandal.

But it was told them, by their lordships, that an article, in that generality would not be sufficient safety unto the merchants, because it would be even in their power, to interpret what was to be accounted a scandal, and what not; and their lordships shewed unto them examples of divers notorious wrongs which our merchants had received in that case, besides that there was no cause why difficulties should now be made to yield to particular provisions; for that in time past, the like had been done, as their lordships made appear unto them by that which had been agreed on in that behalf, with the duke of Alva.

Whereupon, at length, it was resolved by the said commissioners to insert a general article of assurance for that purpose; and to refer the further explanation thereof to some particular articles to be agreed on. Upon these resolutions, their lordships being ready to depart; for that the Spanish ambassador acquainted their lordships with a letter which he had newly received from the constable of Castile, whereby he signified, that touching the motion which had been lately made by the king's majesty, for compounding the differences between the kings of Spain and France, upon the placard of thirty upon the hundred, wherein his majesty offered that himself would be a mediator, that although the king of Spain had given the constable no commission to treat thereupon; yet, if the king's majesty would be pleased to deal in that matter, that he would undertake that the king his master should ratify whatever should be concluded therein.

Monday the 2d of July, their lordships repaired again to the said commissioners, and signified unto them their allowance of the draught of the general article for peace, and touching the cautionary towns which had been confidered by them of their laſt meeting, fave only, that they defired the amendment of fome few words therein; and that, as there was a provifion, that the forces ferving in his majeſty's cautionary towns, fhould not miniſter any aid unto the States; fo alfo, that there might be a reciprocal article, that the archduke's or king of Spain's forces fhould not attempt any thing to the offence of the faid garrifons, which was affented unto by the faid commiffioners.

Then the fenator of Milan exhibited to their lordſhips the general article which was conceived by him for freeing of our merchants from the dangers of the inquifition in Spain, which imported only, that for the better fecurity of the trade there they fhould not be fubject undefervedly to any moleftations in their negociations, unlefs they gave occafion of fcandal.

Their lordſhips took great exceptions both to the weaknefs of the word "undefervedly;" as alfo, for that there was not a direct mention of the words, " for not receiving moleſtation for caufe " of religion," which their lordſhips defired to have clearly expreffed, to give fatisfaction to the king's fubjects, that care had been taken for their fecurity in that behalf.

The faid commiffioners affented to amend the word "undefervedly," but they utterly refufed a long time to have any mention made in the article of matters of religion, and earneſtly infiſted to have the fame to run only in other general terms; for that they could not undertake to prefcribe in caufes of religion, but that there might be a fufficient provifion for the merchants fafety by other private articles.

Their lordfhips anfwered, that it behoved the king's majefty to be no lefs careful to provide, that his fubjects might not be wronged for matters of confcience, that they fhowed themfelves to be careful to preferve their religion; and that there could not be aptly made a reference from the general article to the private, unlefs there were mention made in the general article of the matter referred; and, moreover, that it would minifter fufpicion, that there would follow no due execution of the faid private orders, if it fhould be refufed fo much as to name the thing that was to be provaled for.

Their lordfhips further had fpeech with them, touching the explanation of their meaning in the word "fcandal;" for that, if it were left ambiguous, it might draw his majefty's fubjects into danger, as well for omiffions as commiffions, as they did exemplify in fome particulars.

The faid commiffioners anfwered, that if they fhould exprefs all particulars, what fhould be interpreted to be fcandalous, and what not, the fame would grow to be infinite; and therefore, that they held it beft rather to reft in the general than to defcend to over-great particularities, notwithftanding that they accorded that for the better diftinction, the word "public" fhould be added

unto

unto it; and that they accounted not the use of private prayer by our merchants, either in their shops, or in their chambers, to be within the compass of public scandal, but to be a matter of adherence to trade; and in the end, after much debate, the said commissioners further yielded to pass the general article, with mention, that his majesty's subjects should not be molested, either by land or sea, for matters of conscience, within the king of Spain's or archduke's dominions, if they gave not occasion of public scandal; and that the particular agreements made in that behalf with the duke of Alva, should now also privately be confirmed.

Wednesday the 4th of July, their lordships repaired again to the said commissioners, and the lord Cecil put them in mind of the general article which was agreed on, concerning the inquisition, which was again read and approved by them, and also of confirming of the private articles, which were assented unto by the duke of Alva; but their lordships desired further, that order also might be taken, that his majesty's subjects might not be entangled by any questions or provocations proceeding from their parts, that might minister cause of scandal, by declaring of themselves, being urged by such means; and also, that the consuls of the English might not, in respect of their residence there, for the government of the merchants, be accounted as inhabitants, and thereby made subject to the censures, which were not reputed inhabitants; both which propositions were thought reasonable and agreed unto.

Afterwards their lordships, entering further into treaty of the matter of intercourse, the lord Cecil took occasion upon the articles, which had been before delivered unto them by the commissioners, to signify that their lordships found they had therein made question of things which they thought should never have come in speech, but have passed under silence, namely touching the restrictions added by them concerning the trade of the Indies, which had never been heretofore offered to any other prince, in any other treaty; and it could not stand with his majesty's honor now to admit.

Whereunto the senator of Milan answered, that although they did not hold any thing which had passed in discourse to stand resolved, till the same were absolutely concluded; yet they prayed their lordships to remember, that in the argument of that matter, they had so far forth declared themselves, that they were to stand upon it, being a liberty which the king had not hitherto granted to his own brethren, or any other friends.

The earl of Northampton, in answer unto him said, that he declared his mind so ambiguously, that their lordships understood not thoroughly whether their meaning was, that they could not permit the said trade, or whether they could not but by express words forbid it: that touching the first, their lordships had no desire to move them to grant the same; but touching the latter, that there was no reason that his majesty should be hardlier dealt withal in the point, than other princes had been, especially the cause being of that

APPENDIX.

nature as that therein, there ought to be no restraint. By the law of nature and nations, the sea ought to be common to all men; and likewise among friends, mutual commerce ought not to be forbidden in any part of their dominions.

The senator of Milan replied, that although by nature, in ordinary course, the sea was free to all; yet notwithstanding, the jurisdiction thereof might be prescribed, when a positive act gave first occasion thereof; and thereupon entered into a large declaration, how the king of Spain and Portugal had by prescription attained a right, as he said, in those seas; and touching the other allegation, that liberty of intercourse ought to be yielded unto in each others kingdoms and dominions among friends, he said, that the king's majesty was willing to grant the same in his other dominions, which were great; but, for the Indies, which he had discovered with great charge and loss of men, it was reasonable, that he should restrain the same to his own benefit, to answer so great a charge.

Whereunto the earl of Northampton answered, that neither of these two points which he pleaded of privilege by first discovery, nor of prescription by time, which were all the grounds that the king of Spain could take for that arrogation of the propriety of the Indies to himself, could in any reason stand; because that, for the first point of privilege, we did produce patents granted by Henry VII.; yet in record, to Columbus, &c. for discovering of the Indies *quinto Martii anno Septimo;* and, that further testimony which Ferdinandus

APPENDIX.

Columbus set down in the life of his father, whereunto he might add the answer of Charles I. to the Portugueze ambassador, claiming against him, as the Spaniards did at this day, against us, and all nations, a sole interest in this trade; that it was not found out by their skill, but by mere chance, they being cast upon those places by shipwreck, not guided by foresight or knowledge; besides, that if first discovering might give occasion of any such prohibition, that then the queen's majesty might have restrained their fishing in the Northern seas, which. notwithstanding, the Spaniards took liberty to use; and lastly, that the freedom of intercourse to the Indies could not be prejudicial unto them, but good for both states, our merchants demeaning themselves well in their trade; and touching the point that the king of Spain could not challenge the said right by prescription, the said earl alledged that he could avouch all the greatest doctors of the civil laws and common law to prove, that to prescribe the seas, was against the law of nature and nations; because, by that not only *maria & equora, sed & omnes res immobiles etiam communes erant*, (not only seas, and navigable rivers, and lakes, but whatever things were fixed and immoveable were common.) For though we have a little digressed from their community, so far as concerned the propriety of lands, whose dominion being common by nature, was notwithstanding. by tract of time divided and severed from that community; yet that in the dominion and propriety of the sea it

APPENDIX.

was otherwife, the law of nature and community remaining ftill, as at firft, unchangeable; both becaufe the mobility and fluxibility of that element admitted not fuch anchor-hold of poffeffion; as alfo, becaufe the main ocean was too vaft a fhare to be poffeffed or commanded by any other fovereign than by him that created it; but to omit that heap of teftimonies, which the grave fenate of the learned writers offered in this cafe, his lordfhip faid, he would only avouch one, which, for his underftanding was to be reverenced, and for his integrity to be preferred in this caufe before any, in refpect that he was of council to the king of Spain, whofe intereft was chiefly pinched in his conclufion: the author he alluded to was Ferdinando Vafquieres, who, glancing at the Venetians and Genoefe for affuming to themfelves the exclufive intereft and right in their feveral gulphs, reprobates their tenets in the plaineft terms; and alfo, the opinions of that crowd of Portugueze and Spaniards who efpoufe their doctrines. Vafquieres freely declares his opinion, that the kings of Spain have not any prefcriptive jurifdiction over the great Indian Ocean, and maintains in general, the liberty of the feas againft the idle dreams of the Venetians and Genoefe, and all who abet their narrow and unjuft maxims on this fubject.

The earl of Northampton having quoted at length the words of Vafquieres in the original Latin, of which the fubftance has juft been given briefly in Englifh, proceeds to obferve, that the ground of this writer's opinion was, that reafon which was formerly set down, that no prince was tied to any civil laws from which prescriptions did spring, but resorted to the common law of nature and nations, which absolutely prohibited all prescriptions of those things which God and nature had left in community and liberty. And whereas lawful prescription did require a space of time, *cujus non extat memoria*, (immemorial), that it was evident by the report of records and histories, that the first possession of any place in those parts happened within the memory of man; moreover, that this prescription had been interrupted, which it ought not to be, when right was claimed, might be proved not only by the resort of the countrymen to those parts in time of war, and of the French and other nations in like manner; but most evidently by that answer of the emperor Charles, to the king of Portugal, excepting against his traffic to the East; that trade was open to all nations by sea, that he would be barred of no place where there was hope of gain; and most plainly by this conclusion, when the Portugueze began to speak so big, that it was a phrase fit to affright and terrify faint spirits; for that it lay in him to requite all affronts with double measure: and therefore, that it was best for them to depart peaceably for the present time, and return again *cum facti essent prudentiores*, (when they had learned greater prudence). The said earl adding therewithal, that he would be loath to be conceived, as if in this they went directly to contest or oppose against the scope of greatness of the king of Spain; but only to demonstrate to the said commissioners upon this occasion, how great equity there was in the demand of our merchants, that free trade might be allowed to them by the common passage of the seas; so they wronged no princes in Europe, came not where the king of Spain had regiment or property, nor sought traffic by force, but with freedom, and to the liking of those Indian princes, which experience had taught did invite them, and would be glad of them.

The senator of Milan answered thereunto, that although Vasquieres were of that opinion, yet there were many others that upon good advice, had determined otherwise. and for the Emperor Charles, if he should so answer to the Portugueze touching the East Indies, that it might have been retorted against himself, in respect of his right to the West Indies; that, for the example of the discovery of the northern seas, they had interest in the said discovery as well as we; and, for the controversy between the emperor and the king of Portugal, that the Pope had determined it, distinguishing each part to other by separation of the line.

To this it was answered by the earl of Northampton, first, that it did not rest in the liberty of any prince or potentate under heaven, to limit or stint the scope of traffic or intercourse which nature had left at liberty; for since society was the comfort of men's life, amity the bond of union, and charity the badge of Christ, to take away the ordinary means of settling and establishing those infallible assurances, were the ruin and utter overthrow of that happy work which Chrift would have intended. Above any thing, therefore it was fin to cut off the moft apt occafion of reconciling minds and affections that were fo far fevered both in piety and policy. Again it was alledged that the Pope of all other potentates, was leaft fit, and worft qualified to decide thofe debates, drawing both his priefthood, and the warrant of his pre-eminency from Chrift our Saviour, who in refpect that his kingdom was not of this world, nor to be maintained by the fword, as that of other princes, but was dependent upon another ftring; refufed flatly to decide fome queftion wherein he was elected arbitrator, about the portion of a ftate of inheritance. But fuppofing that a Pope, as paftor, had to deal and moderate in their difputes between the fheep of his own fold, yet as St. Paul refufed plainly to judge of thofe that are without the Church, (*Dei iis qui funt foras judicare*), fo likewife, it might be thought hard by fome princes which were not within the fold, to hearken to the voice of a ftrange fhepherd, (*audire vocem paftoris cujus non fuit*). Laft of all, the uttermoft that either in law or equity could be required, was, that the fentence fhould ftand in full ftrength, only againft thofe that had fubmitted their caufe to the compromife, that is, Spain and Portugal, without comprifing other princes of Chriftendom that were left at liberty; that the work of winning fouls was laudable and excellent; but yet, fince the tafk was over great for one ftate, or two, fo many provinces having nothing to do with Spain or

APPENDIX. 313

Portugal, which were to be drawn by ordinary means into the ordinary way, the safest and soundest course for the dispatch of that labor, as our Saviour himself had taught, was to send in many laborers where the harvest was plenteous, (*multos op rantes ubi meſſis multa*), and not to lay the labor upon one hand or two, which in reason, must be weary before the church be replenished. That many were both resolute, and able to preach Christ crucified, which by obstructions of ready passage were excluded from the scope of their religious industry.

That the bounty of Christ, in giving and granting, as the royal prophet had set down, *terram fiis hominum*, (the earth to the sons of men), was only limited by conscience and equity, with this respect, that it did not take away the right of any other, either by pre-occupation, purchase, gift, or any other means possessed of his part; because, not every thing, but *quod nullius in bonis eſt*, (what is in no man's possession), being either derelicted, or *nunquam acquyſtum*, (never acquired), *occupanti conceditur*, (becomes the property of the first occupier). But in this case we did not seek territorial property, but commerce, and the propagation of faith and charity; therefore, not to be refused.

The lord Cecil said, that to bring the matter to a conclusion, he desired to be satisfied from the commissioners, whether by their commission they were so restrained as that they could not pass that article for common liberty of intercourse, without an express prohibition of the Indies;

which, if it were so, then that their lordships must plainly let them know, that the king's majesty could not admit a condition so much prejudicial to his honor.

The senator of Milan answered, that by their commission, they could not admit any article in another form than to exclude from the liberty of the trade with the Indies: notwithstanding, if their lordships could advise of any means how, the substance being preserved, the king's honor may duly be respected, by the alteration of any other form of words than was proposed, they would willingly assent thereunto; or otherwise, that they were sorry that so much labor had been taken in vain, seeing they could not effect what was desired of all parties.

Hereupon, after further consideration and debating, it was resolved at length by all parties, that in the article conceived for general intercourse, those words should be inserted, *in quibus ante bellum fuit commercium juxta & secundum usum & observantiam*, (in matters wherein there was commerce before the war, agreeably and according to the usage and observance of ancient compacts), and so the article to pass for the kingdoms appertaining to the Spanish king; whereby their lordships thought it fit, rather to leave the matter to the liberty of the other interpretation of former treaties, and the observance and use thereof, than that the instancing of express permission or prohibition, might give interruption to the treaty.

Their conference being ended, the lord Cecil

APPENDIX. 315

signified to the said commissioners, that the French ambassador had acquainted the king's majesty, that he had received authority from the French king his master, to treat with the said commissioners, for the compounding of the difference concerning the impost of thirty in the hundred, and the Spanish ambassador also agreed to have agreed with him thereupon.

Thursday the 5th of July, their lordships repaired again to the said commissioners, and it was moved by their lordships, that they might proceed to consider of the rest of the articles which were delivered by the commissioners of Spain, concerning intercourse of trade, upon the perusal whereof, it was moved by the lord Cecil, that there might be a permission that it should not be lawful for the ships of war of the said princes, to enter into our ports above a certain number; and that advertisement should be before-hand given to his majesty by the said princes, when they should have occasion to send extraordinary numbers of ships of war into those parts, which was thought reasonable, and the same inserted accordingly, into the said articles; and so, with other amendments in some other points, the articles for the trade with Spain were resolved, and agreed on.

Afterwards, their lordships proceeded to consider of the articles which were delivered by the archdukes' commissioners, wherein their lordships finding that among other things, they had specially inserted, the former trade of our merchants into the archdukes' ports, and undertaken to assure the liberty of the same trade.

It was demanded by their lordſhips, whether they intended to enjoin our merchants to trade into their ports, notwithſtanding that the States ſhould oppoſe themſelves thereunto.

The ſaid commiſſioners anſwered, that ſeeing they had allowed of merchants to trade into Holland, it was as great reaſon, that the king ſhould take order, that his ſubjects might be permitted to trade freely into their ports, the archdukes being no leſs worthy to be therein regarded than the Hollanders. And, as it was one of the moſt eſſential points whereof they expected benefit by the treaty, that it did likewiſe import the king's majeſty in his honor not to have his ſubjects trade reſtrained by the ſaid Hollanders.

Their lordſhips anſwered, that it was not the king's meaning to make a difference of reſpect between the archdukes and the Hollanders; but that it was fit to proceed by ſuch degrees, as not preſently to give them diſcontent by any public ſtipulations againſt them, whereby to enter into terms of unkindneſs with them; and for the peace which he made with the archdukes, to hazard to plunge himſelf into a more deſperate war with the others, in reſpect of their obſtinacy, to reſtrain all trade from their ports, pretending that otherwiſe their ruin did depend thereupon; beſides, that as merchants could not be compelled to trade to any places where they ſhould not find it convenient and ſafe for them, ſo that there was no reaſon to tie the king's majeſty to ſtraiter conjunctions upon that point than the French king was by his treaty; but that they might assure themselves, that the king's majesty did effectually desire that his merchants should trade into their ports, and that all good opportunities should be taken for the same.

The said commissioners alledged, that it did not less import the archdukes, that their princes should be relieved by trade; and therefore earnestly insisted, in respect that the benefit thereof was one of the principal fruits of a peace, as had been before declared, that there might be direct provision for the same by articles, as had been proposed.

Their lordships said, that they would be willing to satisfy them, in the effect of that which they desired to endeavour that our merchants might trade into their ports, though it could not be as yet with that fulness as heretofore it had been used; and if the States should impeach our merchants therein, that the king's majesty would shew as conveniently he might, to be sensible thereof, but because it was not fit for him to promise by open act, to take any unkind courses against them, their lordships yielded otherwise to pass the said articles in general and reciprocal terms, that care should be taken by the king's majesty, and the archdukes, for a free intercourse of trade between their subjects in each of their countries, and delivered them a minute of an article for that purpose, whereof the said commissioners desired to have leisure to consider till the day following, and so their conference ended for that time.

Friday the 6th of July, their lordships repaired again to the said commissioners, and their lordships requiring to understand by them how they were satisfied with the article which was delivered to them at their last meeting for a reciprocal intercourse of trade with the provinces of the archdukes.

The president Richardot answered, that they were forced again to represent to their lordships, that it did so much import them to receive benefit by the trade of his majesty's subjects with them, as that they must desire that there might be a direct provision for the same; that it was not their purpose to seek to engage his majesty into a war, but only desired that we would take order, which we might, for relief in that behalf, otherwise that they should receive little fruit by the peace; that they confessed their strength to be too weak by sea, as that they were not able to prevail for the freeing of their ports from the impeachments which the Hollanders did give them; and therefore, that they desired his majesty's assistance therein, which they conceived was not to be refused, seeing it would be good for the subjects of both countries to procure such an intercourse of trade.

The lord Cecil told them, that as the king's majesty would be willing to favor the archdukes in any thing he might, so he was to have care not to do it with prejudice of his honor; as in this case they sought to impose such a condition of inequality upon him as could not be very disadvantageous unto him if he should assent to the same; and therefore, that the article concerning the said matter ought to pass between the king and the archdukes in reciprocal terms.

The earl of Northampton added, that the joining of the king's majesty with the archdukes could not but be both honorable for the said princes, and also effectual to the purpose by the commissioners intended: honorable, in that considerations made between greater and lesser princes ever strengthened the weaker and redounded to their reputation; effectual, for that when it should appear that his majesty had a joint desire together with the archdukes, that the commerce for their subjects should be free, and to that purpose had reciprocally accorded that each of their ports, and the passage thereunto, should be open to the others subjects, it could not but be of great force to work the effect which was designed for the common benefit of trade; and further, his lordship referred unto their considerations, if his majesty should undertake the care solely, as by their speeches they urged, whether, besides the note which ought to be taken of so unequal conditions clean contrary to the common ground, *ubi commodum ibi onus*, (the party that is to reap the profit ought to bear the burden), the same might not be interpreted also, to imply in this point, a league offensive and defensive, and a professing of hostility to all the archdukes enemies, or at least administer cause of jealousy unto the United Provinces; that his majesty would take occasions to damnify them for the archdukes' benefit, which, how inconvenient it were to be done at this time, both in respect of his majesty's honor, and the discommodity also that might grow thereby to the archdukes themselves; the case standing with them to consider duly of it, and then he doubted not, but they would no longer insist on those terms, nor seek to press their lordships further than might be accorded unto conveniently.

Their lordships finding the commissioners not fully satisfied with the aforesaid reasons, it was at length agreed to insert into the said article the words *conjunctim & divisim* (conjointly and severally); which gave satisfaction unto the said commissioners, and the president Richardot in the name of them, yielded great thanks unto their lordships for their honorable proceedings with them in all the course of the treaty, wherein they acknowledged to have received very good contentment, and prayed to be excused from having so much insisted upon the last matter, in respect that the same was also of great importance unto them.

That article being so agreed, their lordships signified unto the said commissioners, that they conceived to have now resolved of all the principal articles of the treaty, and that the king's majesty was not willing to tie himself to longer residence within the city at that time of the year, but to go his intended progress; therefore, they wished that the coming of the constable of Castile might be hastened, with all the speed that might be, which the said commissioners undertook to do, and that he should arrive within twenty days, and because there remained nothing else to be

further

APPENDIX.

further done for the final concluding of the treaty, than only to confider of certain demands which had been made by our Englifh merchants for their better affurance, and to reduce the treaty into form; it was moved by their lordfhips, that for the fpeedier accelerating of that bufinefs, Sir Daniel Dun and Sir Thomas Edmonds might refort unto them for the difpatch thereof, with them in refpect of their lordfhips other employments, at that time, which was affented unto.

It was, moreover, moved by the lord Cecil, that it might be proceeded by the treaty, that if hereafter, upon the king's interceffion, thofe of the United Provinces might be drawn to a reconciliation with the archdukes, there might be a refervation of liberty for the receiving of them upon the king's motion and folicitation in that behalf, which was likewife yielded unto, and fo their lordfhips conference ended for that time.

Friday the 10th of Auguft, the conftable of Caftile arrived at London, being conducted from Gravefend to Dover by the lord Wotton, and the chief gentlemen of Kent, whither the earl of Northampton, attended by divers of the king's fervants, and others, was fent to receive him, who brought him thence to Somerfet-houfe, which was richly furnifhed for him by the king, and order taken for the defraying of him and his train at the king's charges, and fo likewife for all the other commiffioners.

Thofe of Spain being lodged together at Somerset-house, and the archdukes' commissioners at Durham-house.

Sunday the 12th, their lordships and the commissioners went to visit and welcome the constable in the king's name.

Tuesday the 14th, the king's majesty returned from Royston.

Wednesday the 15th, their lordships went to confer with the constable, to make a recapitulation of all the points of the treaty which had been formerly agreed on with the other commissioners; and, for that it was propounded by the merchants to know whether the treaty did import to give them leave to carry likewise the commodities of Germany into Spain, as well as those of this realm, without paying the impost of thirty per hundred; which, although their lordships conceived in their meaning, and according to the words of the treaty to be clear in that point; nevertheless, it was thought fit by their lordships, to speak by accident of that matter, first, with the commissioners, and afterwards as there should be occasion with the constable himself, which was accordingly done: and the said commissioners insisted earnestly upon the contrary interpretation of the said point, for not comprising the merchandizes of Germany to be free from the payment of the said impost of thirty in the hundred: and also, the constable maintained, that he would not yield to the further enlarging of the said article, seeing he had sent the treaty subscribed by their lordships into Spain.

APPENDIX.

Whereunto their lordships replied, that they only defired the explanation, and not the enlargement of the faid article, for that they did not affent to the paffing of the fame, but with the meaning for concluding the aforefaid liberty for the merchandizes of Germany; whereupon that they muft ftill ftand as a thing which deeply concerned the intereft of his majefty's fubjects, and upon thefe terms their lordships departed from the conftable at that time.

Thurfday the 16th, the conftable received audience of the king.

Friday the 17th, their lordships repaired again to the conftable, to agree of the form of the preamble of the treaty, and had again fpeech with him concerning the former queftion of the merchandizes of Germany, infifting as before they had done, that they could not yield otherwife to interpret the faid article with the liberty which had been mentioned; whereupon, after fome further debating of the matter, the conftable in the end agreed to the admittance of that liberty, for free tranfportation of the merchandizes of Germany into Spain, which were fubject by the placard to the payment of the impoft of thirty per hundred; but he defired that their lordships would content themfelves with the promife thereof, under his own hand, without altering any thing in the words of the treaty; for that having fent the treaty into Spain figned by their lordships, it might be reckoned a great lightnefs in him to yield afterwards to the enlargement of the same in any thing; and he undertook that the king of Spain should ratify his said promise, which was accepted by their lordships, and a private article accordingly drawn and signed by him for the said matter, and their lordships also procured him at the same time to sign the private articles for the moderation of the proceedings of the inquisition against his majesty's subjects trading into Spain.

Sunday the 19th, the king's majesty took his oath in the chapel before the constable, and the archdukes' commissioners, for the observation of the peace; and that day all the said ambassadors were sumptuously feasted by the king, at his own table at dinner, in the great banqueting house, and during the time of dinner, order was given for the proclaiming peace at the court-gate and through the city.

Monday the 20th, the constable had a private audience by the king.

Tuesday the 21st, it was appointed that the constable should take his leave of the king, because of his majesty's desire to leave the city, to proceed in his pretended progress; but in respect that the constable fell sick, and was too unable to stir off his bed, the king's majesty was pleased to visit him at his own lodging, and there to bid him farewel; and to do the like to the count of Aremberg who was also indisposed of his gout, after performance whereof his majesty immediately departed from London.

Saturday the 25th, the conſtable and the reſt of the commiſſioners departed from London, the conſtable being accompanied to Gravefend by the earl of Northampton, and from thence to Dover by the lord Wotton. The earl of Aremberg and the reſt of the archdukes' commiſſioners embarked themſelves about the ſame time in the river.

APPENDIX.

B.

(Vol. I. Page 136.)

Sᴉʀ Francis Cottington, in a letter to the lord treaſurer Saliſbury, dated Madrid 5th February 1609, ſays, " The carrying away the Moors of Valentia, who were ſuffered to tranſport all their wealth with them, hath coſt the king, beſides what he ſtill owes, much above 800,000 ducats, as myſelf have feen by the brief of the account in a comptador's houſe. Preda (one of the Spaniſh ſecretaries of ſtate), tells me of much more, which I can alſo eaſily believe.

" Hereupon, it ſeems, the king hath taken a refolution not to ſuffer any one that goes now from Andaluſia, Eſtremadura, and the two Caſtiles, to carry away any kind of gold or ſilver, or prohibited commodities; neither may they, by exchange or otherwise, convey their monies out of these kingdoms; which to prevent, by proclamation all men are prohibited to deal with them in that nature, upon pain of extraordinary punishment.

"The French ambassador, notwithstanding, as it seems, received of them great sums of money upon good conditions; and, for the more safe conveyance of such papers as he gave them, he dispatched his steward in post for France. This was not so secretly carried, but his steward was apprehended in Buytrago, thirteen leagues hence, and brought back prisoner to this court: his mail was taken from him and sent unto the secretary Prada. The ambassador, hereupon, wrote a very angry letter unto the council, in which, as himself tells me, he threatened, if they opened the mail, no messenger or correo should pass from hence through France, without having his letters seized. He went in person to every one of the counsellors of state, and uttered much choler. In the end, as I am informed, they gave him his mail unopened, and the steward is again on his way with it.

"By order of the council, Sylva de Torres, the president of Alcaldies, wrote a letter unto the ambassador, and sent it him with the mail; the ambassador took the letter, and without opening it, threw it into the fire, saying unto the messenger, "Tell Sylva de Torres that this answer I gave him." The ambassador doth much glory

APPENDIX.

herein, but is by many cenfured for his paffionate proceeding. They are here very angry with him; and though they fay little, will, I dare affure your lordfhip, find a trick to tame him, if he remain long among them. The fums of money he hath received, are reported to be fo extraordinarily great, as I dare not report it unto your lordfhip; but Prada himfelf tells me of many hundred thoufands."

In a letter to the lord treafurer, dated Madrid, the 4th of March, 1609, Sir Francis writes thus, " By my former advertifements your lordfhip has underftood that the Morefcoes of thefe parts were prohibited to carry away any kind of gold or filver. This was fo ftrictly executed, as fome thirty-two or thirty-three were hanged at Burgos, for being found with money and jewels. Among the reft, one that had in his albarda, which is like a pad to carry facks on, four hundred ducats in doubloons. Notwithftanding all this warinefs and rigor, they found, that fome by bills of exchange, others in fpecie (artificially hidden), carried away great treafure; whereupon, they have now publifhed, that all fhall carry what money they will, conditionally, that by the way, where they fhall be fearched, they leave the one half to the king.

" Commiffioners are now fent from hence into every province, and to make fale of fuch houfes and poffeffions as they have left, and were belonging to them; by which, it is thought the king shall gather a very great treasure; and doubtless, it cannot be otherwise."

It appears that his Catholic majesty never dreams of applying the confiscations of the Morefcoes to the exigencies of state, but dissipated them with a thoughtless profusion among favorites. From a letter of Cottington's, dated Madrid 16th of May, 1610, we learn that "the king had given unto the duke of Lerma, out of the goods of the Morefcoes, 250,000 ducats; unto the duke of Uzeda, Lerma's son, 100,000; unto the Conde of Lemos 100,000; and unto the Condesa Lemos, Lerma's daughter, 50,000; which is in all 500,000 ducats, all paid already out of the sale of the lands and goods of the Morefcoes."

The following extract of a letter from Cottington, dated Madrid, June 10th, 1610, serves at once to illustrate the state of society in Spain, and the condition of the wretched Morefcoes who remained, after the expulsion of their kindred, in that country.

"Of late there have very few nights passed, in which many people, of all ranks, have not been slain in the streets: whereupon it is here proclaimed, that no man may keep a slave within five leagues of this court; as imagining that those kind of people have committed these murders; and not unlikely, for that few did here serve themselves with other than captive Turks, and Moors; and so the multitude of them were very great."

In what follows, we have an example of the

APPENDIX. 329

viciffitudes of nations; for as we have juft feen the hard fate of the Moors oppreffed by the Spaniards, we fhall there behold a picture not lefs affecting than curious, of the Spaniards, at a former period, oppreffed by the Moors.

Sir John Digby, afterwards earl of Briftol, the Britifh ambaffador at the court of Spain, in a letter, dated Madrid, 2d December, 1617, fays, " Certain inhabitants are here, now fome few months fince, difcovered among the mountains, not many leagues from Salamanca, who dwell in a valley compaffed by impaffable hills. They are, to the number of five hundred perfons, and doubtlefs have dwelt there (they I mean and their predeceffors) ever fince the conqueft of Spain by the Moors, from whom it feems they fled (fome few families of them); and hard it is to underftand how they got down into that valley. They have no other grain but rye, nor other flefh than goats. Fifh they have in brooks and lakes; and the valley is of a good compafs, which was hitherto imagined to be only mountain inacceffible.

" Some fixty years paft, were likewife difcovered in the Pyrenean hills, divers villages, not far from La Pena de Francia, and in the fame nature as thefe are, who are extreme poor miferable fouls, and know neither God, nor any religion."

C.

(Vol. II. Page 288.)

WE learn from a letter of Sir Francis Cottington's, dated Madrid, January 5th, 1610, that the Spanish parliament had been just dissolved, after having been continued for the space of four years. " Many new laws, Sir Francis adds, are published, though not yet printed ; among which it is provided, that no man, on great penalty, may lend his coach, nor any go in coaches of their own without four horses in it, two coachmen, and a gentleman of the horse following on horseback."

The Duke of Lerma appears to have carried his love of pomp or parade to lengths, that to the present age must appear to be ridiculous, which, to his cotemporaries, appeared to be excessive, and which, in his particular circumstances, were certainly imprudent.

" In a late letter," says Sir John Digby (writing to the British secretary of state from Madrid, 9th of June, 1617), I advertised you of 70 long carts sent from hence with stuff, by the Duke of Lerma, unto Lerma; touching which, I must now thus far advertise your honor, that those carts going all together out of town, with a multitude of officers and servants, in great bravery, with trumpets sounding before them, passed by the Palace-gate, that not being the direct way, where the king, hearing the trumpets, inquired the cause of their sounding; and being thereof informed, called for the duke, and gave him a very sharp reprehension, who laid the fault upon his officers, and forthwith turned many out of his service, who had great and painful places. But this, I understood, gives the king so little satisfaction, as he now absolutely refused to go to Lerma, where the duke had made extraordinary preparation for his entertainment. This is so much noted and spoke of in this court, as I have thought it worthy the advertising unto your honor; and peradventure, it may be the beginning of a greater inconvenience to the duke. His plate alone, sent in these carts, besides money, jewels, and stuff, weighed above eight hundred thousand ducats, as I am credibly informed by those who had the charge of it, and have seen it in their books by good account."

It appears from a letter of Sir John Digby's dated Madrid, 28th January, 1619, that the duke of Lerma's annual income amounted to at least six hundred thousand ducats.

We may form some idea of the power and consequence of this minister, and of the pomp and state in which he lived, from the following extract from a letter of Sir Francis Cottington's to the lord treasurer Salisbury, dated Madrid, 19th August, 1619. "I dare assure your lordship, that he (the secretary Aroftequi) and I, before winter pass, may peradventure wait many an hour together, at the duke of Lerma's door, and go back again without getting in. Many times have I feen the conſtable do this, as Sir Charles Cornwallis can well witneſs. I once ſaw the Florentine ambaſſador, being a biſhop, thruſt out of an outer chamber of the duke's. Sir Charles had more free entrance than any man in his time, of what degree ſoever; and yet ſometimes was fain to ſtay. Your lordſhip knows well, that, but by the way of this duke, here is nothing to be done; and therefore, I have written thus largely of his unſufferable greatneſs."

INDEX.

A.

Aersens, Dutch secretary, his disinterestedness and public spirit, i. 249.

Agriculture, decline of, in Spain, i. 7. 70. Expedients for remedying the disadvantages arising from thence, 71.

Albert, archduke, collects his troops and sends them against the mutineers at Hochstrate, i. 118. His marriage with the infanta of Spain, 10. Arrives with the infanta in the Netherlands, 44. Adopts the customs and manners of Spain, 45. Takes the command of his army, and marches against prince Maurice, 53. His bravery, 61. Resolves to besiege Ostend, 74. Desirous of peace, 225.

Aliaga, friar, confessor to Philip, ii. 135. His character and conduct, *ibid.*

Anspach, marquis of, commands an army raised by the princes of the Union, ii. 191. His incapacity, 193.

America, operations of the Dutch there, i. 197.

Arts, progress of, in the Low Countries, i. 198.

Antwerp, a plan of prince Maurice for reducing that city, i. 158. Frustrated by Spinola, 159. Truce concluded there between the United Provinces and Spain, 314.

B.

Barnevelt, pensioner of Holland, sent ambassador into England, i. 126. His character, 227. Recommends peace, 228. 258. 263. Sent ambassador to England, 126.

Bohemia, described, ii. 156 Progress of the war in, 196.

Bohemians, their revolt, ii. 170. Their reasons for deposing their king elect, 181. Skirmishes between them and the Imperialists, 176. Strengthen themselves by new alliances, 181. And chuse a new king, 183.

INDEX.

Bois le duc, Siege of by prince Maurice, i. 119.
Bommel, besieged by the Spaniards, i. 26.
Buccleugh, lord, commands the Scotch infantry in the service of the united States, i. 172.
Borgia, Don Ferdinand de, his character and conduct at the court of Madrid, ii. 141.
Bucquoy, count, commands the garrison of Emmerick, i. 20. His activity, 164. Appointed to the command of an army in the Low Countries by Spinola, 181. To that of the Imperial army, ii. 176. Defeats Mansfeldt, 180. His signal valor, 206.

C.

Calderona, don Roderigo de, count of Oliva, and marquis of Siete Iglesias, his history, ii. 132. His death, 148.
Catholic religion, an object of great dispute in the negociation for a peace or truce between Spain and Holland, i. 282.
Clement IV. pope, advises king James I. of Arragon to banish the Morescoes, i. 330.
Colonna, the historian, an officer in the Spanish army, i. 34. An invention of his, 35.
Comet, anno 1619, alarms the nations, ii. 184.
Commerce, Dutch, i. 201.
Commissioners for peace, on the part of Spain, i. 269. On that of the confederates, *ibid.*
Confederacies, their usual fate, i. 42.
Conspiracies, frequency of, in Italy and Spain, accounted for, ii. 114. Conspiracy against Venice, 116.

D.

D'Aguilar, don John, commands the Spanish force destined to reduce Ireland, i. 92. Delivers up to Mountjoy the forts which were possessed by the Spaniards in Ireland, 98. Is transported with the troops, cannon, and ammunition, in an English fleet, to Spain, *ibid.*
D'Ampierre, count of Lorrain, raises forces in support of the cause of Austria, ii. 180.

INDEX.

D'Ancre, Marefchal, and lady Marefchal, their hiftory and tragical fate, ii. 93.

Defertion of the Italian troops from the colors of Spain, i. 113.

Difcipline, its power over an army, i. 164. And influence in conciliating the good-will of even hoftile countries, i. 165. 193.

E.

Eaſt Indies, the operations of the Dutch there, i. 197. Company of Merchants trading to, 218. Trade to, a fubject of great contention between Spain and the United Provinces, 312.

Edmond, colonel, rifes to that office from the rank of common foldier in the Dutch fervice, i. 187. His military fkill and bravery, 188. And death, *ibid.*

Elizabeth, queen of England, her death, i. 121. And character, 122.

Emmerick, the town of, poffeffed by the Spaniards, i. 16. Taken by the Dutch, 20.

Effex, earl of, his gallantry, ii. 196.

F.

Ferdinand, king of Arragon, fubdues the Moors of Granada, i. 327. The tyranny of that prince reftrained by the Cortes, 331.

Ferdinand, archduke of Gratz, fucceeds Matthias in the government of the Auftrian dominions in Germany, ii. 178. Endeavours to appeafe the minds of the revolters by kindnefs, *ibid.* Raifed to the imperial throne, 181. The vigor and feverity of his character and conduct, 197. 207.

Fifheries, Dutch, i. 199.

Fleet, a Spanifh, fent to cruife againft the Englifh, i. 43. Of eight Spanifh tranfports intercepted by the Dutch admiral Hautain, 161.

Frederic, elector Palatine, oppofes the ambition of Auſtria, ii. 155. Elected king of Bohemia, 183. His fufferings, 208.

G.

Gabor, Bethlehem, prince of Tranſylvania, ſupports the Bohemians, ii. 181. 185.
Germany, ſtate of, i. 23. Princes of, enter into a confederacy againſt the Spaniards, 24. Remiſſneſs of their conduct, 39. Disband their army, 42. War in, ii. 60. Origin of the famous thirty years war in, 153.
Grandees of Spain, diſguſted at the partiality of Philip III. to the duke of Lerma, i. 5. Recover in the preſent reign a confiderable ſhare of their former importance, ii. 224.
Grave, town of, beſieged by prince Maurice, i. 106.
Groll, ſiege of, i. 184.

H.

Heemskirk, admiral, commands the Dutch fleet, i. 241. Attacks and defeats a Spaniſh fleet, riding at anchor in the bay of Gibraltar, 245. His death, 246.
Henry IV. king of France, a ſaying of his concerning James I. king of England, i. 128. *note*. His conduct towards the United States, after the peace of Vervins, 235. His great plan, ii. 4. Prepares to take the field at the head of a powerful army, 9. His death, 12. And character, 13. Effects of his death, *ibid*.
Henry, Frederic, prince of Naſſau, ſent ambaſſador to England, i. 126. His diſtinguiſhed prudence and capacity when only twenty years of age, 170.
Herrings, art of ſalting, invented, i. 199.
Hochſtrate, taken by a body of Spaniſh deſerters, i. 114.
Houtman, Cornelius, conducts a ſmall Dutch fleet into India, i. 206.

James

INDEX.

I.

James I. king of England, his character, and accession to the crown of that kingdom, i. 125. His prejudices against the United States, *ibid*. Concurs with the French king in promoting peace between Spain and the United Provinces, 240. His conduct with respect to the affairs of his son-in-law, the elector Palatine, ii. 187.

Jeannin, president, sent ambassador, to the Hague from France, i. 239. Admitted to an audience of the United States, 286. Presents a memorial to the United States, 295. His success in reconciling the United Provinces to a truce with Spain, 305.

Intermarriages, between the royal families of France and Spain, ii. 22.

Ireland, Catholics of that kingdom, supported by Spain, i. 72. Invaded by the Spaniards, 90.

Isabella, infanta of Spain, married to the archduke, Albert, i. 10. Her arrival in the Netherlands, and entry into Brussels, 44. Animates and exhorts the Spanish troops, 52. Her firmness and constancy, 66.

Italy, Spanish levies there, excite jealousies, i. 58. Engineers brought from Italy by the Spaniards in their war in the Low Countries, 101. Liberties of, in danger, ii. 50. 68.

L.

Lerma, duke of, the favorite of Philip III. king of Spain i. 4. His profusion, 8. Courts the ecclesiastics, 9. His lenity and moderation, 43. The motives which induced him to agree to a truce with Holland, 150. His fall, ii. 135. And character, 135.

Lemos, count of, his character and conduct at the court of Madrid, ii. 141.

Lesdiguieres, marechal, his character, ii. 81. Magnanimous resolution of, 86. Marches to the assistance of the duke of Savoy, 96.

INDEX.

illustrious foreigners from different nations, 77. Capitulates, 152.

Oxford, earl of, his gallantry, ii. 195.

P.

Panic, unaccountable, nature of, and important effects, i. 171.

Parties and disputes in the United Provinces, i. 291.

Peace, negociation for, between Spain and England, i. 49. Interrupted by disputes concerning precedence, 50. Negociation for peace between Spain and the United Provinces, 197. Wished for by the courts of Brussels and Madrid, and why, 222. 225. Retarded by the bigotry and pride of the court of Spain, 285. Parties in the United Provinces for and against, 291. Treaty of, between the Spaniards and the duke of Savoy, ii. 58.

Philip II. king of Spain, Birth and education of, i. 1. His character, 2. His attachment to the duke of Lerma, 4. His marriage, 9. His reluctance to acknowledge the independence of the United States, 305. His religious scruples on this subject, 307. Ratifies the preliminary articles for a truce with the Dutch, 320. His illness, ii. 220. Death, 223. And character, 224. Review of his reign, *ibid.*

Pilsen, tower of, reduced by count Mansfeldt, ii. 176.

Poland, king of, aids the Austrians, ii. 187.

Portuguese, their adventurous spirit, i. 209. Their settlements in India, *ibid.* The corruption of their governors in India, 210.

Prague, city of, described, ii. 157. Battle of, 202. Important consequences of this battle, 205.

Prohibition, of trade, between Spain and the United Provinces, i. 213.

Property, of individuals, restored by the truce between Spain and the United Provinces, i. 281.

INDEX.

R.

Reformation, origin and progress of, ii. 157.
Reputation, loss of, followed speedily by a loss of power, i. 162.
Review of the reign of Philip III. king of Spain, ii. 224.
Rhinberg, reduced by the Spaniards, i. 15. Retaken by prince Maurice, 76. Siege of, 185.
Ribera, patriarch of Antioch archbishop of Valencia, his memorial to the king of Spain against the Morescoes, i. 341.
Rohan, duke of, his passionate grief at the death of Henry IV. ii. 15.
Rosni, marquis of, sent ambassador to England from France, i. 127.

S.

Sandoval, fortress of that name, built by Mendoza the governor of Milan, ii. 55.
Savoy, dukes of, their character, ii. 17. Charles Emanuel, duke of, his character, *ibid*. Endeavours to revive the league against the house of Austria, 20. Obliged to make submissions to the king of Spain, 26. Revives his pretensions to the sovereignty of Montferrat, 34. Invades Montferrat, 39. Endeavours to secure his conquests, 40. His conduct a subject of great mortification to Spain, 43. Takes the field against the Spaniards, 65. Engages with them, 68. His illness, 81. Maintains his independence on Spain, 85.
St. Andrew, a fort of that name in the isle of Bommel, i. 38. Besieged by prince Maurice, 47.
Serrano, Spanish governor of Sluys, makes an attack on the isle of Cadsant, i. 144. Is repulsed, 145.
Sluys, harbour of, affords a commodious retreat and shelter to the Spanish fleet, i. 110. Its importance, 145. Besieged by prince Maurice, 146. Capitulates, 148.
Spain, its exhausted state, i. 6. Troops of Spain employed

INDEX.

in the Low Countries, 12. Their Licentiousness, 21.
And barbarity, 22. Its ambition accounted for, ii. 1.
Its surprising indifference about the warlike preparations
of Henry IV. of France, 11. Gallantry of the Spanish
nation, 31. Her political schemes disordered by the
ambition of the duke of Savoy, 33. Award of, respecting the dispute concerning Montferrat, 47. Effects of
the award, 50. Supports the cause of Austria, 185.

Spaniards, their character, ii. 123.

Spinola, Frederic, with a squadron of Spanish gallies,
cruises on the coast of Flanders, i. 110. Suffers great
disasters, 112. Is killed, 113.

———— *Ambrose*, marquis of, his immense fortune, i. 111.
His great ambition, 112. Is raised to the command of
the Spanish army, 137. Pledges his private fortune for
money to pay his troops, 139. Sets out for Madrid to
confer with the Spanish ministers, 155. Obtains a promise of regular remittance of money of them, to dispose
in the manner he should judge most expedient, 157.
His plan for conducting the campaign of 1605, 162.
Departs from the common maxims of war, 164. His
great abilities, 176. An object of jealousy to the Spanish
ministers, 177. Invades the Palatinate, ii. 190. Falls
sick, 179. A false report of his death, matter of joy
to the United States, *ibid.*

T.

Thorn, count, his history, ii. 165. Excites a revolt in
Bohemia, 167. His character, 174. Appointed to the
command of the Bohemian army, 175. Advances against
Bucquoy, 176. Draws near to the Danube, and threat-
ens Vienna, 179. Recalled to oppose Bucquoy, 180.
His conduct in the battle of Prague, 200. 207.

Trade, of Holland, extended to both Indies, and to the
coast of Africa, i. 214.

Trejo, cardinal Don Gabriel de, signal instance of his gratitude and magnanimity, ii. 149.

INDEX.

Truce, concluded between Spain and the United States, i. 314. Conditions thereof, *ibid.*
Tyrone, earl of, raises a rebellion in Ireland, i. 91.

U.

Ulm, treaty of, ii. 189.
United, States of the Netherlands resolve to invade Flanders, i. 50. Spain attempts to reduce them by operations at sea, 111. They approve the conduct of prince Maurice in protecting the Spanish mutineers, 117. Assisted by queen Elizabeth of England, and king Henry IV. of France, 102. Their interference in the operations of war injurious to the public interest, 162. Their operations in the East Indies and America, 197. Dissatisfied with Philip's ratification of the preliminaries of peace, 295. Their strong suspicion and jealousy of Spain, 270. Refuse to give up their trade to India, 312. Conclude a truce with Spain, 314. And are considered as a free people, 318. Their own success, and the symptoms of languor in the Spanish monarchy awaken their ambition, ii. 61.
Uscocchi, history of, ii. 107.
Useda, duke of, his character, ii. 135. Becomes the favorite of the king of Spain, *ibid.*

V.

Valencia, barons of, remonstrate against the expulsion of the Morescoes, i. 361. Their humanity to the Morescoes, 372.
Valtelline, described, ii. 210. Revolt of, 212.
Venice, senate of, takes part with the duke of Savoy in opposition to the Spaniards, ii. 53. War between that republic and the archduke of Gratz, 108. Maintains its independence on Spain, 128.
Vere, Sir Francis, renowned for his military prudence and capacity, i. 77. Appointed by the United States to the command of the garrison of Ostend, *ibid.*

INDEX.

Vere, Sir Horatio, leads an English regiment into Germany to the aid of the Palatine, ii. 191. His bravery, 195. Remarkable saying of, 196.
Vercelli, siege of, ii. 88.
Victor, Amadeus, prince of Piedmont, his reception at the court of Madrid, ii. 50. Surprises the capital of the principality of Masserano, 83. Reduces Crevalcor, *ibid.*
Villa-Franca, don Pedro de Toledo, marquis of, appointed governor of Milan, ii. 71. His character, *ibid.* His warlike operations against the duke of Savoy, 78. Averse to peace, 101.

W.

Wesel, its inhabitants abolish the exercise of the catholic religion, 15. Laid under contribution by the Spanish general, *ibid.* Besieged by Spinola, ii. 63.
Wisemberg, or White-hill, described, ii. 202.

X.

Ximenes, archbishop of Toledo, persecutes the Morescoes, i. 327.

FINIS.

www.ingramcontent.com/pod-product-compliance
Lightning Source LLC
Chambersburg PA
CBHW031850220426
43663CB00006B/564